Sociological perspectives on modern accountancy

Robin Roslender

London and New York

First published in 1992
by Routledge
11 New Fetter Lane, London EC4P 4EE

Simultaneously published in the USA and Canada
by Routledge
a division of Routledge, Chapman and Hall Inc.
29 West 35th Street, New York, NY 10001

© 1992 Robin Roslender

Typeset in Times by LaserScript Limited, Mitcham, Surrey
Printed and bound in Great Britain by
Mackays of Chatham PLC, Chatham, Kent

British Library Cataloguing in Publication Data
Roslender, Robin
   Sociological perspectives on modern accountancy.
   I. Title
   657

Library of Congress Cataloging in Publication Data
Roslender, Robin, 1949–
   Sociological perspectives on modern accountancy/Robin Roslender.
   p. cm.
   Includes bibliographical references and index.
   1. Accounting – Social aspects. I. Title.
   HF5657.R656   1992
   657 – dc20   91-32486
                                                          CIP

ISBN 0–415–02575–3
      0–415–02576–1 (pbk)

For Alison and Jennifer Louise

Contents

Acknowledgements

The experience of writing the first text interfacing sociology and accounting has been a rewarding one. It provided me with the opportunity to discover how much I knew, and didn't know, about these disciplines after many years of involvement with them. More importantly, it has made me aware of how much I owe to the many different groups of people who have contributed to my intellectual development to date. So in the first instance I am indebted to Chris Rojek at Routledge for the opportunity to write the text and for his support and encouragement during the first two years of the project. During the past fifteen months Elisabeth Tribe has had the unenviable task of ensuring that I finished the manuscript in a finite time period. This she managed to execute with a combination of good humour and firmness. Without it I am quite certain that I would still be far from finished. I hope that in the process I didn't cause her any more lost sleep than I experienced.

I was very fortunate to have undertaken my formal training in the department of sociology at Leeds University between 1970 and 1977. It was Christie Davies, now of Reading University, who first excited my interest in the mysteries of the discipline, these being further explored with other members of the faculty including Zygmunt Bauman, Alan Dawe, Dennis Warwick and Ken Watkins. During my post-graduate days I was also fortunate to have been a member of the "Scribblers Club" with its commitment to developing a radical role for sociology, one which I continue to espouse. However, it is to Ian Varcoe that I owe my greatest debt. Ian was responsible for supervising my doctoral work during this time and in subsequent years. In particular it was his insistence that one devotes the necessary time to the planning and structuring of any project which has continued to serve me so well in all of my endeavours.

After leaving Leeds I moved to Napier Polytechnic in Edinburgh where for twelve years I taught a wide range of courses, most of which can just about be termed sociology. However, very early in my time there I discovered that although I had learned a lot about doing sociology, I needed to know rather a lot more substantive sociology for teaching purposes, and quickly. So began my informal training, something which continues to this day. During these years I was lucky enough to be in the company of John Cooper, Robin Fincham, David Lindsay, John McKie, Dick Williams and Howard Wollman who collectively taught me much of my sociology. As we were involved in teaching on vocational courses it was inevitable that we worked closely with colleagues in other disciplines in an attempt to fashion an interdisciplinary learning experience for our students. For some of us this was to become our principal pedagogical objective and in this connection I have benefited from the chance to work with and learn from my colleagues John Troy and Jim Murray, and from Allin Cottrell now of Wakeforest University, Winston-Salem.

From the beginning, one of my regular teaching assignments at Napier was behavioural science to accounting students, initially on the HND programme and subsequently on the undergraduate accounting degree. This meant that when I began to sit in on professional accounting classes in 1985 I knew most of my teachers, and they knew me. During the next few years they succeeded in taking me from a situation of no meaningful understanding of accounting to the final professional level of the Chartered Association of Certified Accountants' examination programme. In many ways it is their collective enthusiasm for accounting which has inspired me to write this text in the way that I have. While I am indebted to every member of the teaching team for their assistance, several of them have been particularly supportive: Jeff McLachlan, Douglas Sievewright and David Young, and John Dyson with whom I continue to research and write.

The move to Stirling and to a lectureship in accountancy which has given me the chance to teach accounting was principally the idea of Irvine Lapsley and Charles Ward, both of whom have supported me during the writing of the text, finishing the professional examinations and learning much more about accounting and accountancy. My colleagues are slowly coming round to the idea that I might have something useful to say in their fields and I have certainly found them very helpful in providing me with material and references for the text. Much of the second part of the text was developed in the course of teaching on the department's final year honours programme in the 1990 Spring semester, for which I am indebted to my students. During my time in the department I have come to rely on the contribution which Elissa Elings makes to my work. Fortunately for her, in this instance she was responsible for only the bibliography, which was produced as effortlessly as ever.

Among the broader community of academic accountants the contributions of a number of friends and colleagues must be acknowledged. Trevor Hopper has been extremely supportive over the years together with Rob Gray and David Hatherley, all of whom have read and commented on parts of the text. David Otley, Tony Puxty and Peter Armstrong have helped convince me of the need to bring the two disciplines together in some way, as well as providing me with a literature I have been able to incorporate in the following pages. The work of the critical accountants such as David Cooper, Tony Tinker, Marilyn Neimark, Cheryl Lehman and Hugh Willmott has certainly made my task less onerous. Of course, this in no way means that they or any of the aforementioned bear any responsibility for the innumerable weaknesses of the present text. These are the result of my own inadequate learning and not their exemplary instruction.

And so I come to the more personal acknowledgements, those to the family. During the past eleven months there has been a new member of the household to keep me company in my study on many occasions, Jennifer Louise. Lively by day and peepy at night, Jenni already shows an unhealthy interest in books and playing about with the keyboard. Surely an author of the future! Finally my greatest debts are to my wife Alison who has been more tolerant of my inaccessibility, irritability and general detachedness during the past three years than I could reasonably expect. Without her constant support, this project would never have been possible in the first place, let alone completed. For this as well as for the other things too numerous and important to list I will be eternally grateful.

Robin Roslender
Stirling

Introduction

The subject of this text is modern accountancy, which is to be considered from a sociological perspective. The logical starting point is to map out the chosen subject, modern accountancy, before saying something about the particular disciplinary perspective, sociology, from which it is to be viewed. Only then will it be possible to set out the precise subject matter of the text itself. These are the three topics which form the content of this introductory chapter.

MODERN ACCOUNTANCY: A BRIEF OVERVIEW

What is modern accountancy, or more precisely how is modern accountancy conceived of in the following pages? At its simplest it is viewed as an important institution of modern society. Its importance and influence have increased very rapidly in the post-war period and look set to continue in the future. Nevertheless, it is an institution about which comparatively little is known, particularly from a sociological perspective. For these reasons modern accountancy is a highly relevant subject for study at the present time. Having designated it as an institution, it is now necessary to outline what this particular concept means. In the British context the term is commonly applied both to concrete entities such as the Bank of England, the London School of Economics, Glasgow Rangers Football Club, or established events such as Trooping the Colour, the Edinburgh Festival, or Wimbledon. All of these are undoubtedly important entities with their respective histories and traditions, functions and roles, but they are much more restricted phenomena than an institution such as accountancy. The sense in which the term institution is being used here is the much broader one of constituting a major component of a society's socio-cultural structure, i.e. as a *social institution*. In this way accountancy is being seen as the equivalent of the other major social institutions such as the family, religion, work, education, art and literature, and science and technology, all of which have been studied extensively by sociologists. Accountancy is viewed here as being similar to these institutions, sharing with them the characteristic of being at the very heart of society as it is presently constituted. Rightly or wrongly, it is viewed as being something to be developed and ever more widely diffused because of its perceived contribution to society's longer term well-being. By comparison with the other social institutions, accountancy has only recently assumed this status and in this way it is much less substantial than either the family or religion, which date back to the very beginning of social existence, or science and technology which have a more modern origin. As things presently stand, however, there is every reason to believe that in time it will become as much a component of the established order as they have.

What does this institution encompass that gives rise to accountancy's growing significance in modern society? What is its constitution? To begin with it involves a set of practices which are commonly termed accounting, the process of identifying, measuring and communicating economic information to permit informed judgements and decisions by users of this information (AAA, 1966). Accounting is conventionally sub-divided into financial accounting and management accounting (including cost accounting), the complementary elements of accounting as it exists in business enterprises of all sorts. Both of these embrace an extensive range of practical techniques which may be used at various times in the course of managing any business. There is also a very clear link between them and what is taught and learned in the name of accounting in schools, colleges, universities and of course 'on the job' itself. However, there is normally a good deal more to learn when studying for an accounting diploma or degree, or to become a member of a professional accountancy association. In the first instance there is auditing which also exists as a specialised occupational role, one commonly filled by qualified accountants.

Auditing complements accounting but it is clearly quite different to it. To extend the term accounting to auditing is rather unhelpful. To see both as constituents of accountancy is a much more useful standpoint to adopt, however. In this way it is possible to add to the list of constituent parts of accountancy two other common elements of accounting knowledge: taxation and finance. Most accountants probably have very little concern with tax matters since these are normally left to more senior staff or specialist groups. At the same time, taxation is not solely the concern of accountants, being of equal importance to those who staff the Inland Revenue or the Internal Revenue Service. These individuals are far more likely to spend their working day performing tax computations. In this way the institution of accountancy clearly extends beyond the sphere of accountants and their various activities. This is also the case in finance where accountants regularly find themselves working in association with and sharing the knowledge of economists, corporate strategists, lawyers and bankers in the pursuit of profitable investment opportunities. The list of accountancy's constituent parts can be extended of course: information systems; accounting theory; quantitative techniques; organisation and management studies, etc. All have their respective contributions to make to the effective performance of accountancy at the present time, thereby complementing accounting more narrowly conceived, i.e. financial and management accounting.

The institution of accountancy extends far beyond this collection of its constituent parts. It also embraces those who perform its many activities, the various accountancy practitioners and, in particular, accountancy professionals. Accountants are presently prominent among the growing legions of professional workers who are employed in a wide variety of work in many different types of organisational setting and subject to many differing organisational and managerial arrangements and regimes. Without their individual and collective endeavours there would not be such an institution as accountancy. Then there are the various professional accountancy associations, each one with its own history, philosophy, internal structure, etc. As well as providing the means to enable individuals to gain the professional qualifications which are required to practise accountancy, a number of these organisations have been highly influential in determining what society recognises or perceives as accountancy. Their success in promoting the interests of their members engenders strong support for any policies designed to retain, or ideally extend, the influence which the professional accountancy associations have. Without doubt they are major players in the modern accountancy institution. In recent times they have begun to share this role with the largest of the professional firms including the so-called 'Big 6', the richest and most powerful of the international chartered accountancy corporations. These firms employ tens of thousands of accountants worldwide, provide accountancy services to the entire spectrum of clients and as a result are normally viewed as the market leaders. On this basis they have enjoyed great success in shaping the constitution of large areas of modern accountancy in the same way that a handful of mega-corporations such as Boeing or IBM have shaped contemporary science and technology.

Accountancy is also crucially concerned with the outcomes of accounting, the actual practice of, say, budgets which are imposed on subordinate staffs rather than negotiated with them, operating capacities which are rationalised as a result of an objective strategic management accounting exercise, or wage claims which are lost due to the downward revaluation of fixed assets or the need to provide for the rising level of default on Third World debt. In the same way that science and technology are as much about the 'greenhouse effect' or the search for geologically appropriate burial sites for 'safe' nuclear waste, so accountancy commonly involves lost jobs, restricted choices and reduced safety standards, all of which may, quite knowingly, make the world a much worse place today, tomorrow, forever perhaps. One of the interesting features of accountancy's relatively short history is that unlike most of the other major social institutions it has not been able to successfully promote its 'good' side to the public while managing to 'talk down' its inevitable shortcomings. It could be that the latter are presently so problematic that it is preferable to remain silent on these matters. On the other hand accountancy has had the misfortune to come to the fore in an enlightened age, and perhaps suffer from being the scapegoat for many of the evils which have been perpetrated by the much longer established institutions mentioned above. In this scenario, the obstacles which face those who are seeking to develop and promote alternatives within modern accountancy may prove insurmountable.

By now the distinction which in effect has provided the structure both for these opening comments and the text as a whole should be quite clear. Accounting *per se* is only a very limited, although very vital part of accountancy which as a major institution of modern society has many important and at the same time problematic constituent parts. This text is not an attempt to study modern accounting. For one thing the focus would be too narrow and it would seem to omit many of the more interesting questions that might be asked of accountancy. In addition this is what conventional accounting texts are about, the vast majority of which seem to get by successfully without needing to adopt anything other than a 'technical' accounting perspective. Anyone hoping to find in the following pages sociologically informed insights on the head office method of maintaining branch accounts, the temporal method of foreign currency translation or the repeated distribution technique of allocating service centre costs will find little of interest here. However, analyses of the future prospects of the accountancy profession, the organisation and management of accountancy workers, the practicalities of devising alternative accounting paradigms, the status of accounting theory or the processes of auditor socialisation, all topics which increasingly appear to attract the attention of academic accountants, form part of the substantive content of the following chapters.

The text was conceived of as a study of modern accountancy from the perspective of a quite separate discipline, a study which was sufficiently interesting to a number of friends and colleagues to warrant a prolonged period of research, reflection and regular writing. Whether it has been a worthwhile exercise, or whether in the last analysis there is a more pressing need for, and a greater potential value in producing conventional accounting texts is clearly an important question. Not wishing to avoid it, some thought is given to the promise and the pitfalls of thinking about accountancy in the final chapter. Siting it at that point allows anyone who has read this far, and wishes to proceed, the opportunity to assimilate more fully the varied content of the following pages before they arrive at any conclusion. For the moment it is more important that attention switches to an account of sociology, the disciplinary perspective which has provided the basis for the project.

SOCIOLOGY AND THE SOCIOLOGICAL PERSPECTIVES

Sociology was the name the French scholar Auguste Comte gave to the new, positive science of society which he commended to his peers in the first quarter of the last century. He envisaged a discipline which would be comparable with mathematics, astronomy and physics, at that time the most advanced of the sciences. By adopting the same scientific approach, i.e. positivism, he claimed that sociology would be able to provide the knowledge, explanations and understanding needed to bring about the development of a well-regulated social order. Thus from the outset sociology, like all social theory before and since, was bound up with the issue of social change. A generation later Karl Marx reaffirmed the link between social and sociological analysis and social change, although unlike Comte he saw it contributing to the development of a more emancipatory social order than capitalism offered to the masses. The establishment of sociology as a respectable academic discipline occurred in Europe in the thirty years after 1890, sometimes termed the classical period of sociology. The key figures in the process were Max Weber and Emile Durkheim, and to a lesser extent Vilfredo Pareto, Georg Simmel and Ferdinand Tonnies. It was at this time that sociology became recognised as a thoroughly *critical* discipline, in the sense of being concerned with the study of society in a full and even-handed way, setting out the positive side, highlighting the negative, identifying the benefits and assessing the costs of the various social structures and processes. In this way those who were active in promoting the discipline were seeking to reassure a sceptical audience that sociology was not simply the handmaiden of political theorists but offered a means of promoting the scientific study of societies and all of the benefits this would give rise to.

The development of sociology in Europe continued until the mid-1930s after which time it was to become a predominantly American endeavour for the next thirty years or so. During this period it became increasingly dominated by a form of theorising known as *structural-functionalism*, and the general theories of Talcott Parsons in particular. At the same time it became a much more empirical discipline in line with the general traditions of American scholarship. As a result its critical edge was rather blunted while its links with social change tended to exist in name only. In many ways this was the era of the sociology of the status quo, the scientific study of the prevailing consensus. In Europe, however, a new generation of sociologists were rediscovering the work of the discipline's founding forefathers, its critical emphasis and its links with political theory and practice. At the same time they also found a great deal in the prevailing consensus to subject to critical scrutiny. The events surrounding the Vietnam War raised a growing range of political questions which sociologists were very willing to provide answers to. As a result the discipline in the late 1960s was a highly charged mass of critical and radical ideas which looked set to help change the world (Gouldner, 1971). The discipline was successful in attracting many of the best students who in those liberal times were infatuated by the possibilities of change. By 1970 it was sometimes difficult to differentiate between Marxist theory and sociological analysis, although a range of other alternatives to structural-functionalism were also widely supported. When the euphoria of the late 1960s had died away, sociology set about the task of establishing a balance between its analytical, critical and radical traditions and between theoretical and empirical factions in an attempt to create a mature science of society which would fulfil the promise of the classical period. This has largely been successful although sadly not in the case of British sociology. For a period during the 1980s it was effectively an intellectual pariah, vilified by Conservative governments and trivialised by influential sections of the media. As a consequence it is fair to conclude that it has an unfavourable reputation in many circles. In recent years there have been signs of an improvement in British sociology's prospects, although perhaps at some cost to its longer term integrity.

Having outlined the history and general character of sociology it is necessary to move on to consider the development of the discipline since the classical period. In general it has developed as a series of sub-disciplines such as the sociology of the family, religion, work, art and literature, i.e. the various social institutions listed earlier. However, it has extended far beyond these and given rise to the sociology of almost every facet of society including the sociology of the bicycle, the sociology of scientific communications and, inevitably, the sociology of sociology. The degree of development of the various sub-disciplines varies considerably, reflecting both their status within the discipline as a whole and the interest they generate among sociologists. The development of theoretical sociology is carried on within the sub-disciplines but there has always been a tradition of general theorising involving the leading sociologists of the day. Among the contemporary theorists Giddens and Habermas command the same attention as have Comte, Marx, the classical sociologists, Parsons and Alfred Schutz before them. However, most sociologists readily identify themselves as specialists who pursue their interests in narrow fields and who are content to keep abreast of developments in their own sub-disciplines. Keeping up to date with the overall development of sociology is not a serious consideration other than in the most general way. This situation applies to any mature discipline and to some extent is the inevitable consequence of the emergence of the intellectual division of labour which has characterised the past three hundred years or so.

Given this structure, what is it that unifies all of these researchers, scholars and writers working in their own fields to create the content of sociology? Essentially it is the perspective they have on society which informs the particular questions they ask; the connections they investigate or seek to establish; the interest which they have in structures and processes, meanings and motivations, power and knowledge; the nature of the explanations they offer and those they choose to exclude. These are learned in the course of studying sociology, either formally as a student, or perhaps as an accounting academic interested in the insights which sociology can offer on the social, organisational and behavioural aspects of accountancy. These are the principal elements of what might be best described as the *sociological perspective*.

To talk in terms of *the* sociological perspective as if it were a unified perspective is, however, quite misleading. In fact nothing could be further from the truth because sociology has always been characterised by its multi-perspective constitution. As well as developing as a series of sub-disciplines, it has also developed as a series of different ways of viewing society, each of which offers only a partial perspective on society, one way of seeing among many potential ways. This goes some way to explaining why many who are new to sociology often find that the discipline seems not to fit together in some neat way, and why its literature often appears uneven, contradictory, open-ended, fragmented, etc. Equally it explains why sociology is able to provide the range of insights that it does and why it continues to excite the interest of many leading academics in other disciplines including accounting. In the same way that most sociologists specialise in particular sub-disciplines, many also tend to favour and employ a specific way of seeing or perspective on society. They are normally able to defend their chosen perspective against criticism from other viewpoints while being able to appreciate the various merits of the many alternatives on offer. Again this is a feature of their training as sociologists, the purpose of which is to ensure that they are theoretically and methodologically self-aware and thereby able to contribute to the development of sociology in a professional way. This desired self-awareness takes time to achieve of course and for this reason the American Sociological Association takes the view that it is only after the award of a doctorate that a sociologist should be admitted to the profession of sociology. In this way it is adopting a similar stance to every major professional accountancy association presently in existence. Without wishing to disagree in any way with the conclusion that it takes a great deal of time (and application) to become a professional sociologist (or accountant), it is possible to convey to non-sociologists the principal features of the discipline's multi-perspective under-pinning, which are fully acknowledged in the title of the present text.

Sociology is not unique among the social sciences in embracing different viewpoints; in psychology there are behaviourists and Freudians while in eco-nomics there is a long-established division between Keynesians and supply side theorists. Accounting theorists hotly debate the respective merits of normative and positive theorising while in financial accounting the historical cost con-vention is based on only one of a range of valuation principles. However, in the case of sociology there are seemingly more perspectives to contend with and, more importantly, many of them appear to be quite fundamentally opposed to each other. Perhaps the best place to begin is with an account of two key oppositions which exist within sociological theory and which constitute the basis for the many perspectives which characterise the discipline and its literature. The first opposition is between a sociology based on a *holistic* approach to under-standing and one which is based on an *atomistic* approach. In the less arid terminology of the layman, this means seeking to understand society from the 'top-down' and from the 'bottom-up'. So for example the role of education in society can on the one hand be understood as serving various purposes or functions for society: socialisation, training, occupational replacement, provid-ing opportunities for social mobility, etc. By doing so effectively, education functions to ensure that society continues to exist, at least in this respect. By implication it is the reproduction of the society (= the whole) which is of prime importance from this perspective since every constituent element of a society can only be understood in terms of the total entity. What does education mean to the individual, how does s/he view it? This is the basis of the complementary perspective which considers the role of education in society viewed from the 'bottom', from the perspective of the participants. This way of seeing society focuses specifically on the meanings which participants give to the different elements of society. In the case of education these may include: it provides opportunities for qualification and social mobility; it keeps the young off the streets; it is a legal obligation to be in school up to the age of sixteen; it offers a means to develop talents and to sharpen intellects and so on. The meaning of education is in fact a complex of meanings not all of which are consistent with the holistic view that education is an essentially positive element of the social structure.

It is obviously a truism that in order to understand the rich tapestry of education it is necessary to consider it from both perspectives. No respectable sociologist would ever claim otherwise. However, this is rather easier to agree with than to put into practice and as a result sociology has tended to adopt a workable compromise. To understand this it is necessary to return to the holistic–atomistic opposition and rethink it in terms of a continuum. At the extremes it is possible to be concerned with only functions or meanings but this could only give rise to a highly restrictive range of insights. Moving down the continuum allows a balance to be struck between incorporating the importance of meaning into understanding society while still emphasising the primacy of structure. Conversely moving up the continuum from a concern solely with participants and meanings provides a means of understanding the vital role which they play in the processes of constructing and reconstructing society and its constituent structures. Ideally a perspective which combines a balanced emphasis on both structure and process, and meaning and function, would be sited somewhere in the middle of this continuum. In many ways this would be as restrictive as adopting one of the two extreme views since it would inevitably be extremely bland. In practice most sociologists find themselves favouring a move toward one of the two extremes of the continuum in an attempt to resolve the opposition between the holistic and the atomistic approaches to understanding society. As a consequence they produce a range of accounts of the same social reality which reflects both its complexity and the value in seeing it in different ways.

The second opposition, and its associated continuum, is between a sociology which embraces a *descriptive* emphasis and a sociology which embraces a *radical* emphasis. In simple terms it is an opposition between a sociology which is content to describe society as it is and a sociology which is more a form of political practice than it is an academic discipline. Once again these two extremes would give rise to highly restrictive forms of sociology and in practice very little if any extant sociology is purely descriptive or purely political rhetoric. However, there are examples of sociological work which can be placed along the continuum between them. At the descriptive end there is a great deal of analytical and taxonomic work characteristic of American scientific sociology after 1945. This was the era of *value-free* sociology when a concerted attempt was being made to provide an objective sociology in the manner of the natural sciences. Much of this sort of work was and remains both technically sound and insightful. The problem is that sociologists who embrace this approach elect not to offer any comment on what they observe and analyse, preferring to leave their sociology at the level of exposition rather than moving on to some form of critique. By implication, those who adopt a critical perspective have opted to move beyond description to some form of social commentary. At its simplest a critical socio-logy is one which looks beyond what can be observed to what lies behind it and in turn offers some comment on it. It is useful to think of a critical sociology in terms of degrees of criticism. First there is the most liberal form of criticism that only amounts to raising the most obvious points for comment although not necessarily wishing to take any action in support of these. This liberal critical position would also mark the mid-point on the continuum as a consequence of its inherent intellectual blandness. Moving along the continuum there is the more comprehensive mode of criticism which tends to suggest some sense of deep concern but in the last analysis an unwillingness to take any action. Next is the more radical critical position where insight, concern and action are interrelated in a sociology which is committed to political change but which still retains the hallmarks of rigour and scholarship which are necessary to distinguish it from political rhetoric.

This is the form of *radical sociology* which in the later 1960s promised to dominate the discipline and thereby make a major contribution to changing society. It is most commonly conceived of in terms of left-wing radicalism, hence its identification with *Marxist sociology*. However, in the era of the 'radical right' it is necessary to acknowledge that it is entirely conceivable that a right-wing radical sociological tradition could emerge and make its contribution to changing society. This is very much the implication of the recent critique of contemporary sociology offered by Marsland (1988). Radical or Marxist sociology accepts Marx's own dictum that it is insufficient that 'philosophers' merely understand society, their role is to change it. For Marx one of the fundamental features of capitalist society was that it is a class society and consequently to understand society it is necessary to recognise the existence of classes, and more importantly, the conflictual relationship which inevitably exists between them. The class struggle was for Marx the central social process, a perpetual threat to stability, the essential motor for change. Any consensus in capitalist society could be achieved only at the expense of the masses and was thereby not a true consensus at all but a set of arrangements devised mainly to serve the interests of the dominant alliance of classes. Marx saw that the role for people like himself, committed to the scientific study of a society which appeared grossly unfair, was to demon-strate the many negative features of such societies and to do so in a way which would hasten their replacement by a more acceptable set of social arrangements. This outlook still survives within radical sociology although it no longer seems to appeal to such a wide constituency within the profession.

These two oppositions and their respective continua can be interfaced as shown in Figure 1. By doing this, four *fields* for situating the various sociological perpectives are created.

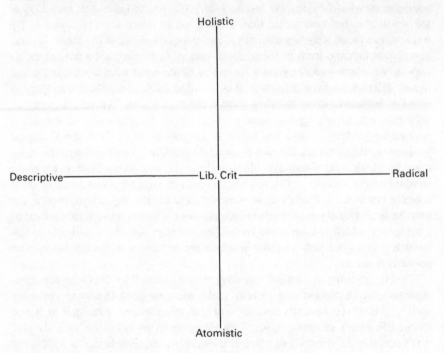

Figure 1 Fields for situating sociological perspectives

Within these four fields a great number of potential sociological perspectives are conceivable, each offering its own characteristic perspective on society. Not all have actually emerged of course, but it is possible to situate some of the more influential perspectives as follows (cf. Burrell & Morgan, 1979). In the top left field the best known example is the *structural-functionalism* associated with Parsons. By comparison, the functionalist perspective associated with writers such as Merton was rather less holistic in orientation and more critical in tone. In the top right field the *radical structuralist* and *labour process* perspectives are more holistically oriented than the *critical theory* perspective which is associated with the Frankfurt School. All three are heavily reliant on Marxist theory. A number of perspectives can be situated in the lower left field including *social exchange theory*, *phenomenological sociologies* including *ethnomethodology* and the *action frame of reference*, and *symbolic interactionism* which emerged in the late 1950s in American sociology as the first major alternative to the structural-functional orthodoxy. In time it has been developed into a more critical perspective which is sometimes known as the *negotiated order* perspective which has a greater interest in power and its constituent processes. In this way it shares an affinity with what some have termed *radical Weberianism*. Finally, in the lower right field development has been much less evident although some radical phenomenology has surfaced together with the beginnings of a *hermeneutic sociology*.

Each perspective has something to offer in the way of understanding society which is why they all find some support among sociologists irrespective of current fads and fashions. They are all part of the discipline's constitution although their existence has ensured that the literature of sociology is perhaps more fragmented, contradictory and inconclusive than that of other disciplines. This should be seen as a measure of the value of sociological analysis, not a sign of weakness or immaturity. Without these many perspectives it would not be possible to begin to understand in any meaningful way the complexities of society nor to produce the rich tapestry which is contemporary sociological analysis. In this light, the choice of title for the text was perhaps the easiest thing about it. Any serious sociological study of accountancy must reflect the discipline's multi-perspective character, hence the use of the plural term 'perspectives'. Inevitably this has resulted in ideas and issues being integrated into the text which the writer might be highly critical of in other contexts. However, in the interests of extending the institution of accountancy's knowledge of itself, insights which come from a range of sociological perspectives, and occasionally from beyond the discipline, are readily included in the following pages.

THE LOGIC AND PLAN OF THE TEXT

The present text was never conceived of as simply an attempt to assemble the elements of a sociology of accountancy. There are three reasons for this. Firstly from the outset it was clear that insufficient relevant literature existed to make this possible. As a consequence it was inevitable that much of the content of such a text would need to be created, or even contrived, an exercise which held little appeal for this writer. Thirdly, and most importantly, since the text was being written for accountants rather than sociologists, it was necessary to consider subject matters which might be of some interest to them, an imperative which also seemed to preclude a unitary sociology of accountancy approach for the whole project. So from the outset it was clear that the text should have two parts. The first of these would be a modest attempt at presenting a sociology *of* accountancy which would consider various topics and issues of interest to accountants in a fairly conventional way. The second part would be rather more innovatory, being an attempt to offer some elements of a sociology *for* accountancy. Here the *sociological imagination* would be deployed to provide a measure of insight on a selection of topics and issues presently of concern within some of the principal branches of accountancy. Rather than simply looking at accountancy as a sociologist, this part would involve the writer applying his own sociological imagination to these topics and issues in order to contribute to a better understanding of them. As a student of accountancy for some time prior to the commencement of the text, the writer felt reasonably well-placed to undertake this challenge. The passage of time has seen comparatively little departure from the original proposal. The text remains divided into these two parts, and the eight chapters which they contain have been the subject of fine tuning rather than major overhaul. As a consequence the intervening time has been spent in ensuring that the text enhances the future for both of the disciplines which it has elected to interface.

The first chapter in Part I is concerned with the accountancy profession. The first section consists of a lengthy review of the literature of the sociology of the professions, which provides a basis for determining the nature of the contemporary profession and its members. In the second section the focus switches to a discussion of the structure and organisation of the profession both in the UK and abroad. Particular attention is paid to the development of the various professional accountancy institutes and associations which have come to play such a major role in the fortunes of the modern profession. The third section is concerned with the recruitment and socialisation processes associated with the profession and its various professional bodies and includes a critical analysis of the educational and training experiences of their student members. In keeping with the rest of the text, the final section of the chapter focuses on an associated topic, in this case an assessment of the validity of the public's image of the accountant. The underlying purpose of this and subsequent final sections is to provide a provocative conclusion to the chapter which also reinforces a number of the main points made in the previous sections. Chapter 3 is concerned with the nature of the work roles which contemporary accountants are engaged in. To simplify things this work is differentiated into three principal types by sector: public practice, industry and commerce, and public sector accountancy. In the section on the public practice role attention is focused on the need for specialisation, the consequences of the growth of larger firms and the challenges which a changing business environment might have for those who work in this sector. In the case of the corporate accountancy role the main issue which is addressed is the increasing formalisation of accounting practices in large-scale organisations and its consequences for the growing ranks of accountants employed there. The intrusion of political pressure in the public sector, particularly in the UK context, is the main issue considered in the third section of this chapter. Finally the chapter concludes with some thoughts on the significance for the profession and its members of the emergence of the accounting technician role given some of the developments which have been identified in the previous pages.

Accountants' work experiences are the focus of the fourth chapter, which builds directly on the previous one. Initially an account of the social organisation of work informed by the writings of Marx, Taylor and Braverman is sketched out. The idea of work as labour process and its essentially negative consequences for those who experience work in this way are outlined in this section. The question of whether accountants experience their work as a labour process is the issue discussed in the second section. Research on the work experiences of both white-collar and other groups of professional employees is discussed before offering some tentative conclusions on the question. Next the promise of information technology for the accountancy profession is scrutinised, again drawing on the experience of other occupational groups. Similar, unpromising conclusions are suggested. In the final section of this chapter the thorny issue of whether accountants are management is debated at some length. In the course of this section the question of the class identities of professional workers such as accountants is considered with some provocative conclusions being offered. These are in accordance with others suggested earlier in the chapter. The final chapter in Part I is concerned with the relationship between the institution of accountancy and ideology. The first section offers an anatomy of the ideology concept. This is followed by a section which reviews the way in which recent studies of accountancy have identified its ideological qualities. The greater part of this literature has emanated from the *critical accounting* tradition rather than sociology itself, a fact which indicates how seriously the link between accountancy and ideology has been taken by some within the profession. The third section is concerned with the ideological status of some of the alternative ways of accounting which have been proposed during the past twenty years, including social responsibility accounting, social audit and, more recently, environmental accounting. In the concluding section another much vaunted but hitherto unsuccessful alternative form of accounting, human resource accounting, is subjected to further critical scrutiny in the light of developments which have suggested that it may be about to experience a major revival in its fortunes.

Part II also has four chapters in which sociology is deployed to provide some insight on topics and issues which are presently of some concern to the accountancy profession. Each of the four chapters focuses on a particular branch of accountancy: Chapter 6 is concerned with financial accounting, Chapter 7 with management accounting, Chapter 8 with finance and Chapter 9 with auditing. All have the same structure; each begins with a brief account of the particular branch of accountancy in question with the intention of establishing a measure of common ground between sociology and accountancy. These accounts have been purposefully devised to serve as a basis for the remainder of their respective chapters. It is hoped that their contents will be sufficiently familiar to those with a background in accountancy to carry them through the remaining sections of the different chapters.

In the case of financial accounting the particular foci for attention are theory and theory construction, questions of methodology and the conceptual framework project. These appear to constitute a form of 'black hole' into which an enormous amount of intellectual energy has been directed over time with very little discernible advance. The second section of Chapter 6 is given over to a critique of a series of oppositions which normally form the content of the theory debate in financial accounting. The various points which are raised in the course of this critique are the result of thinking through similar issues in the case of sociology. In the following section Robert Merton's seminal work on the relationship between anomie and deviance is presented as an example of the sort of theoretical work which those working in the social sciences should seek to emulate as far as possible. In the final section attention switches to the contribution to the theory debate made by Watts & Zimmerman and in particular the claim that their work should be viewed as part of the sociology of accounting choice. In the past decade a good deal of management accounting research has been carried out using sociological perspectives. The second section of Chapter 7 considers some of the reasons why there has been such an interest in employing sociological perspectives in this branch of accounting research. In the third section some of the research which has been produced by this tradition is subjected to a critique, the purpose of which is to draw attention to the partial nature of any insights which can be gained from employing any particular sociological perspective. In this way it builds directly on the earlier discussion of the various perspectives on offer within the discipline. The final section of the chapter focuses on the emergence of the 'new' management accounting which has appeared in recent years and in particular the work of Johnson, Kaplan and Cooper. The contribution which a training in sociology can make to the development of the necessary analytical and critical skills is briefly discussed.

Chapter 8 is concerned with finance, which to date has been heavily influenced by economics. Against this background it was decided to suggest some potentially fruitful links between topics in finance and parts of the literature of sociology. Agency theory is the focus for the second section of this chapter. It is a theory intimately concerned with the consequences of the separation/divorce of ownership from control in modern capitalist enterprises, an issue which has also interested many sociologists and as result a sizeable literature has been built up to complement that on offer in finance theory. Much practical financial management involves making decisions but the study of decision-making is rarely discussed in finance texts. In the third section the main elements of the literature of behavioural theory are outlined in an attempt to provide a critical perspective on decision-making practices. The concluding section focuses on a contemporary issue of interest to sociologists studying organisations, the context for most financial management, corporate culture. Part II concludes with a chapter on auditing which is viewed from an interactionist perspective. In section two the principal elements of role theory are outlined and in the following section these are applied to the practice of auditing. Among the issues which are considered in the course of these two sections are the socialisation of auditors, their role playing activities and the processual and negotiational aspects of audits. Many of the points which are raised should be comparatively easy to integrate into the main body of auditing thought. This should come as no suprise since auditing, like management accounting, is as much concerned with social, organisational and behavioural issues as it is with technical ones. The final section of the chapter discusses the prospects for internal auditing, a variant of auditing currently attracting a great deal of interest from management and which could emerge as a major branch of accountancy in its own right.

The concluding chapter of the text has three sections, the first of which is a summary of the main points raised in the previous chapters. The other two sections are in effect a pair of short, fairly quirky but no less valuable essays, one on accountancy, the other on sociology. The former is a response to the perfectly valid question of how does thinking about accountancy in this or any similar way help to make someone a better accountant? The essay on sociology is an attempt to demonstrate to sociologists the value of moving to a more insider type of role than one which seems content to observe and comment from the sidelines.

Part I

The sociology of accountancy

Chapter 1

The profession

The initial requirement of any study such as this is to provide a sociological analysis of the professional nature of modern accountancy. In the first section the professions and professionalisation are discussed in a general way and at some length. This provides a basis for considering the nature of the profession and its members. It is followed by a discussion of the organisation of the profession in the UK and abroad which focuses on the many institutes and associations of accountants. Recruitment and socialisation are considered in the third section, particular attention being paid to the educational and training experiences of student members. In the final section a light-hearted description of the public's image of the accountant is sketched out. This is subjected to some criticism in an attempt to highlight some of the points which have been made in the previous pages and to provide a broader basis for the rest of the text.

PROFESSIONS AND PROFESSIONALISATION

The sociology of the professions is a well-established field and as such it has attracted contributions from some of the discipline's major figures. In the past decade or so it may have become a little less productive (cf. Atkinson & Delamont, 1990) but nevertheless it has a rich and voluminous literature which can only be touched upon here. Many of the foundations were laid in the work of Emile Durkheim, one of the founding fathers of sociology at the turn of the twentieth century. In his view, professional organisations in the form of moral communities based upon occupational membership were a prerequisite for the process of orderly transition to a new social consensus (Durkheim, 1957). In his earlier works he had described the breakdown of the established order of central Europe in the wake of the rapid industrialisation of the later nineteenth century. He took the view that in order to avoid total social disintegration, a state which he termed *anomie*, a new form of social and moral order must be found (Durkheim, 1933). As he approached the end of his life he came to believe that professional ethics could serve as the fount of a new moral order. A similar view was embraced by the English social philosopher Tawney who saw in professionalism a major force which was capable of opposing the rampant individualism of the acquisitive society. He believed that the professions promised to advance the community interest and for this reason they should themselves be promoted (Tawney, 1921).

During the inter-war years commentators such as Carr-Saunders & Wilson (1933) and Marshall (1939) wrote approvingly about the contribution which such occupations were making to society. The twin themes of altruism, or other orientation, and the service ethic were widely addressed as the case for the professions grew stronger. For this reason it was hardly suprising that when the sociology of the professions began to emerge as a distinctive field within American sociology such occupations were characterised in a highly positive way. The twenty years following the end of World War II saw American sociology dominated by the structural-functionalist perspective which required the sociologist to study how the various structures or institutions of society were functional (or not functional) for the broader society. Any institution was a legitimate field of study and most attracted attention over time. Among these were the professions, of course, the objective being to demonstrate their functional relevance to society at both the general level and in the context of the professional–client relationship. Structural-functionalism's leading theorist, Talcott Parsons, was himself very interested in the professions, especially the medical profession, and as a result he discussed them on many occasions. He argued that they were of great importance to society because of their collectivity-orientation which he contrasted with the self-orientation which he believed characterised business and commerce (Parsons, 1954). At the level of practice Parsons drew attention to the way in which the professions give primacy to the valuation of cognitive rationality as applied to a particular field, a feature which he sees to be consistent with the functional imperatives which characterise modern societies (Parsons, 1968). The same issues were addressed by another structural-functionalist, Barber, who argued that it was because the professions recognised their importance to society but did not capitalise upon it that they were functionally relevant to society. By implication those occupations which were not so community-oriented were not accorded the same freedom of action as the professions and were not to be viewed as functionally relevant in the same way (Barber, 1963).

Most of the sociology of the professions produced during the 1950s and early 1960s did not assume this abstract theoretical form, however. Instead writers tried to explain why some occupations were viewed as professions, and some were not, by identifying the defining characteristics of a profession. This more middle-range approach to theorising about the professions is best seen as complementary to the general theory issuing from writers such as Parsons or Barber since it remains firmly within the structural-functional tradition. There are many examples of this sort of approach but perhaps the best known is that offered by Greenwood in 1957. In his view there are five defining characteristics of a profession, the first being that they have a basis in systematic theory. This implies that it requires a prolonged training process to develop a professional competence with the result that qualification as a practitioner normally occurs many years after leaving high school and only as a result of success in an extended formal examination programme. On the basis of this formal accreditation of competence the professional is recognised by the public to have the authority to practise in a particular field. Writing in the American context Greenwood has in mind the situation of licensing which exists on a much broader scale than in the UK. Recognised authority, the second characteristic of a profession, is embodied in a licence to practise in a particular field to the exclusion of all other parties. By implication only where an occupation attracts a licensing arrangement can it be described as a profession. The third characteristic identified by Greenwood is what he terms community sanction. By this he has in mind such situations as consenting to a doctor's request to remove one's clothing and to undergo an examination. Most people accede to such requests because they recognise the doctor's need to carry out examinations under such conditions. For Greenwood only a minority of occupations are accorded similar rights and privileges. Because such professions are in a position of possible exploitation it is necessary that they are responsible for policing their members. This is achieved by ensuring that all members are aware of and abide by the codes of ethics which true professions must have. So for Greenwood the possession of a code of ethics is the fourth characteristic of any profession. Finally he identifies that these codes constitute only a part, but a major part, of the culture of any profession. By a culture he has in mind the many dimensions of the lived experience of people in such occupations as medicine or law, the same characteristic which had attracted Durkheim's interest half a century earlier.

One of the implications of Greenwood's or similar trait models such as those of Cogan (1953) or Goode (1960) is that it might be possible for occupations to gauge just how professional they presently are and how it might be possible to improve the collective situation of practitioners. In the status conscious early 1960s this is more or less what happened in America, prompting a leading sociologist to discuss the possibility of everyone becoming professional to some degree. Wilensky's 1964 paper was both an extension and a critique of the existing characteristic of a profession literature. He identifies a typical sequence of events based on the development of eighteen occupations generally recognised as being professions – the *natural history of professionalism*. This history takes the form of a five stage process: initially a full-time occupation emerges and in time practitioners set up a training school of some description. The third stage sees the foundation of a professional association which begins to lobby in order to achieve the legal protection it recognises it will benefit from. Finally the association adopts a formal code which serves to guide its operations in the future. Wilensky then goes on to say that the passage of time has seen an increasing tendency for occupations in pursuit of professional status to depart from this sequence of events and that it is now of historical rather than contemporary interest. This is of relevance to the popular view that to some degree all occupations were becoming professional, a thesis which Wilensky wishes to refute. Drawing on the evidence of contemporary quests for professional status, he concludes that 'the whole effort seems more an opportunistic struggle for monopoly than a "natural history of professionalism"' (Wilensky, 1964, p. 157). At the same time many of the 'new' professional occupations do not have a great deal of autonomy nor exhibit much of a service ideal, irrespective of their intellectual integrity. This is particularly so for those occupations associated with large-scale organisations and bureaucracies. For all these reasons Wilensky concludes that it is unlikely that many occupations will be able to attain the status of the *established professions* and so the professionalisation of everyone is not about to happen.

Wilensky's paper was published at a time when a growing number of sociologists were becoming aware of the various problems entailed in the adoption of a structural-functional perspective for the study of society and its constituent parts. In the context of the professions it was already apparent to other writers that there was little value in attempting to generalise about them. After reviewing the work of twenty-one authors who had attempted to define the essence of the professions Millerson concluded that not one trait was common to all, nor did any two characterisations concur (Millerson, 1964). In the same year Rueschemeyer asked whether it was possible to talk in general terms about even medicine and law, the two most commonly cited professions. Three years earlier Bucher and Strauss had identified a number of divisions within the medical profession which they presented as being far from the united professional community implicit in the functionalist orthodoxy. These two writers were also leading figures in one of the alternative theoretical perspectives which was beginning to gain support in the early 1960s. Known as symbolic interactionism, the focus of this perspective was at the level of the individual rather than on the broader social whole (as in structural-functionalism) with particular emphasis upon the role played by signs, imagery, impression management, etc., in structuring social reality. Their paper was an example of the insight which this alternative perspective could provide. Other influential interactionist writers such as Becker (1962) and Hughes (1958) advocated a critical approach to the study of any profession. No longer should claims of altruism, community interest or commitment to the service ethic be taken at face value. These were powerful images or symbols which could be used in a variety of ways. Very soon students of the professions influenced by interactionism assembled a literature which served to debunk many professional claims and practices (e.g. Carlin, 1966; Freidson, 1970). This led one writer to describe any sociologist who chose to adopt a functionalist perspective on the professions as a 'dupe' of the established professions and thereby not performing much useful sociological analysis at all (Roth, 1974).

One of the most commonly identified negative practices of the professions, and at the same time a key factor in successful professionalisation, is the phenomenon of *social closure*. Introduced into the literature of sociology by Max Weber, social closure is the process whereby one social collectivity seeks to exclude other groups from access to some desirable reward. In the case of the professions social closure refers to the ways in which professions go about ensuring that potential competitors are excluded from performing particular categories of work and are thereby unable to obtain the rewards associated with that work (Parry & Parry, 1976). One of the key techniques of social closure is *credentialism* (Parkin, 1979). A credential is some formal measure of competence such as a professional qualification which is accepted as being the basis for performing certain sorts of work. If a profession is able to convince society that it is necessary to have a particular qualification in order to carry out certain work it can control access to that work and more significantly to the rewards associated with it. As well as excluding other groups, credentialism can also serve as a mechanism to restrict the supply of competent practitioners, a charge which has often been raised against the professions. Other writers interested in the relation of professions to the market have focused on the idea that the process of professionalisation can be understood as a *collective mobility project* which if successful can enhance the life-chances of individual participants in significant ways (e.g. Larson, 1977).

In his paper Wilensky talked of the established professions and of newer professions developing different structural forms. This line of analysis was later to be successfully pursued by several writers including Elliott and Johnson. Elliott (1972) identified two types of profession: *status professions* and *occupational professions*. The former are comparatively rare and in Elliott's view are unlikely to increase in number. They are long-established and tend to have had a history during which their contribution to society has become increasingly more focused. Whereas in earlier days members were men of letters and often offered a range of services, their counterparts offer specific but highly valued services. The status of these professions is based partly on their traditions and partly on their contemporary functions. By contrast the occupational professions are much more recent in their origins, many having been called into existence by the industrialisation process of the later nineteenth century. Both their modernity and specificity contribute to their lack of status. Many of the occupational professions may have grounds for expecting a much higher status but since status is accorded by the public it is their view which is crucial. This is why Elliott, like Wilensky before him concludes that there is little chance that many new status professions will emerge in the present day.

Johnson offered an analysis of the professions based on the existence of three different power relations involving the practitioner and the client (Johnson, 1972). The first is where the professional defines the needs of the client and the manner in which these needs are to be catered for. The practitioner is in control of the situation, and more significantly this control is accepted by the client. In order to ensure that this control is not misused such professions go to great lengths to police their members' activities. It is this *collegiate control* situation where the profession imposes a form of collective self-control that reassures the public that it will not suffer by accepting the loss of power entailed in any consultation with such practitioners. For Johnson this is the sort of arrangement which has given rise to much of the existing literature. It is not the typical situation of the professional although it was in the past. It is typified by the sole practitioner or small partnership arrangement characteristic of the legal and medical professions. At times Johnson comes close to concluding that these are the only true professions but in identifying two other forms of practitioner–client power relations he effectively identifies two further types. The first are those involved in the opposite form of relationship, where it is the client who defines both his/her needs and how these are to be met. There have been two principal variants of this relationship which Johnson terms *oligarchic* and *corporate patronage*. The former is associated with traditional aristocratic societies such as seventeenth and eighteenth century England or Renaissance Italy when the rich were the patrons of a range of individuals including artists, musicians, couturiers and on occasions architects and physicians.

Corporate patronage is the contemporary variant where it is the large-scale corporation which is the client and professionals such as engineers, systems analysts or, in Johnson's view, accountants, who perform the services as defined by clients. Most although not all of these practitioners are 'housed' professionals in the sense that they are employees of corporations and thereby involved in applying their expertise to 'local' corporate matters. They are employees rather than the independent practitioners associated with the exercise of collegiate control. Their numbers have increased rapidly with the growth of industry and more recently business and commerce. They have also become more manifold as new needs have been defined. In this way it is possible to see that Johnson's corporate professions are very similar to Elliott's occupational professions, both being significantly different from traditional, independent, (high) status professions. However, Johnson identifies a third form of practitioner–client power relation which he believes to be significantly different. Here the state is involved as a third party which mediates between the client and practitioner. This relationship of *mediative control* is exemplified in the case of a social worker: the client is the individual or family in need of support of some kind, to be provided by the professional social worker. Precisely what can and cannot be provided in the way of assistance is set out by the state and both parties must recognise this and abide by it. Their relationship is overseen by the state which prescribes the manner in which the professional is to work and the rights which individuals have to be assisted by such professionals. This arrangement is common to all state professionals including teachers, health visitors and the medical professionals employed within state health services such as the British NHS. Although these professionals are employees in the same way as corporate professionals, their employers are not their clients. Their situation is neither one of patronage nor collegiate control.

Johnson's typology offers a starting point for discussing what sort of profession contemporary accountancy is. In his view it is subject to corporate patronage, with a large proportion of accountants actually being employed in corporations while many independent firms carrying out auditing services are becoming increasingly dependent on a few large clients (Johnson, 1972, p.66). Industry, business and commerce certainly account for the greatest proportion of qualified accountants but in recent years a growing number have been employed in the public sector as it has expanded. The majority of these perform the same sort of work as their colleagues in the private sector. They are not state professionals in the sense that teachers or social workers are since they do not have relationships with clients which need to be mediated. For this reason they too can be designated corporate professionals who are subject to the patronage of their public sector employers. This still leaves those accountants who are engaged in public practice – should they also be designated as corporate professionals? Sole practitioners and partners in small public practice accounting firms have clients, are available for consultation on the same basis as lawyers or doctors in private practice and have similar power to control their relationships with their clients. While auditing is a major element of their work, and as a result may give rise to a situation which might formally be identified as patronage, in most cases it is likely that the practitioner controls the performance of this and the various other accounting services to clients. For these reasons collegiate control is still very evident in the public practice. This type of (chartered) accountant may not have quite the same status as doctors or lawyers but in the public's view it still ranks as a highly desirable occupation. The position of accountants working in the larger accounting firms is, however, less clearcut. While sole practitioners and partners in any public practice are involved in a traditional form of relationship with their clients, the individual accountants who carry out the work in larger practices do not have clients as such. Since they work for the firm they are in a situation little different to their counterparts in the public and private sectors, being identifiable as corporate professionals. However, they are corporate professionals who work in environments in which collegiate control is also strongly evident. In the following chapters these accounting roles and work experiences are subjected to much greater analysis.

The profession as a whole has long practised credentialism as an exclusionary social closure strategy. At the level of the profession as a whole there is a long history of protracted training periods, high examination standards, equally high failure rates and a steady turnover of aspiring accountants. There have been suggestions of the professional associations operating a quota system to restrict numbers and to retain for members their high levels of reward and attractive career prospects. There is certainly a shortage of accountants in the UK at the present time but rates of qualification do not appear to be increasing although the numbers involved certainly are. However, for much accounting work outside of public practice there is no reason why an individual must be qualified. This might be expected to give rise to an attack on the restrictive practices of the profession but only does so in a minimal way. Qualified senior accountants are still very unlikely to offer opportunities to individuals who are not qualified or in the process of qualification. To do so would be to commit a form of professional suicide. Alternatively, companies could choose not to employ any qualified accountants and avoid having to pay out high salaries to such people. For some reason few opt to do so, seeming to accept that a formally trained accountant is more likely to understand the mysteries of accounting than an MBA or business studies graduate. At the same time, simply being qualified is not an automatic passport to any job since some categories of accounting work are restricted to certain types of accountant. In the UK auditing can only be undertaken by appropriately qualified members of one of the three institutes of chartered accountants or by certified accountants. This is a case of intra-professional exclusion, these organisations having secured legal protection of their highly lucrative auditing work. Members who belong to other organisations cannot carry out audits unless they are also willing to qualify as members of one of the four. The main difference in the training programmes of the two groups is the extent of auditing studies (and experience) each prescribes, itself another form of credentialism. Finally, at the level of the individual vacant post, exclusionary forces are evident where an advertisement asks for a particular qualification often more in line with the preferences of the person who wrote it than the demands of the job.

These practices all say something about the ethics of the profession and the motivations of its constituent parts. The functionalist writers might not have viewed accountancy as a true profession but many people do, both inside and outside it. The reason for this difference of opinion may be that nowadays professional status is measured in personal financial terms rather than altruism or service to society. This is quite opposite to the view embraced by Durkheim who believed that self-interest, invariably the basis for financial success, and professionalism could never go together.

PROFESSIONAL ACCOUNTANCY ASSOCIATIONS

In a study of contemporary professional organisation Millerson (1964) identified four types of professional association. The first are those organisations which exist to confer status on their membership, the *prestige associations*. These are few in number and many of their members already have high statuses, prestige associations serving to increase this. It is not possible to join such an association, membership being by invitation, e.g. of the Royal Society with its highly prestigious FRS designation. *Study associations* are more numerous and individuals with the necessary qualifications can apply for membership. The principal function of these organisations is the pursuit of scholarly activities and for this reason they are common in the scientific field, an example being the Faraday Society of chemists. The third type of professional organisation is by far the most common nowadays, the *qualifying association*. Here the principal emphasis is on the education and training of the new members of a profession. Although the provision of vocational higher education has increased rapidly in the last thirty years most of these associations still retain their dominant role in the field of professional qualification. The professional accountancy associations are examples of this type as are the British engineering institutes.

The final type, the *protective association*, is comparatively uncommon in the professions, being concerned with the performance of a protective function similar to a trade union. One well known example actually is a trade union, the National Union of Teachers, but the most famous is not, the British Medical Association. Although any qualifying association can engage in a range of protective activities, their Royal Charters or constitutions normally forbid them from behaving in a union-like way. This is why in the late 1960s the British professional engineering associations formed a separate association, the United Kingdom Association of Professional Engineers (UKAPE), as a response to membership pressure for greater protection (Roslender, 1983a, 1983b). It is also one of the reasons why the various accountancy associations indicate to their members that association membership is not incompatible with membership of an appropriate trade union. Trade union membership among accountants is not common, which suggests that the ways in which the associations presently operate provide a sufficient degree of protection against third parties.

In Britain the qualification function is very pronounced among the various professional accountancy associations. One way in which this can be seen is in terms of the distinction between the primary and secondary register associations (Renshall, 1984). Six major bodies with a combined membership of fewer than 200000 presently constitute the primary register. These are the Institute of Chartered Accountants in England and Wales (ICAEW); the Institute of Chartered Accountants of Scotland (ICAS); the Institute of Chartered Accountants in Ireland (ICAI); the Chartered Association of Certified Accountants (ACCA); the Chartered Institute of Management Accountants (CIMA) and the Chartered Institute of Public Finance and Accountancy (CIPFA). All have established reputations for producing accountants of the highest calibre who are able to find employment throughout the world. These six associations also endow their individual members with high levels of professional status which is normally reflected in both their salaries and career prospects. The secondary register is constituted by organisations which have impressive names including the Association of International Accountants; the Society of Company and Commercial Accountants; the Association of Authorised Public Accountants and the Association of Cost and Executive Accountants. All offer a qualification of some description and in the past have proved particularly popular with foreign students. Although these qualifications have never been recognised by the international accounting community the existence and persistence of such organisations illustrates the importance of a qualification within the profession. These second register bodies should not be confused with several other bodies including the Association of Accounting Technicians (AAT), the Institute of Internal Auditors (IIA) and the Institute of Company Secretaries and Administrators (ICSA), each of which offers a qualification of recognised value.

By far the largest of the British associations is the ICAEW which as a result is often referred to as 'the Institute'. It currently has 84000 active members and 8000 retired members. The Institute received its Royal Charter in 1880 when its

membership was fewer than 600. It was formed by the amalgamation of four associations which had emerged in the previous decade in London (1870), Liverpool (1870), Manchester (1873) and Sheffield (1877). In 1885 a rival association was formed by accountants excluded from the Institute, the Society of Accountants which later became known as the Society of Incorporated Accountants (Willmott, 1986). In the early days the conflict between the two bodies was often hostile although they were aware of threats which other bodies posed to both of them. The Institute grew steadily in its first sixty years from 578 in 1880 to 2702 in 1900. In 1920 it had 5343 members and by 1940 this had increased to almost 14000. The Society had also attracted a sizeable membership many of whom were employed in the same sort of work as Institute members. During the next fifteen years both organisations experienced much slower growth as potential recruits found other careers open to them. This together with a fear that the public might begin to question the disunity of the profession was sufficient to persuade the two bodies to begin merger talks. The outcome was the winding-up of the Society in 1957, its 11335 members becoming Institute members. This was a successful stategy if subsequent growth is taken as an indicator: in 1960 membership of the new Institute numbered 33867 increasing to almost 50000 in 1970. In 1977 membership stood at 65362 rising to 71677 five years later and to a total of 91762 by 1989. Taking the active members alone the Institute accounts for half of the qualified membership of the six first register associations.

If the Institute is by far the largest of the six first register associations, the Scottish Institute has the distinction of being not only the oldest of them but also the world's first accounting association. Although the ICAS was only established in its present form in 1951, it dates back to January 1853 when the Society of Accountants was formed in Edinburgh. It was granted its Royal Charter in 1854 when it had 54 members. The following year saw the Glasgow Institute of Accountants and Actuaries gain its Royal Charter, the Aberdeen Society of Accountants emerging in 1867. It was these three organisations which amalgamated in 1951, with Glasgow and Aberdeen surrendering their Charters and the Edinburgh Society's name being changed to the ICAS. The Scottish Institute also has the distinction of having invented and adopted the designation 'CA'. Although all six organisations are now chartered bodies only the members of the ICAEW, ICAS and ICAI are entitled to term themselves 'chartered accountants'. And of these only Scottish Institute members can use the CA designation. Currently there are 12000 CAs and 1750 student members. Like all British accountants they are employed throughout the world. Although a much smaller organisation than the Institute, the ICAS has experienced a more impressive rate of growth in the past decade. It has long been recognised as a leading force in the development of professional education and training programmes. During recent negotiations regarding the possibility of a merger with the Institute the ICAS was extremely confident about not losing its identity despite its resultant minority status in such an organisation. In the event, while ICAEW members voted for the merger ICAS members rejected the proposal and look set to retain their independence for the foreseeable future.

The third of the institutes of chartered accountants is the Institute of Chartered Accountants in Ireland which received its Royal Charter in 1888. Its membership is drawn from both Northern Ireland and the Republic, the ICAI having offices in both Dublin and Belfast. During its first sixty years in existence membership grew very slowly standing at 443 in 1940. Twenty years later it had almost quadrupled in size to 1656 members. By 1980 it had again more than doubled its membership to 3880 and presently it has almost 7000 members together with 2000 students in training. Like the ICAS it is responsible through the Centre of Accounting Studies for all of the tuition which its student members receive in respect of their professional examinations. However, the ICAI has worked closely with the tertiary education sector to devise a set of educational programmes designed to maximise the benefits to be gained during both full-time pre-training study and a training contract. In general it seems to be the most radical of the three bodies, a characteristic which its director of education recently attributed to its modest size (Lynch, 1990).

The three institutes of chartered accountants presently share their monopoly of the audit function with the Chartered Association of Certified Accountants. Better known as the ACCA, the association traces its origins back to the London Association of Accountants founded in 1904 as a rival to both the Institute and the Society (Willmott, 1986). In 1938 the LAA joined forces with the Glasgow-based Corporation of Accountants which itself had been formed in 1891 as a rival to the Glasgow Institute. The name of the new organisation was the Association of Certified and Corporate Accountants (hence ACCA) which in 1941 became strengthened by a further merger with the Certified Public Accountants (1903) who had in 1932 amalgamated with the Central Association of Accountants (1905). In 1974 the ACCA dropped the reference to corporate accounting in its title, becoming simply the Association of Certified Accountants. It retained ACCA for its associate membership designation and did so again when it adopted the Chartered Association title in 1984. The ACCA has always sought to develop an international reputation and it is fully active in well over a dozen countries around the world. Among its activities is the provision of examination facilities which allow the indigenous population to study in their own countries, something which the other three organisations have never been able to do for logistic reasons. One consequence of this is that the ACCA has a massive student membership many of whom are based overseas. This student membership is also believed to be very dynamic in that it is constantly in flux with many new members joining each year and quite sizeable numbers drifting out of the Association without qualifying. Presently the ACCA has 36000 qualified members of whom around two-thirds are resident in the UK. It has well in excess of 75000 student members compared with the Institute's 17000. For this reason it is perhaps reasonable to conclude that the ACCA is *the* British qualifying association.

The Chartered Institute of Management Accountants was the name adopted by Britain's management accountants as they launched their new, more progressive image in January 1987. CIMA originated as the Institute of Cost Accountants Ltd in 1919 amid controversy and some acrimony, particularly on the part of the Institute who seemed suprisingly threatened by the rise of these 'cost clerks' (Loft, 1986). This name was soon changed to the Institute of Cost and Works Accountants by which it was to remain known until the mid-1970s when it was granted a new Royal Charter as the Institute of Cost and Management Account-ants. The ICWA grew steadily, having 830 members in 1930, 1430 in 1941 and almost 3300 in 1951. By 1971 membership had reached 12000 rising to over 19000 in 1980 and topping 25000 in 1985. Presently CIMA has around 30000 members and fellows; however, if its 'passed finalists' are included (being those who have completed only the examination programme and not their logbooks) its qualified membership would probably be greater than that of the ACCA, making it the second largest association. Like the ACCA it has a large student member-ship, currently in excess of 47000 (including passed finalists), and in recent years it has become more attractive to a wide range of intending accountants. One reason for this is the success with which it has projected itself since the CIMA concept was developed in the late 1980s. Of particular note has been the promo-tion of a wide-ranging management and professional development portfolio. Equally there has been a succession of salary surveys which indicate the longer term benefits of qualifying with CIMA. At this point in time at least, CIMA seems to be the most progressive of the six associations.

The Chartered Institute of Public Finance and Accountancy offers a pro-fessional training which is geared toward accounting in the public sector although it does not hold a monopoly position in such work. Its origins can be traced back to 1885 when a group of local government accounting specialists decided to establish a forum for discussing matters of common interest and concern. By 1901 the forum had become so successful that it was incorporated as the Institute of Municipal Treasurers and Accountants. In 1959 it was granted a Royal Charter which was to serve it until 1973. With a membership in excess of 8000 and in the context of a rapidly expanding public sector a Supplemental Charter was granted to the newly named CIPFA which permitted it to extend its established remit to the whole of the public sector. In the intervening years CIPFA has experienced a number of pressures the most obvious being the attack on the public sector after 1979. One consequence has been a steady increase in the number of retired CIPFA members since 1980, standing at 2000 in 1986 compared with around 8000 employed members in the same year. Conversely the number of student members has continued to rise in the 1980s. Today almost all of these students are home-based unlike in earlier times when the IMTA provided a range of facilities for training overseas. These were discontinued after the mid-1970s as the institute sought to develop its training programme for the broader UK public sector. As the 1980s drew to a close CIPFA looked set to continue to grow at a much more modest rate than its counterparts. This prompted its leadership to support a proposed merger with the Institute in 1990, the latter having already failed to merge with its Scottish counterpart a year earlier. The merger plans were rejected by the Institute's membership although subsequently the two organisations have agreed to establish a 'framework for cooperation'. So for the present even in the absence of a monopoly, CIPFA retains a significant grip on public sector finance and accountancy.

While no other country has so many major accounting associations several have at least two. In Canada most accountants are members of either the Canadian Institute of Chartered Accountants (CICA) or the Society of Management Accountants of Canada (SMAC). The former was founded in 1902 and has always had links with the Institute including a reciprocal membership scheme. Like the Society it is a federal body being constituted by provincial associations. At present it has 40000 members and 10000 students and like its British counterparts it is essentially a qualifying association. Management accountants formed their first association in 1919 calling it the Canadian Society of Cost Accountants. After a succession of name changes the Society adopted its present title in 1976 but retained its previous membership designation 'registered industrial accountant' until 1985 when members became 'certified management accountants'. There are 18500 CMAs together with 20000 student members, a balance which resembles CIMA's with whom SMAC liaises but has no reciprocal membership arrangement. A third, much smaller organisation also exists, the Certified General Accountants Association founded in 1908.

In Australia there are two associations one of which is practice-based, the Institute of Chartered Accountants in Australia (ICA), the other being both more broadly based and larger, the Australian Society of Accountants (ASA). The ASA was formed in 1952 as a result of the merger of the Commonwealth Institute of Accountants founded in 1886 and the Federal Institute of Accountants founded in 1894. With a current membership of 54000 the ASA is much bigger than the ICA which has around 16000 members. Although the ASA is a qualifying association like its British and Canadian equivalents, it is much less reliant on a formal examination system as a means of providing admission. Its comprehensive educational and development programmes will be reviewed in the next section. The ICA was founded by Royal Charter in 1928 and has always been an association of practising chartered accountants. The two organisations cooperate on a range of matters including the issue of public practice certificates to ASA members by the ICA and the reciprocal arrangement for ICA members to become certified practising accountants (AASA CPA) if they wish to develop their career in other branches of accountancy. The New Zealand Society of Accountants (NZSA) was created by an 1908 Act of Parliament. At that time there were two associations, both of which were well supported, the intention being to recruit from these and in time create a single unified association. In the case of the New Zealand Accountants and Auditors Association, founded in 1898, relations were generally amicable and in 1950 it merged with the NZSA. The Incorporated Institute of Accountants of New Zealand (1894) was less inclined to merge however, and it was only in 1972 after some further legislation on the part of the NZSA that it ceased to exist. In 1944 a third association had emerged, the New Zealand Institute of Cost Accountants, which was concerned to raise the standard of industrial accounting. It cooperated with the NZSA from the outset and when it was formally dissolved in 1966 it was simultaneously reconstituted as the cost and management accounting division of the Society. Membership of the NZSA stood at 14500 in 1987 having increased from 11400 in 1980 and 8800 in 1970.

The world's largest accounting association is the American Institute of Certified Public Accountants (AICPA) with over 260000 members and an estimated 100000 examination candidates each year. Founded in 1887 as the American Association of Public Accountants, the AICPA was known briefly as the Institute of Accountants in the USA. In 1917 it became the American Institute of Accountants, the name it retained after merger with the American Society of Certified Public Accountants in 1937. In 1957 its present name was adopted. Despite its size and influence, in order to practise in the USA it is necessary for AICPA members to register with the individual State Boards of Accountancy, an arrangement unknown in Britain. The National Association of Accountants is the next largest body with over 90000 members, many of whom are also CPAs. The NAA is principally a body of management accountants like CIMA or SMAC. A plethora of smaller associations also exists such as the 17000 strong National Society of Public Accountants most of whom are in private practice and are not CPAs. Alongside these is a distinctly study association, the American Accounting Association with a membership of 14000 many of whom are academics. The 'Triple A' does not perform a qualifying function, having been established to consider research and educational issues.

There is only one organisation of professional accountants in Japan, the Japanese Institute of Certified Public Accountants (JICPA). It was formed in 1949 as a result of the enactment of the Certified Public Accountants Law the previous year, a statute intended to ensure that Japan's professional accountant cadres compared favourably with those of the USA and the UK. In 1953 JICPA was incorporated under the Civil Code of Japan which still provided the opportunity for Japanese accountants to remain outside of the institute. However, after 1966 all accountants in public practice had to be CPAs which entailed that they had to be members of JICPA, and since most Japanese accountants are involved in this type of work, most are members. JICPA has had control of the professional training function since its inception and is very much a qualifying association. It also encourages post-qualifying education and has developed a programme of lectures and seminars to complement the provision which most of its members' employers have instituted on a voluntary basis. In recent years JICPA has been growing rapidly: in 1975 it admitted its 5000th member, in 1980 its 6000th. Five years later another thousand had been admitted and in 1988 membership stood at 8200 with an additional 1600 junior CPAs. Of these over 97% are employed in public practice with only a small number employed in private undertakings. This identity of accountancy with public practice is also the case in the broader

European context. It also results in smaller associations as compared with the ICAEW, CICA or ASA. In France the Ordre des Experts Comptables et des Comptables Agrees has a membership of no more than 11000 while its German and Dutch equivalents are only half this size. As Renshall points out, the meaning of public practice in these countries is more restrictive than in Britain and normally does not include taxation, management consultancy, or other services, the accountant normally being the performer of the traditional accountant and auditor functions (Renshall, 1984).

RECRUITMENT AND SOCIALISATION

Any individual who becomes an accountant experiences a process of *professional socialisation*. The same can be said of anyone who becomes a doctor, an engineer, or a probation officer. Indeed anyone who assumes an occupational role experiences a process of socialisation which results in the individual's embracing a particular occupational identity as an element of the broader occupational culture. Professional socialisation is only one variant of this commonplace social process which the vast majority of adults undergo during their lives. Individuals who fail to become what they set out to be, be it a toolmaker, teacher, or accountant, have not been able to cope with their occupational socialisation process in some way. Those who are successful, however, do not become identical in every respect; rather they have been able to integrate the demands of their chosen occupational role with their own individual human capital. Learning to be an accountant or any other type of specialist is only one aspect of an individual's *secondary socialisation* experience. Most people become spouses, parents, grandparents, etc., as well as house owners, members of clubs or societies, occasional sportsmen and so on. Once again few if any individuals are successful at everything they become involved with. The experience of failure is itself an important learning process which equips people for their future endeavours. In this way it is similar to the *primary socialisation* that all infants, children and adolescents experience in their early years. If there is a difference between the two, it is that in the case of the adult there is perhaps a little more freedom to choose which experiences to embrace, a privilege rarely extended to the young.

The traditional route to qualification as an accountant was from school to some form of apprenticeship, perhaps in a public practice office or in the accounts department of a company or local authority. It was the employer who was responsible for recruiting the aspiring accountant while the professional associations provided the means to formal qualification. The task of socialisation was shared between them with the employer introducing the young recruit to the world of practical accounting in a tried and tested way while the associations made progressively more demands on them in the examination room. The need to work and study at the same time was, arguably, the principal feature of the traditional socialisation process. On the one hand it was intended to inculcate a sense of responsibility in the individual while simultaneously introducing them to a culture of endeavour and application. The period of qualification was normally a lengthy one and failure was (and remains) commonplace. Once qualified it was expected that the individual would then continue to follow a career in the profession which in turn would involve extensive participation in the socialisation of succeeding generations of accountants. It is still possible to follow this route in the case of the ACCA and CIMA but it is now necessary to have some form of post-school accountancy qualification to become a student member of the other four associations. Coupled with the increased opportunities to take a degree in the past twenty-five years, the profession as a whole has become increasingly characterised by its graduate entry.

It is not possible nor would it be desirable to become a qualified accountant without a period of appropriate employment experience. In the case of the English, Scottish and Irish institutes, it is necessary for a graduate to obtain a training contract with a recognised firm of accountants. Following the success of the pilot scheme introduced by the Irish institute in 1983, both the ICAEW and the ICAS are proposing to introduce the Training Outside Public Practice (TOPP) initiative in 1991. In the case of the ICAEW and ICAS a training contract is normally for three years during which time the necessary examinations are taken and, hopefully, passed. The situation with the ICAI is slightly more complex. Three year contracts are available to graduates who have then gone on to take one of several post-graduate diplomas in accounting. Without the latter the contract will extend for an extra six months. As an incentive, the possession of a diploma reduces the burden of the professional exams to be taken during training. Four year contracts are still available in association with the ICAEW and ICAI to those without degrees. In both cases it is necessary for the school-leaver to complete a pretraining or commencement course which in the Irish context normally extends to two years nowadays. Thirty per cent of ICAI students are non-graduates as compared with 10% in the case of the English Institute while in Scotland only a tiny minority of students do not have a degree.

If a graduate has a 'relevant' degree, one which has a curriculum acceptable to a chosen institute, then only two sets of examinations are taken. In the case of ICAEW students these are PE1 and PE2 while ICAS students face the Test of Professional Competence parts 1 and 2. By contrast, an ICAI student with a 'good' business degree and a post-graduate diploma in accounting faces only the Final Admitting Examination, although this cannot be taken until two years into a contract. Possession of any other type of degree necessitates satisfying the ICAEW or ICAS examiners in some form of foundation or conversion course from which varying exemptions may be gained depending on how much, if any, relevant study has previously been undertaken. So an aspiring chartered account-ant with a degree in music will have three sets of examinations to pass in three years as well as learning the practical side of the profession. Traditionally it has been possible to ease this load slightly by taking a one year conversion course before looking for a training contract. This gives a graduate with a non-relevant degree a chance to catch up and to compete with those in possession of relevant degrees on a more equal basis. However, the financial pressures which now exist on young graduates inevitably mean that the extra year is a costly venture. More and more graduates take on the burden of three years of professional study with the view to qualification at the earliest possible time. All three institutes allow their students some opportunity to retake failed examinations, although there are fixed time limits. As a result the three year training contract can become just that with a partly qualified chartered accountant in a situation of professional limbo, ever conscious of the need to pass the examinations while falling behind in the career stakes. Success in final examinations together with the satisfactory completion of the training requirement allows the student to use the title chartered accountant. A further period of post-qualification training is required before a practising certificate is awarded which empowers the holder to audit company accounts, i.e. to sign audit reports.

CIPFA's education and training system is similar in form if not in content, being distinctly public sector oriented. A graduate with a relevant degree is required to follow a three year training programme which is approved by the institute. During this time three sets of examinations are attempted although provision exists for individuals to obtain some exemptions if they can demonstrate the necessary level of competence. Those with 'specially relevant' degrees sit only the final examinations and can become full members after completing two years of approved service. Provision exists for those with accounting or cognate degrees to obtain subject exemptions at levels 1 and 2, while non-relevant degree holders must successfully complete a graduate conversion course before beginning their three years of formal training. Non-graduates may enter training by successfully completing the institute's foundation course or they may offer an alternative equivalent qualification such as an HND in accounting. CIPFA monitors the training of all its students very closely and has as one element of its final examination programme a project which the student carries out in the context of their own organisation. In this way the two aspects of the student's professional socialisation are arguably more fully integrated than is the case for their chartered accountant counterparts.

Both the ACCA and CIMA provide the school leaver with the opportunity to work and study for the entirety of their professional socialisation. This involves the student in a tortuous programme of private study, correspondence courses or perhaps day release as the means to qualification. At the same time both associations also permit the greatest divorce between work and study since it is possible to follow full-time courses in polytechnics and similar institutions which prepare students for final level examinations. In order to gain full associate membership, however, it is necessary to demonstrate three years of acceptable employment experience with further training for a practising certificate. In recent times an increasing number of student members of the ACCA and CIMA have opted for the middle way, entering employment after taking HNCs, HNDs or degrees, relevant or otherwise, and gaining a measure of exemption in the examination programme. They have decided to complete their examinations by part-time study while gaining the necessary employment experience required for associate membership. CIMA is currently debating the value of a predominantly graduate entry, following the Scottish and English institutes. If this becomes a matter of policy CIMA will in all probability also adopt a standard three year training programme with qualification at 24. Conversely, the ACCA has recently reaffirmed its commitment to open entry by promoting an open learning programme in association with the Open College. This is consistent with its being the most qualification oriented of the British accounting associations as outlined in the previous section. However, in the home market it seems inevitable that an increasing proportion of ACCA student members will use the Association to complete their professional qualifications having spent some time in further or higher education. This in turn will result in the majority of the ACCA's UK new members qualifying in their early twenties with three years of practical experience in line with their counterparts from the other five associations.

Qualification at the age of 24 after periods of both full-time and part-time study and a programme of on-the-job training has its benefits and, of course, its costs. On the positive side a growing number of young accountants will have been studying accounting for a minimum of six years. And those who have taken a degree of any sort should possess the sort of outlook which a successful career in accountancy increasingly demands. The downside is that the study element of the socialisation process has been divorced from the training element for up to half of the six year period, and more significantly in most cases it is the requirement to study which has been experienced first. By the time the aspiring accountant is in the final stages of secondary education, passing examinations in order to move on to the next stage will have become a fact of life. The experience of a further period of examination-oriented study to take a degree or diploma will only serve to reinforce the impression that passing examinations is what qualification is about. When the new recruit begins to learn the practical aspects of accountancy the professional examinations are both a known and an unknown quantity. They are known in the sense that they are consistent with previous experience, and in particular the culture of skimming, cramming, satisfying examiners, etc. The unknown is how to manage this and work at the same time. In theory maturity should play a major role here since the individual is now twenty or so years old. In practice it may well be too late since they are so used to a one-dimensional existence that they will not be able to accommodate quickly enough. This goes some way towards explaining the persistence of high initial failure rates among graduate entrants to the profession in recent times. It is not that they are intellectually weaker than previous recruits to the profession. Nor is it simply a case of a mismatch of their abilities and the technical skills which the professional examinations continue to test. The problem lies in the difficulties associated with replacing a well-established professional socialisation process with one which appears more substantial but which in fact abandons the basis of previous success.

Those who are able to come to terms quickly with their new circumstances tend to do so in a fairly standard way. They work hard as a matter of course with excessive attention to time-management. It seems as though little time is misused which in many ways reflects the adage often cited in respect of accountants that time is money. As far as the professional examinations are concerned it is normal to see the worst features of learning almost universally practised. Reliance on study manuals and question and answer books rather than conventional textbooks is extensive. Revision schools, rote learning, question spotting, cue cards, staying up all night, etc., are all commonplace (cf. Power, 1988). In the same way as this wordprocessor stores these paragraphs in its memory for as long as it is switched on (unless they are purposefully saved) so the various knowledges needed to pass particular examinations are learned and quickly forgotten. Failure is accepted almost as a matter of course and resitting examinations part of the price to be paid for a lucrative career in the longer term. Total failure can occur in the case of chartered accountants if they run out of time. They may choose to switch to the (supposedly easier) ACCA or CIMA where the time limits are more relaxed, students being able to take their examinations until their funds run out or their employer's patience does.

On the work front few concessions are made regarding shorter hours or less work while studying. Where day release is provided it is usual to find students doing five days work in four and if necessary working the designated day. Block release and study leave, as provided to trainee chartered accountants, normally means only this with students working right up to and following the designated periods with heavy overtime being commonplace. The content of much of the work is generally consistent with the overall situation. In the case of many chartered and certified accountants very routine auditing work is the staple diet which serves to fill the gaps between examinations. By comparison the challenge of a night wrestling with a couple of past examination questions is understandably appealing. The socialisation of auditors will be considered in more detail in Chapter 8. At the same time, the last thing a finalist wants is a highly demanding job which will result in a further reduction in the limited time available for study. It is for this reason that outside of public practice it is not uncommon to find senior accountants who are part-qualified but whose professional expertises are commensurate with their levels of seniority. Their case demonstrates that although the traditional process of professional socialisation was generally successful and has many lessons for the present day, it was not without its own inherent problems.

THE PUBLIC'S IMAGE OF THE ACCOUNTANT

In this section the British public's image of the accountant is set out in a fairly light-hearted way and then subjected to critical enquiry. The purpose of the exercise is to highlight some of the points which have been made in the previous sections and to provide a broader foundation for the rest of the text. The following description is intended to be neither entirely accurate nor exhaustive. However, it is offered in the belief that it does reflect the way in which many members of the public view accountants and also because it provides a useful means to extend the analysis of the modern accountancy profession which has been developed in the previous three sections. Five interrelated elements of the accountant's public image can usefully be identified: accountants are chartered accountants; as individuals accountants tend to be rather conservative; in their employments accountants are powerful and influential figures; invariably accountants are hard working and well-rewarded; and finally, accountants are usually men. Each of these elements will now be scrutinised.

The identity of accountants as chartered accountants is hardly suprising given that well over half of the qualified accountants in Britain are of this designation. At the same time few people can be unfamiliar with the traditions of public practice and the chartered accountants employed there. The low public visibility of the ACCA coupled with its traditional association with public practice inevitably makes it hard for the public to distinguish 'certified' from chartered accountants. Public sector accountancy and CIPFA are equally unknown quantities with the much-publicised need for this sector to adopt a more conventional approach to financial management only serving to further blur any distinction between accounting in this sector and in general. The term 'in general' is of crucial significance: what is meant by it? If only half of qualified ICAEW members, 30% of qualified ICAS members and 26% of qualified ACCAs are currently employed in public practice it certainly does not mean this sector. At least 60% of accountants are to be found in industry, commerce and finance engaged in a wide variety of jobs some of which may resemble chartered accountancy but most of which certainly are quite different. The acceptance of TOPPs programmes by both the Scottish and English institutes is further evidence of the limited value of the accountant/chartered accountant identity in the years to come. Within public practice there is a growing differentiation of accounting functions as various management consultancy, project management, recruitment and information technology specialists take their place alongside the establishment of auditors, tax planners and insolvency practitioners. An increasing number are not qualified chartered accountants, something which no longer debars them from assuming partner status. On these various grounds, it may be concluded that whatever basis there may have previously been for identifying accountants as chartered accountants, the future value of the identity is extremely suspect.

Most people view accountants as individuals in a very uncomplimentary way. They are seen as dull, boring, flat, unexciting, grey, rather conservative people. This is very much how they were portrayed in a classic sketch by the Monty Python team in which just such a character seeking a new career as a lion-tamer undergoes an assessment to be told that he has precisely the qualities necessary to be an accountant. The joke is that he is in fact an accountant already. In another sketch this image is reinforced when John Cleese points out that being an accountant he has no opinion. More generally, many of the accountants seen on television, a major source of imagery, are still pretty close to this identikit picture. They look rather old and grey, dress in highly conventional ways and generally speak in a reserved, monotonous fashion which is unlikely to provoke much enthusiasm in the listener. It would be difficult to deny that the profession itself does not seek to promote such an image to some degree. Qualities such as integrity, caution, exactitude and pragmatism are commended to trainees (Hastings & Hinings, 1970). But it also encourages them to be independent and objective at all times, to develop an inquiring mind and a critical outlook and generally to adopt a thorough approach to any work they are called upon to do. Sociologists interested in the study of science and the development of scientific knowledge have long since drawn attention to the highly positive value of these latter qualities in scientists (Merton, 1973). If scientists are viewed very favourably by the public, why not accountants displaying the same approach to their work? A major part of the explanation is that while science with its laboratories, experiments and discoveries is perceived as a glamorous, exciting world, accountancy with its book-keeping, financial controls and penny-pinching ethics is not. This is not an accurate image of modern accountancy of course, but it is one which most people have of it and of the sort of individuals who perform it. Only when its true nature, and variety, is established will it be possible to begin to dispel the rather conservative image which the public has of accountants.

If accountants are viewed as being fairly innocuous in themselves, by contrast in their employments they are viewed as powerful and influential people. Irrespective of the negative view the public has of the nature of the work they undertake, it has great significance in the broader order of things. Companies are believed to be run by accountants who decide on plant closures, cost cutting programmes and investment proposals; they devise budgets and monitor their operation, determining subsequent adjustments and amendments; and on a more personal basis it is accountants who normally agree expense claims. In short, what accountants say usually goes is a truism in modern corporate life. The foundations of the power and influence of accountants lie not in their personal or professional qualities but in the value which senior management place on the information which accountants provide. If senior management are considering the closure of a particular plant they will ask their accountants to provide them with the financial information necessary to make the decision. When the decision is made managers use the accountants' information to *legitimate* their actions. From the outside it can appear that the information is the basis for the decision, whereas on many occasions senior management have already made their decision and simply use the information to explain or underscore it. Where senior management themselves are from an accounting background, a situation which is common in the UK, they will be predisposed to favour accounting solutions to their commercial problems. This situation is less likely to give rise to possible conflicts between the accounting and finance function and senior management, and logically may lead to an enhanced role for accountants. It also begs the question why have accountants become so powerful and influential in the first place? The answer is that they have always been able to provide the sort of information necessary to legitimate the actions of senior management and in turn realise the interests of shareholders (Armstrong, 1985). It is interesting to contrast this situation with that which has characterised West Germany in the post-war years. Here science, engineering and technology have been much more influential in shaping the nation's culture. Senior management is widely permeated by individuals with such educational and professional backgrounds. There are comparatively few accountants employed in industry and those who are invariably find themselves viewed as book-keepers. It need hardly be added that in Germany accountants are not regarded as powerful and influential professional employees (Child, Fores, Glover & Lawrence, 1983).

Accountants are renowned for their capacity for hard work, something which they experience as soon as they undertake their professional training and which seems to stay with them for the rest of their working lives. In the public's view they are very well rewarded for their efforts, being able to command high salaries and receive attractive perks in comparatively secure positions. Generally speaking the public is properly apprised of their situation. According to one of the major recruitment firms, a newly qualified chartered accountant in public practice can expect to earn around £25000 in London at the present time while someone with four years post-qualifying experience can expect a minimum of £29000. If the same individual immediately moves to industry or commerce on qualification both salaries are likely to be marginally enhanced. CIMA and ACCA members can expect to earn a little less on qualification but should catch up in the next four years. In the case of the young Scottish CA, public practice offers about £16000 on qualification and industry or commerce £19000. CIMA and ACCA members again have to content themselves with a little less at first, catching up over the next four years. As a result employment in London will still provide an extra £5000 p.a. along with a greater likelihood of a company car, private health care, a mortgage subsidy, a share participation scheme and pension provision. The only employment package plus on the Scottish scene is the greater provision of bonuses. These are obviously heavily aggregated figures and it is interesting to compare them with the appointments pages of both the accountancy press and the national and local newspapers. Better still, talk to well-qualified, experienced accountants who are looking for new jobs about the salaries on offer for those situations which are genuinely vacant. Between the two extremes of Scotland and London there is a range of variation with salaries tending to rise as one moves further south. Most accountants will also agree that the general quality of life also tends to deteriorate the further south you go nowadays: traffic jams, long distance commuting, densely packed housing estates, the erosion of the green belt and a general lack of solitude. None of this is likely to improve in the short term which means that to compensate it will be necessary to increase the regional salary differentials of accountants still further, perhaps even to the point where it will no longer be economic to employ such expensive labour. But will any alternative be available?

Finally, having this far studiously avoided using the term 'he' when talking about the accountant, it is fair to say that in the popular image accountants are usually men. This is not hard to understand when the extant female membership of the profession is reviewed. In the case of the ICAEW, ICAS, ICAI and CIPFA this presently stands at 10–11%. CIMA admitted its one thousandth female member as recently as 1986, women currently accounting for less than 7% of membership. The ACCA has marginally the highest level of female members, standing at 12% in 1988. By comparison the average female membership of the professions in the UK presently averages 17.5%. It is also interesting to note that over half of the 'home' membership of the Association of Accounting Technicians are women. On the other hand female representation among student membership is very much higher having risen dramatically in recent years. The ICAEW reports that almost a third of its students are now female as were 31% of its new admissions in 1989. The ICAI has a 30% female student membership while the ICAS claims that in recent years around 40% of those in training are women. CIPFA has a similar level of female students which is still rising.

Despite this impressive change in women's participation in the accountancy profession, they are unlikely ever to be more than a sizeable minority unless men decide to abandon it for some reason. This seems highly unlikely in general but what already appears to have happened is that men have gifted some of the least rewarding jobs in the profession to their female colleagues. As in most other professions a sexual division of labour is becoming evident (Wainwright,1984). In a recent paper Humphrey, Kirkham & Ciancanelli (1990) demonstrate that while 26% of male ICAEW members were partners in public practice only 12% of women fell into this category. Conversely 34% of female members were employees in public practice as compared with only 13% of men. And while 42% of men were employed in industry and commerce (cf. 26% women), 26% of women were engaged in 'other work' (cf. 8% men). The implication is that while three-fifths of female ICAEW members are presently consigned to lower status jobs only one-fifth of the men are there with them. Further analysis of the data suggests that although in their early years men and women are more equally distributed between the different types of work, it is the men who succeed in making their careers away from the less prestigious, more routine functions of the accountancy profession. The fact that many more women are being trained as accountants now takes on a broader significance. Why are they being recruited? Is it because the men available are now so academically weak that women must (grudgingly) be drafted in to replace them which in time should result in more women assuming senior positions in the profession? Or is it more a case of 'room at the bottom' rather than at the top. Is the nature of much accounting work changing such that many of the new, less demanding and rewarding jobs will be admirably suited to highly qualified women with a need for part-time/flexi-time employment to accommodate their child-rearing responsibilities, leaving the best jobs, careers and the control of the accountancy profession in the hands of their male colleagues?

Chapter 2

Contemporary accounting roles

In the previous chapter attention was focused on the broader accounting profession. The nature of the professions was discussed first with a number of points of contact between accountancy and the professions being established. Attention then turned to the various bodies which have emerged in Britain and internationally to organise the profession. Particular interest was focused on the growth of these institutions in recent years and in the case of the UK bodies, on their current recruitment, educational and socialisation practices. The broad anatomy of the profession established, the chapter concluded with a brief and necessarily selective analysis of the image of the profession in contemporary Britain. Of the many points which this wide-ranging introductory chapter raised, perhaps the most useful one to begin exploring further is the diversity of the modern profession. In the following sections accounting in public practice, in industrial and commercial organisations and in the public sector are all reviewed, the chapter concluding with some consideration of the emergence of the accounting technician role.

PUBLIC PRACTICE: TRADITION AND CHANGE

Traditionally accountants have always worked in public practice, a slightly misleading term in that many of the practices which accountants carry out there are anything but public. Just to confuse things, the equivalent term for similar medical work is 'private practice' which in the British context differentiates it from the public medical work undertaken by doctors in the National Health Service. Even more confusingly, the term public in the context of accounting practice is used in the same sense as it is in the context of the British education system where 'public schools' are an institution in the fee-paying sector which has existed alongside the State system since the major reforms of the later nineteenth century.

Public practice is the recognised domain of chartered accountants in Britain with about half of the ICAEW's active membership currently employed there, 60% of them being either sole practitioners or partners. Admittedly the proportion of Scottish and Irish chartered accountants employed in practice is rather lower although it is still greater than the ACCA's 26%. Comparatively few

CIMA or CIPFA members are found in public practice offices due mainly to their present non-acceptability in British company law as auditors, a crucial element of much practice work. Traditionally individuals with such backgrounds had subsequently qualified as chartered (or certified) accountants although this is no longer so necessary in view of the changing nature of public practice work. As well as auditing, public practice has always encompassed a great deal of basic financial accounting work including the preparation of accounts for small businesses together with taxation services and the provision of financial planning advice to clients. Another aspect of practice is the insolvency function. Although long established, it accounts for no more than a thousand specialist practitioners at the moment. In recent years a growing number of accountants employed in public practice have found themselves involved in the much broader sphere of management consultancy, a development which has brought them into competition with non-accountants. This promises to be an area with significant growth potential but one which necessarily involves a move away from the basics of financial accounting. At present, however, it is fair to conclude that as well as being the domain of chartered accountants, public practice still entails a vast amount of essentially financial accounting work although the situation is showing some signs of change.

Under current British company legislation all limited companies of whatever size together with other business entities such as charities, trusts, trade unions and friendly societies are required to have an annual audit when their accounts are subject to scrutiny by a qualified accountant who is independent of the enterprise. While only one in six of ICAEW members in practice currently claim to be active solely as auditors, there is every reason to believe that auditing is still the most common work engaged in by public practitioners, especially those in early career. Auditing remains a financially attractive proposition for those who engage in it, which is the principal reason why the four British institutes whose members are able to act as auditors are anxious to retain their monopoly of this work. There have been suggestions that some of the Big 6 are concerned about the returns on their auditing labours but at least one of the more powerful of them believes that a good auditing image can only result in attracting a greater proportion of the more profitable business.

The origins of auditing are normally traced back to ancient Egypt but in the form of an independent scrutiny, the essence of present-day auditing, they are a result of the rise of the joint stock company from Elizabethan times onwards. Such ventures involved the investment of money by individuals seeking a handsome return on their stake, the task of providing this being left to what are nowadays called directors who had often conceived of the venture and were in need of extra funds. The task of preparing whatever financial statements were provided fell to the directors with the inexpert shareholders very much in the dark. Not surprisingly the early history of the joint stock company was one of scandals and swindles, the South Sea Bubble affair of 1720 being the most spectacular incident. As industrialisation quickened pace in the second half of the eighteenth century, the sums invested became much larger and the risks of misappropriation greater. Pressure for statutory controls grew and after more damaging frauds the Joint Stock Companies Act 1844 included the requirement that all incorporated companies must have their annual financial statements audited in the interests of fairness to shareholders. No specified form of audit was mentioned nor was it laid down that they had to be carried out by professional accountants. The most common practice was for shareholders to elect from amongst their numbers an auditor who was called upon to provide a 'full and fair view' of the balance sheet as well as to detect the existence of any frauds. The Companies Act 1856 removed the compulsion to have an audit but introduced a model set of articles of incorporation which included a balance sheet format and a series of audit requirements. Company directors could substitute their own articles but this might make attracting funds difficult and besides, shareholders had quickly become accustomed to the protection afforded by the previous act. Adopting the provisions of the 1856 Act and those of a second act six years later virtually necessitated the employment of a professional accountant, the latter act being known as 'the accountants' friend'.

Between 1862 and the reintroduction of the compulsory annual audit in the Companies Act 1900 the standards of auditing and accounting had risen so that while the profession did not yet possess a legal monopoly of the audit function, the annual review of the balance sheet and the underlying records of a company was increasingly coming to it. In that year Ernst and Whinney derived over half of their total income from such work. It was to be almost a full half century before the profession was granted a monopoly of the work of auditing the annual financial statements of all companies. The Companies Act 1948 required that audits be performed by qualified professional accountants, the Board of Trade being the government department which determined the precise nature of qualification. It was only in the Companies Act 1976, however, that the Department of Trade mentioned by name for the first time the three institutes of chartered accountants together with the ACCA as the only bodies whose members were recognised in law as being able to carry out auditing work (together with two smaller groups of practitioners). The 1948 Act itself instituted several changes which in part explain the emphasis on formal qualification. A profit and loss statement was now to be presented along with the balance sheet. All published accounts were now to contain a minimum level of financial information disclosure. Where appropriate, group accounts were to be produced for the first time. Finally, as might be expected, the duties, powers and responsibilities of the auditor were clearly laid down for the first time, the emphasis being upon the quality of a company's published results rather than on the detection of error or fraud. It was this act which first required the auditor to form an opinion as to whether these accounts offer a 'true and fair' view of a company's situation. Subsequent acts in 1967 and 1976 were concerned in part with amplifying or extending the provisions of 1948, further strengthening the position of the auditor. The most recent Companies Act 1989 is more concerned with the regulation of the auditor. Improvements in the education and training of auditors are being sought, the four accounting bodies being designated 'recognised supervisory bodies' to achieve this objective. And for the first time 'bodies corporate' are empowered to perform audits, provided that they are controlled by suitably qualified persons. The broader implications of these changes have been fully appreciated by all concerned.

As long as there is a statutory requirement for an annual audit those empowered to perform such work have a captive market. It is a very lucrative market since there are no restrictions on fees although the existence of competitors, be they other public practitioners or bodies corporate, does provide some measure of protection for companies which cannot readily afford to pay escalating fees. It would be no defence for an outgoing auditor to reveal to a new auditor that the reason for not being re-appointed was the client's concern with the level of fee being sought, if this were excessive. The full extent of market captivity is best illustrated in the case of the small to medium size client company. While large corporations probably use accounting firms for little other than their statutory audit and a measure of management consultancy, many small companies are not in a position to carry out much of their own general accounting. Since they must become associated with professional accountants for an audit, other services could follow not least because of the convenience factor. Hence the view noted earlier about the value of a good audit image. There is presently no limitation placed upon the auditor, as a professionally qualified accountant, also performing a range of accounting services for audit clients. It is assumed that the professionalism and associated personal qualities of the individual will ensure the proper performance of the various tasks. Any conflicts of interest will be resolved in an objective fashion. The preparation of the necessary financial statements is the most obvious additional service which may be undertaken, which task usually involves the accountant in translating the rudimentary in-house records into the standard formats required by law. The performance of this function will inevitably inform the view that proper records are in fact kept, something which is covered in the audit specification. However, any competent accountant should suggest to a client early in their association that the maintenance of proper books of account is in the interests of all parties. As part of this work the accountant will become involved in preparing the information required for taxation purposes. This in turn shades into the advisory function where clients may be encouraged to make the fullest use of available taxation benefits or have explained to them the fuller financial implications of plans which they might wish to pursue. Such advice may extend far beyond the boundaries of (financial) accounting as the practitioner becomes involved in consultancy of a more general nature regarding, for example, the introduction of manufacturing technology and information systems, the development of staff, formulating business strategies or the financial restructuring of entire companies.

This multifaceted service to small to medium size clients has certainly been the traditional image of public practice, especially in the case of small accounting firms, and explains why over 60% of ICAEW members in practice claim to be engaged in 'general practising services'. It has many positive features. The work is likely to be varied, producing a succession of challenges and new experiences, depending on the client base of course. This is particularly so in the case of the open-ended consultancy role. The financial rewards involved are potentially very attractive supplementing those which come from the far less appealing but 'bread and butter' audit activity. At the same time the small accounting firm providing a consultancy service faces a downside. The number of problems or questions which clients have is rising while the solutions become more complex. The amount of information necessary to provide a satisfactory sevice to clients is probably beyond the comprehension of the small numbers of staff involved. The consequences of providing poor advice have also to be borne in mind although this applies equally to all aspects of a firm's activity. Pressures such as these are likely to cause many small firms to tread warily in these new and expanding areas even to the extent of taking on more auditing and basic accounting work than they might otherwise do.

Up to this point very little has been said about the minority side of public practice in terms of numbers employed but the dominant force in terms of public image and fees paid – the large firms. Recent history has seen the Big 9 become the Big 8 and now the Big 6 through a series of much-publicised mergers but beyond these massive corporations there are many more large accounting firms with multi-million pound turnovers and sizeable staffs. All make a great deal of their money from providing their auditing services to the entire spectrum of clients but currently it is management consultancy (and insolvency) which is showing the greatest growth. The basis for their success in this sphere is the availability of funds to develop and support the necessary range of specialist consultancy services which they have sold to clients old and new. Increasingly life in one of the large firms, after qualification, is as a specialist. This is really nothing novel since they have always provided careers for accountants in auditing, taxation, insolvency, financial planning, etc. Nowadays the range has simply expanded to include such specialisms as information technology management, personnel recruitment, project management, financial management, external training and in some cases what might best be termed cost and management accounting. One consequence has been the necessity to recruit growing numbers of staff who have no auditing nor indeed formal accounting training to work alongside those trained in-house who have somehow managed to avoid a career in auditing or taxation.

Some of those involved have already recognised the difficulties that these changes will result in in the long term. The large firms are likely to remain under the control of senior partners from the auditing establishment. Career progression in the broader organisation is likely to be restricted although the rewards available as specialists are likely to remain attractive. This reflects the importance which both buyer and seller will continue to place on a broadening range of consultancy services. In their day-to-day work these specialists can expect to find themselves making limited inputs into the efforts of the multidisciplinary teams who increasingly provide consultancy services. Worse still is the possibility of having to sell clients the latest 'product' which the firm has developed. In many ways the fate of the management consultant in a large firm will be little different to that of the career auditor. The solution? Abandon public practice to set up small specialist consulting firms known in the financial press as 'boutiques' which operate on the basis of the old adage that small is beautiful. These should complement the existing ranks of small general accounting practice firms, leaving the highly lucrative auditing function to the big battalions who have worked so hard to control it. Some things change, some stay the same!

INDUSTRY AND COMMERCE: THE FORMALISATION OF ACCOUNTING

In Britain the greatest number of accountants work in this sector or more correctly, group of sectors. It includes manufacturing industry, the traditional base of the country's economy, commerce with its established retail, banking and insurance industries all of which have grown rapidly in recent years both in size and diversity, plus the service industries whose boundaries appeared to extend daily in the enterprise culture of the late 1980s. Although mention of the latter brings to mind small-scale operations and contemporary notions such as customised services and added value, the general pattern of development of the manufacturing, retailing, banking, leisure industries, etc., has been the emergence of large-scale organisations, groups and holding companies, and multinational corporations. In this respect many accountants in industry and commerce find themselves employed in environments quite different to those traditionally associated with public practice. More significantly, these accountants are normally involved in the performance of activities which in many senses are only formally related to those of the public practitioner. For this reason it is desirable to use the term *corporate accounting* to distinguish the work of accountants in industry and commerce from that of accountants in public practice. The intention of the following paragraphs is to provide a very general outline of the nature of corporate accounting and in particular to draw attention to the ways in which it has been *formalised*, resulting in the work itself being concerned with the application of what are termed *accounting formulae*.

In discussing public practice it was suggested that traditionally at least it was the home of chartered accountants and financial accounting and that to date both management accounting and management accountants had played only a very minor role in this work. It must not be imagined that by contrast industry and commerce are the sites for the practice of management accounting nor the domain of those with a formal qualification in that branch of accounting. The number of ICAEW members who work in this sector itself exceeds the present total qualified CIMA membership. The reality of the situation is that large-scale industrial and commercial organisations are locations where all types of accountant are engaged in a wide range of activities in environments quite different from those of public practice. One major difference is that accounting is only one of the management functions and it is often integrated with finance to create the accounting and finance function. Those who are part of this function are required to work in continuous association with colleagues responsible for the other management functions: marketing; personnel and industrial relations; research, design and development; computing and data processing, as well as operations management specialists and the corporate strategy group. Normally the accounting and finance function will be headed by a senior officer of the company, often titled the finance director, who will not only manage the accounting and finance function but will sit on the board of the company as an executive director and thereby be involved in the task of managing the broader entity. Depending on the size of the organisation, there will be a defined organisational structure within accounting and finance, as in each other function. This structure is in place to ensure that the totality of the work of the function is carried out in an orderly and an equitable way. The division of accounting and financial work is designed to promote the efficient performance of the work of the function. At the same time it provides a means whereby senior staff within the function can manage the performance of that work. As a result all those who form part of the structure of the accounting and finance function will have a clearly specified set of tasks to perform which require them to take responsibility for particular elements of the broader function. In this way everybody knows quite clearly what they are responsible for and what they should be doing at any specified time.

It is in these general ways that corporate accounting can be said to be formalised. The term is used to draw attention to the operational consequences of organisation, specialisation and specification and to do so in terms of structures and processes rather than in an experiential way. Formalisation is to be seen as the corollary of the importation of the general principles of management control into the practices of corporate accounting. Consideration of the experiential dimension is deferred until the following chapter. It is now necessary to offer some details on the patterns of formalisation starting with the more financial accounting aspects of corporate accounting.

Once each year every company must produce a set of financial statements which are subject to the scrutiny of an auditor. The three basic statements are a balance sheet, a profit and loss account and in the case of most companies some form of funds statement. Small and medium-sized companies are permitted to lodge modified statements with the Registrar of Companies but this still necessitates the production of full accounts for the audit itself. In the case of any efficiently managed company such statements are not simply produced at the year end but are available on a regular basis for purposes of management's various control needs. Although it might be argued that the profit and loss account is ultimately the most critical of the three, much day-to-day financial accounting has a balance sheet emphasis. Starting with the element of the balance sheet *tangible fixed assets*, it is established practice to maintain some form of fixed asset register. This 'document' serves as a record of the holding of such assets which means that all fixed asset purchases are to be recorded together with any disposals, transfers, or assets scrapped. In contrast to questions set in financial accounting examinations which involve a limited number of fixed asset movements, in real businesses such movements may run to thousands each year. It is not only movement that needs to be monitored. All assets have values associated with them and these are constantly changing either as a result of depreciation or revaluation. Because companies are given life by imperfect human beings some fixed assets appear unknown to accountants while others, not suprisingly, disappear. Department managers decide to stop using machinery and maintenance throw it out without anyone telling their colleagues in accounting. Modifications are made impromptu with revaluation implications, or worse grant or taxation consequences which are never conceived of by non-accountants. For these reasons it is not uncommon for accountants to leave their desks to go out and about to check the accuracy of their records or to send out requests to departmental heads for information. All of this activity requires the development and implementation of procedures which to the outsider may appear unnecessary, costly and on occasion inconvenient. To the person who is responsible for maintaining the fixed asset register it is an equally tiresome chore made worse by the fact that it is invariably the same individuals who create problems. But the register has to be accurate for audit purposes if nothing else. So the procedures have to be gone through constantly by whoever is responsible for this task.

Moving to current assets and initially to *stock*. This can account for a large part of a business's health and again the accountant is interested in the existence of these assets. More significant perhaps is the value of these assets since mere existence is not a guarantee of value. The relevant accounting standard, SSAP9, requires stock to be valued at the lower of cost or *net realisable value*, which entails that the accountant needs to be in possession of information as to the cost of any stockholdings including the likely costs of their completion together with some information on their current market value. If the latter is lower than cost, it will be necessary to write down the value of this stock with all of its broader financial implications. This requires that all costs are continuously monitored and that this is done accurately. A similar exercise on market values will need to be undertaken perhaps in conjunction with colleagues in marketing and the corporate strategy group. This of course shades into management accounting but for the moment the point to be made is that in accounting for stock the operational reality is one of procedures involving constant monitoring and the regular provision of information on costs and values. Turning to *debtors*, few modern business enterprises can survive without extending some form of credit to their customers and as a result the level of debtors in any financial statement is likely to constitute a significant component of a company's health. While credit can boost sales, it can equally well be the cause of a company's collapse. For this reason it is crucial to keep a constant and informed eye on the extent of debtors and more importantly the composition of their debt. Allowing a lot of customers only limited amounts of credit may prove less risky than being understanding to an old customer who is experiencing financial difficulties. In practice this means that accountants are constantly involved in monitoring the debtors' register, investigating any unusual occurrences and checking new credit applications all of which will involve following procedures laid down in the interests of maintaining financial control.

Cash at bank and in hand is often a comparatively small figure in a balance sheet but its size should never be taken as a measure of its importance. To have too much of this most liquid of assets can be indicative of a company's financial mismanagement as such spare funds may be profitably invested, even for short periods of time. Some companies will always have a substantial amount of cash, retail organisations for instance, but they may also require such levels of funds to pay their own creditors. It is part of the accounting function to ensure that any undertaking practises proper financial management. This might mean that any spare cash is transferred to head office so that the company or group as a whole is able to practise effective financial management. On occasion it may be necessary to 'borrow' cash from head office to avoid unnecessary overdrafts. In the case of a small operation the accountant may have to decide how much to invest and for how long without jeopardising the financial situation of the company. Whichever is the case any decisions can only be made if procedures exist to keep a careful check on cash. This may involve calling the bank at a particular time of the day, followed by a report to head office of the close of day balance which may then be followed by cash movements if necessary. It is these procedures and associated guidelines which constitute the means of controlling this asset. Failure to carry out these routine activities may prove unproblematic when no action is in fact required but equally very costly if there is a need to act. So the daily routines must be followed and the control which is being sought is thereby achieved.

Constant monitoring of debts payable to *creditors* is the other side of the coin to monitoring debtors. While it is obviously beneficial to delay payments to trade creditors there are dangers too: supplies may be threatened; suppliers who have offered advantageous terms may be forced out of business; a number of creditors may decide to act in concert and cause a measure of financial embarrassment. Thus it is desirable to keep a close watch on the level and composition of a company's trade creditors, with mechanisms for ensuring both regular payments and those which may be necessary in the case of emergencies. These payments must also be made only for actual quantities of supplies received which in turn requires the establishment of effective procedures for recording the receipt of supplies and monitoring the prices which are charged on invoices received. One creditor in particular demands payment on appointed days, the State. Payments of value added tax (VAT) must normally be made quarterly on or before dates laid down by HM Customs and Excise; a company is not permitted to pay only when it has the funds available unless it is prepared to face the wrath of the collection agency. Similarly any income tax, advance corporation tax or National

Insurance contributions must be transferred on appointed days. Since these sums will tend to vary from period to period this means that accountants sometimes have to take cheques to the bank to pay into the relevant accounts. Should they forget, a polite telephone call may be received by way of a reminder of the outstanding debt. Shareholders may not be so zealous but they too expect to receive their dividend income when it is due to them. They also expect that the appropriate taxation adjustments will have been made so relieving them of what might be regarded as an irksome task. Retaining their goodwill can be an important consideration, especially if further share issues are being contemplated. Although it is not always an accountant's job to undertake the various tasks involved in attending to the demands of the various categories of creditor, ensuring that the work is carried out on time is often part of their function.

The purpose of this extended, and in places laboured, analysis of corporate financial accounting is to impress upon the reader that a great deal of it involves following procedures which have been devised for ensuring the efficient control of a particular set of activities. This involves the maintenance of comprehensive, accessible and accurate records which must constantly reflect the financial reality of the business. It is essentially these procedures and routines which form the constituent elements of accounting systems nowadays. These procedures, routines and systems with their extensive reliance on regular monitoring and updating processes are the embodiment of the adoption of *formalisation* as the means to establish effective management control within corporate accounting. According to Child, formalisation is marked by:

> established written policies, procedures, rules, job definitions, and standing orders which prescribe correct or expected action, and then to back these up . . . systems for the documented recording of what has taken place in the way of communication and performance.

> (Child, 1984, p.153)

An alternative way of making the same point is to say that the formalisation of corporate accounting results in its becoming the application of predetermined accounting formulae to the various tasks at hand in the interests of efficiency and effective management control. To ensure that the accounting and finance function is able to carry out its designated work in an effective, efficient and economic manner, it has been judged necessary to introduce into it practices already widely employed in other functions. In this way it is possible to describe the formalisation of corporate accounting in more pejorative terms as evidence of its increasing bureaucratisation. The experiential consequences of this process will be considered more fully in the next chapter.

In order to consider the formalisation of corporate financial accounting the balance sheet has been discussed. Moving on to management accounting, the emphasis switches to the profit and loss account. This approach has been adopted purely for heuristic reasons and it should not be imagined that financial accountants in industry and commerce look after the balance sheet while management accountants work on the income statement. In most cases any individual accountant, irrespective of qualification or designation, will probably be involved in both areas of activity to some degree, reflecting the integration of the different aspects of corporate financial management. A profit and loss statement is constructed around the concept that in a specific time period the sales of product X brought in revenue £Y (either cash or credit) and cost a total of £Z to produce. Of this latter sum £a was for labour, £b was for materials, £c was for depreciation and £d for a variety of overheads, etc. In simple terms the difference between the revenue and the various costs involved is the profit of the entity, which is then subject to taxation. Only after the deduction of the appropriate sum for the payment of tax is there an amount which is available for distribution to those who have a stake in the business. Normally only a comparatively small amount is actually taken out of the business in this way not least due due to the fact that the profit figure which the account shows is a notional one. Because it is prepared on an *accruals* basis, the income statement of a business can depart quite substantially from financial reality which in some respects would be better represented in terms of actual cash position. Many apparently highly profitable businesses have collapsed overnight as a consequence of their lack of cash funds, one of the more spectacular recent cases being Laker Airways in 1982. This is not the place to debate the respective merits of accruals and cash flow accounting. Whichever basis is adopted, the final profit figure offers an account of the activities of a period which will have been carefully, constantly and comprehensively modelled and monitored by those accountants responsible for the provision of internal or management accounting information to those responsible for the successful financial performance of the business, i.e. the directors and their most senior managers.

The simplest way to begin to characterise management accounting for present purposes is to take the example of a manufacturing company which produces a single product and which is active in an industry where there are many competitors. Top management will normally be aware of the broad state of the market and so be able to offer a general picture of the relationship between price and demand. Normally a lower price results in a greater level of demand with the possibility of increased turnover and possibly higher profits. If there is evidence of demand in the market then it may be desirable to increase production. All things being equal, this normally results in a reduced unit cost and increased profit. The first major consideration for the company is whether it is feasible to increase production given the present operational capacity of the business. If not, is it worthwhile to invest in new machinery which would necessitate further borrowing from the bank and increased costs. Extending the scale of operations may call for a larger overdraft more regularly which will introduce further indirect expense. The management accountant is commonly faced with such problems and is requested to provide the information required to make the necessary decisions. The normal procedure is to model the possible scenarios and additionally to assess the probability of particular outcomes in such a way that senior management are provided with sufficient information to enable them to make an informed decision. It is not management accountants who ultimately decide but those to whom they report, usually by way of their own senior staffs. Their task is to 'cost' the plans and projects of their employers, senior management, using a range of techniques learned in the course of their training and employed on a day-to-day basis. These are the various management accounting formulae which complement those of corporate financial accounting. They exist as the embodiment of formalisation in the context of corporate management accounting.

In carrying out an exercise on the feasibility of increasing production it would be expected that the accountant draws up a financial plan for the projected expansion. Such a plan is known in accounting as a *budget* in much the same way as in everyday terminology. However, corporate accounting budgets are very much more complex, comprehensive entities being made up of a number of *functional budgets* drawn up in close consultation with colleagues in the other management functions. The initial budget which needs to be established is the sales budget which will indicate the expected level of sales (at an agreed price) on a period by period basis for the coming year say. There is no use in simply saying that in the next year 60000 units will be sold as this might mean 49000 in the first month and a thousand each month for the rest of the year. Ideally the monthly projections should be established which allows the easier development of the production budget for the year. Knowing projected production schedules allows the accountant to devise purchasing budgets for both materials and labour in conjunction with managers in operations, industrial engineering and personnel. Additional budgets will need to be drawn up for all the various overheads involved in the proposal including both production and non-production expenditures. Again the accountant will need to liaise with colleagues in other functions on a regular basis. As far as possible it is desirable to establish a full projection of all of the costs in order to be able to present an accurate picture to senior management. The normal way in which this is done is to integrate all of the functional budgets into a *master budget* which includes a projected profit and loss account for the year together with a projected balance sheet at the year end and in many instances the most important important of all budgets, a cash budget. Drawing up such a budget allows senior management to see very easily the cash flow implications of the proposal in question. Taken together with the other elements of the master budget, it provides them with a basis upon which to make the necessary decisions about proceeding with the proposal or alternatively the basis upon which to begin to restructure the proposal should it presently appear problematic.

Budgets are not used only for the purpose of making decisions such as the above. They are employed whenever a company is planning any sort of future activity. On many occasions budgets are used in association with the set of techniques known as *standard costing* which have been devised to achieve increased control at an operational level as opposed to a budget which serves as a broader plan at a more tactical level. Developed in the early part of the century standard costing has served to secure effective financial control in manufacturing industry ever since. One element of the planning and control information which the accountant will normally provide to the senior management of a manufacturing company will be a standardised costing for each product at a specified level of activity. This is an estimate of the cost of a unit of output which reflects existing information on costs supplemented with any relevant additional information regarding the period ahead. A standard cost is built up from knowing the number of hours it is expected to take to produce a batch of output and thus the unit time of output and then establishing an expected hourly wage rate. Similarly, the amount of materials to be used in making a unit of output is calculated and costed using the information available together with informed estimates of price movements. For each unit it is necessary to include an amount for the cost of both variable and fixed overheads which may have been estimated already, i.e. predetermined overhead absorption rates, or may need to be established at this point. The result is a set of expected unit costs which are to serve as the standard or benchmark for subsequent actual cost comparison. Although this exercise might appear to the outsider both highly esoteric and skilful, if the company has an established management information system the provision of a standard cost for any product should largely be a formality, as should be the drawing up of any budget. Where there is a range of products then a range of standards will need to be produced, again a routine operation.

Since standard costs are essentially estimates, the actual production of a commodity may involve quite different patterns of expenditure. An unforeseen shortage of labour may necessitate offering much higher wages to attract a workforce; a batch of low cost, good quality material may result in less wastage than was planned for and much lower unit costs; constant interruptions to production due to machinery not performing as in the past can all drastically alter the actual cost profile of a product, either positively, negatively, or both simultaneously. As a result in order to achieve effective financial control it is necessary to monitor actual costs and more importantly to understand fully the reasons for and significance of any departures from standards. This is the purpose of what is usually termed *variance analysis*, the basis for on-going financial control and an activity which regularly engages the accountant. On the one hand it is necessary to pinpoint the origins of variation in order that corrective action may be taken, i.e. to get labour, material, or overhead costs back to standard. If it is not possible to take such action then the standard itself will have to be amended with consequences for unit profitability and ultimately the forecasted profit for the period. As ever the accountant is responsible for the collection and codification of the appropriate information and then reporting to senior management on a regular basis and in a specified manner such as *exception reporting* where only 'problems' are highlighted. In this way it is readily apparent that like budgeting, standard costing and variance analysis are further evidence of formalisation within corporate accounting. They require accountants to be constantly involved in devising, monitoring, investigating and amending their cost estimates in the pursuit of greater financial control. They are accounting formulae designed to promote efficiency and effective management control in the sphere of internal or management accounting.

When the actual profit and loss account is finally drawn up at the end of a period of time, it will reflect the existence of close control and the monitoring of all of the actual costs and revenues during the period. Procedures will be in place to ensure that all of the costs and revenues are recorded and that this is done accurately and at the appropriate time. This task is often carried out by accounts clerks rather than accountants but it is the latter who are responsible for devising and implementing the accounting procedures, routines and systems involved. The various information which is generated and reported is also used to formulate future plans, budgets, standards, etc., and in this way makes a contribution to the perpetuation of the business, ideally as a more economic, efficient and effective entity.

Although the previous paragraphs have used manufacturing as the means to illustrate the nature of corporate management accounting and its attendant formalisation, commercial undertakings employ similar accounting formulae. A bank, for example, is trying to make a profit by offering its services to various types of customers. It will need to be able to accurately predict the demand for these services and thus to estimate its revenue in future periods. Providing services necessitates expenditure which must be controlled if the bank is to make a profit. So like the small manufacturing company above, banks need to draw up budgets, implement them, monitor them and periodically amend them to reflect actual activity. It may not employ techniques such as standard costing or variance analysis but it must be in a position to be able to investigate any significant departures from budget in the interests of effective financial control. Retail stores will also need to be able to plan and control their expenditure in the pursuit of profit as well as being able to predict their revenues with great accuracy. However, in their case the fact that they normally buy in all of their merchandise, whether from group companies or outside suppliers, necessitates careful planning and control of all purchases. If demand holds up and operating expenses match budget, difficulties in sourcing stock at the planned price will play havoc with profit margins. So retail accountants must work very closely with their colleagues in the buying function to devise accurate and reliable purchasing budgets. Inevitably there must be procedures and routines in existence which enable accountants to report any significant changes to senior management and to demonstrate their consequences so that corrective action may be taken as soon as possible. Finally in the hotel industry management accounting formulae have become increasingly important as senior management have sought the best use of their assets, balancing the requirements of the seasonal tourist trade with the weekday needs of business customers and the demand for short stay packages in the family market. The price structure operated by any sizeable hotel reflects the application of the principles of variable costing in much the same way as in manufacturing companies. And in the kitchen the operation of 'portion control' systems is evidence of the adoption of the principles of standard costing and financial control.

This discussion of corporate management accounting is not intended to be in any way exhaustive. In practice it is normal to find corporate accountants engaged in a wide range of work activities. The above are only indicative of some of the most fundamental of these. The main point to be taken from these pages is that whatever the task, it is normally the case that accountants in industry and commerce are involved in routines, are following procedures and are operating accounting systems. In this way they are engaged in the application of accounting formulae designed to promote greater management control. This is the reality of the formalisation of accounting in the industrial and commercial sector.

ACCOUNTING IN THE PUBLIC SECTOR: THE INTRUSION OF POLITICS

Many observers view the existence of a sizeable, healthy public sector as a characteristic of an advanced society and a highly desirable one at that. Being one of the advanced societies, the UK has experienced a massive growth in both the size and cost of its public sector for most of the post-war period. As a result the public sector is a major employer of all types of labour including professional accountants. The greater part of CIPFA's active membership is employed here together with an equal number of accountants from the other professional bodies which means that about 10% of all accountants are engaged in public sector accounting of some description. The UK has one of the most extensive public sectors, whose geography is extremely varied, and any brief overview can never do justice to this variety but for present purposes the following division into sub-sectors is instructive.

First there are the many public corporations, each of which has its own unique nature and characteristics. It is possible to identify a broad category of public corporations known as the nationalised industries whose numbers have been reduced in recent years as a result of the policy of de-nationalisation or *privatisation* pursued by successive Conservative administrations during the past twelve years. Among those which still remain in public ownership are two of the first industries to be nationalised, coal-mining and the railways, both of which entered public ownership for strategic reasons in the immediate post-war period. The Atomic Energy Authority, the British Broadcasting Corporation and the Bank of England are three examples of the variety which exists among public corporations outside of the nationalised industries. Next there are the many branches of central government employment ranging from well-known government departments such as health, education, defence, the environment, etc. to specialised agencies including a number of auditing bodies which will be considered later. Central government is sometimes referred to as the Civil Service, a title which clearly distinguishes it from the many local government undertakings which provide services of a more immediate and infrastructural nature: highways, schools, public health, care for the elderly, etc. In addition there are a number of public sector institutions which are responsible for enhancing the quality of life in a more general way, two of the more important being the universities and the National Health Service. Like all public sector organisations they have their own characteristic administrative arrangements. Accountants employed in such industries, undertakings or administrative organs are in great part engaged in the sort of work considered at length in the previous section and in essentially the same manner. The public sector inevitably has its own procedures, routines and systems since it too is highly formalised. Indeed some would say it is too formalised. The present section does not seek to describe the similarities between the public and private sector accounting practice, however. Instead it focuses on some of the distinctive features of contemporary public sector accounting and in particular the specifically political constraints which affect the performance of this work.

To say that the public sector, unlike the private sector, receives its funds from the public purse is a misleading truism. It is certainly the case that the greatest part of the money which it costs to run central government's various ministries and undertakings is raised through levying a range of taxes on the rest of society and as long as this sub-sector continues to exist this will remain the case. Conversely, it has always been the intention that the nationalised industries and most of the other public corporations aim to be self-financing. For all the political rhetoric of the past decade, the cost to the Exchequer of this sector has been comparatively small if often rather unevenly spread. As the size of this sub-sector has decreased in recent years, its financial cost to the public purse has become more realistic, i.e. smaller. In the case of the remaining nationalised industries, the imposition of *external financing limits* has served to restrict their power to raise funds for investment purposes which in turn has made them appear even less worthy of support. Turning to the NHS and the universities, these have traditionally been funded by *transfer payments* from central government departments but as the cost of enhancing the quality of human life has risen rapidly, both have been obliged to devise means of generating a proportion of their own income not least to counteract the effects of a squeeze on funds from central government. It may well be the case that expenditure on these institutions has increased markedly in real terms under successive Conservative administrations but has it risen sufficiently to match the escalating costs of maintaining the level of service let alone improve it? Faced with a growing gap between income and expenditure and the difficulties involved in increased income generation at least in the short term, the only possible outcome is a reduction in the quality of patient care or intellectual labour.

The situation of the local authorities is arguably the most complex and controversial of all the public sector bodies. Traditionally the money for local government expenditure has come from four sources. The greatest part has been in the form of transfer payments from central government which are nowadays known as the *rate support grant*, the purpose of which was to provide the basis for a common standard of services across the country. Local authorities have always been able to raise a sizeable proportion of their funds by means of the

'rates' which the support grant supplemented. If a local authority decided to
increase its expenditure it was obliged to raise its rates, a decision it was called
upon to justify to its electorate on a regular basis. Continued support for a high
spending local authority was viewed as a mandate for the continuation of such a
policy. An alternative source of funds for increased expenditure was borrowing
from third parties which normally had an effect on the rates bill as such borrowing inevitably gives rise to increased charges to cover interest payments. The
fourth source of funds for local government is the charges it makes for the use of
its facilities. The payment of rents for council houses is the most obvious
example but funds have been raised from renting out educational and sporting
facilities, providing services to house buyers, local bus services, etc.

Since 1979 local government, like almost every other public sector body, has
experienced a serious attack on its funding. In fact many commentators agree that
it has suffered more than most because of the inevitable conflict between three
successive Conservative administrations and the power which the Labour party
has retained at a local level. Rate support grant was slashed as central government
sought to reduce public expenditure. The freedom to raise extra funds in the form
of increased rates was countered by rate-capping. The cost of previous borrowing
began to increase as a proportion of committed expenditure which in turn served
as a mechanism to reduce further borrowing. Faced with a general financial crisis
most local authorities had little option but to reduce services, sell assets, increase
charges, entertain competitive tendering for a wide range of contracts and so on.
The introduction of the community charge or 'poll tax' in England and Wales in
1990 (1989 in Scotland) was intended to achieve further central government
control but the initiative was soon recognised as politically inept and is presently
being reformulated. All of the indications are that a greater proportion of funds
will be provided by central government and thus be even more subject to their
control.

This is the backdrop for the practice of contemporary public sector accounting. For over a decade the whole of the public sector has been characterised as
wildly profligate, spending the money of others with little attention being paid to
efficiency, quality, value or some similar emotive notion. In addition to mounting
a debilitating financial attack on the public sector, successive Conservative
administrations have sought to establish a new philosophy of a distinctly commercial sort in the financial management of the sector. As a consequence,
accountants in all branches of the public sector now find themselves called upon
to practise their professional activities in a way which is very much more public
than is the case for their counterparts in either public practice or industry and
commerce. Unless the political climate within the UK changes dramatically in
the near future, public sector accounting will increasingly become a matter of
publicly accountable accounting.

The manner in which many of the ground rules of public sector accounting
have changed in recent years can be discerned from considering two examples of
the increased demand for public accountability: quality of service targets and

value for money audits. The former are performance measures which are readily
communicated and equally readily digested by a populace sensitised to the
inefficiencies of the pre-1979 public sector. They are increasingly evident to us
with television adverts informing us what percentage of public telephones are
currently serviceable, newspaper articles which tell us how many inter-city trains
were on time as they report the latest round of fare increases, and government
Ministers enthusing about falling waiting lists in the NHS or the rising proportion
of young people now in higher education. When these are seen to be improving
the conclusion is that the recent attention paid by the government to the management of such public entities has had the desired effect – they are now more
efficient and their use of the funds available to them is to be applauded. Much of
this information has always been available or at least it could have been provided
if requested. Such information is much 'softer' and thus more readily understood
than 'hard' figures on rates of return on capital or sectoral analyses of growth in
turnover. Both come from the same source of course, the accounting function.
There is nothing inherently wrong with accountants generating information
which can be easily understood by the general public, but two important observations are perhaps in order, however. The first is that it is ironic that there seems
to be little enthusiasm on the part of the government to have similar information
made available by the private sector although some companies have recognised
the value of this type of reporting. Secondly there is the more fundamental
question of whether even traditional accounting can capture the special nature of
public service provision, let alone comparatively trivial performance measurements.
Or is it simply a clear-cut case of ideological ends justifying populist means?

Value for money (VFM) audits are an import from North America where they
are also known as 'expanded scope audits' or 'comprehensive audits' in consequence of their broader emphasis as compared with the conventional financial
audit (Jones & Pendlebury, 1988; Sherer & Turley, 1991). Their introduction in
the UK has both complemented and extended the long established system for
carrying out financial audits throughout the public sector. In the case of central
government the National Audit Office (NAO), established in 1983 to replace the
former Exchequer and Audit Department and headed by the Comptroller and
Auditor General, is responsible for both financial and VFM audits. Local government auditing was formerly the responsibility of the Department of the Environment's District Audit Service in England and Wales. In 1982 a new body, the
Audit Commission for England and Wales, assumed responsibility for this function which was now to be performed by both the Commission's own staff and the
private sector, the intention being to eventually split such appointments on a
50/50 basis. In Scotland all local authority audits for periods commencing after
31 March 1983 became the responsibility of the Accounts Commission, continuing the traditional arrangement whereby Scotland had its own external audit
service. The two pieces of legislation which instituted these new arrangements
also required the auditors to review aspects of value for money as part of their
annual audit programmes.

The nationalised industries are audited by private sector firms in much the same way as any corporate body. The appointment of the auditors is the task of the relevant Secretary of State to whom the final audit report is directed as the individual responsible to Parliament for that industry. This gives rise to some concern about the independence of the auditor and has led to the suggestion that any reports should in fact be presented to the Comptroller and Auditor General. This in turn might provide a sounder basis for performing VFM audits in the case of the nationalised industries, a requirement which presently does not exist although a similar sort of enquiry can be conducted by the Monopolies and Mergers Commission on the instructions of the Secretary of State for Trade and Industry. Finally in the case of the NHS it is the Secretary of State for Health in England and the Scottish, Welsh and Northern Ireland Secretaries who are by law required to employ auditors to audit health authority accounts. Traditionally these have been civil servants but since 1981 some of the work has been performed by private sector firms who have been specifically charged with performing a measure of VFM work. The Comptroller and Auditor General is required to examine, certify and report on the consolidated accounts of the NHS which means that the NAO performs the audit work which it believes is required. VFM was strongly commended to the NHS in the 1983 *Report of the DHSS/NHS Audit Working Group* as a means effect savings which could then be passed on to patients in the form of improved sevices. One noticeable consequence of this has been the growth of the internal audit function at the local level.

The VFM concept is appealing for many reasons, not the least of which is that it is easy for the public to understand. In essence it is an attempt to establish whether a particular public undertaking is operating in a manner which makes the best use of the resources it consumes. It is a means of establishing accountability in the public sector where the absence of free market forces can easily give rise to financial and indeed general mismanagement, the cost of which is ultimately borne by the public. By introducing VFM audits it is possible to measure the performance of those who are charged with managing the public sector in the public interest. VFM asks three simple questions: is a particular undertaking operating *economically*, *efficiently* and *effectively*? The first question is acknowledged to be uncontentious since most people would accept that it is in everyone's interests to obtain inputs of the right quality at the lowest cost. Unfortunately many enquiries have established that this is not always the case and have highlighted numerous opportunities for reducing public expenditure. The definition of efficiency used in the context of VFM appears equally uncontentious: producing the greatest useful output from the given level of inputs. This would certainly hold in the case of manufacturing industry or even in the various civil service bureaucracies. But in the case of hospitals this means as large a throughput of patients as possible while educational institutions show their efficiency by producing more leavers with more qualifications to their name. The complementary question is who judges whether they are 'useful output'? This leads neatly to the third question, that of effectiveness. Are public undertakings achieving the desired results? This time the complementary question is essentially the same: who determines what the 'desired results' are? Answer: the same body which has zealously promoted the VFM philosophy in the UK, three successive 'radical' Conservative administrations committed to fundamentally changing British society.

Drawing these ideas together, it is clear that the situation of today's public sector accountants is an uncomfortable one. This is the case both for those who carry out the various tasks involved, including VFM work, and those responsible for its management. At a time when many believed the advent of new technologies in the manufacturing industries heralded the beginning of a leisured society with a growing public sector amply funded by the wealth these technologies generated, quite the opposite has occurred. Less funding has been made available resulting in new forms of 'creative accounting' which must not, paradoxically, lead to further reductions in funds. New forms of accounting information are being devised not so much to enlighten the public as to convince them of the benefits of the new approach to public sector finance while value for money is a euphemism for constant cost-cutting and, some believe, the eventual dismantling of the public sector. So instead of accounting in conditions of comparative control, the public sector accountant is firmly embroiled in a situation where control lies with ranks of unseen political ideologues.

THE EMERGENCE OF THE ACCOUNTING TECHNICIAN: THE DIVISION OF PROFESSIONAL LABOUR

It would be wrong to leave the account of contemporary accounting roles at this point implying that these only extend to the work carried out by qualified members of the six major associations in the public and private sectors and in public practice. The recent past has also seen the emergence of the complementary role of accounting technician throughout all of these sectors. With the emergence of the accounting technician has come the promise of a clear division of labour within the profession in future periods, one which it is claimed will be to the benefit of both parties. It is possible, however, to present a less optimistic view of the situation so far as many professional accountants are concerned. This is because with the emergence of the accounting technician as an identifiable role within the profession, at present firmly established at its base, has come suggestions of changes which portend something rather different for the future than may have been envisaged.

Adopting a very simplistic view of the division of labour between accounting technicians and professionally qualified accountants, the role of the former is that of a junior functionary engaged in the performance of essentially routine, technical accounting tasks such as book-keeping, maintaining cost cards or payroll records, aspects of internal audit, etc. In this way the emergence of the accounting technician role has been little more than the modest upgrading of a range of semi-professional clerical tasks which have long existed in the context of the broader accounting and finance function. Turning to the qualified accountant, part of their role would logically see them supervising this routine technical work and those who perform it. The more demanding technical work would normally fall to them and probably engage them for most of their time. It is also qualified accountants who would normally provide management with information rather than technicians. It is for reasons such as these that the Association of Accounting Technicians (AAT) describe their members as 'support staff' and expect them to demonstrate a much more modest level of competence in order to satisfy their examination and membership requirements. However, the same body understandably advertises the fact that some of its membership are to be found in managerial positions within public practice, industry and commerce and in the public sector, thereby demonstrating that accounting technicians also have a career path available to them. Accepting this to be so, a more complex picture of the division of labour within contemporary accounting practice begins to emerge. Qualified accountants are employed in positions of a 'senior' nature within the accounting and finance function, part of which involves a variety of sub-functions such as book-keeping, internal audit, customer credit, etc., which may be managed by experienced technicians who may (or indeed may not) be qualified at a lower level than their professional counterparts. The latter do not in fact find themselves called upon to manage those to whom they are senior in the technical sense. Their relationship with each other is that of being called upon to perform different aspects of the broader accounting and finance function.

These three groups: qualified accountants, accounting technicians and senior accounting technicians are joined by a fourth group, those qualified accountants who oversee the work of other qualified accountants. These are the individuals who convey the information provided by the latter to the higher echelons of management on a regular basis. In the same way as senior technicians manage technicians, senior accountants manage accountants. In many cases, however, these senior accountants also manage the two grades of technician. Such individuals are responsible for ensuring that a specified part of the broader workload of the function is completed successfully. To achieve this objective a division of labour is introduced among the different groups with the least demanding tasks being allocated to the technicians while qualified accountants tackle more problematic aspects. The role of the senior technician is to supervise less experienced staff and perhaps resolve some of the technical problems which may arise rather than pass them over to accountants. The team is managed by one or more 'managing' accountant whose function it is to integrate the different contributions. Two observations may usefully be made at this point: firstly, there are two divisions of labour operative here, one which distinguishes the easier from the more difficult tasks as between accountants and technicians. There is also the division between those who are engaged in some extent of management and those who are subject to it, senior staff and subordinate staff. Secondly, while there is a clear chain of command from the most senior accountants down to the technician, the qualified accountant does not appear to figure on it. Like technicians these employees do not manage anyone but they cannot be identified in the same way since they are usually engaged in more demanding work and are generally better rewarded for their skills. Most are also better rewarded than their senior technician counterparts but do not have the same managerial role to perform.

This already complicated picture is not yet complete since two further groups must be considered: trainees and part-qualifieds. The former group may embrace both trainee accountants and technicians but for the present it is the former which is of interest. Trainee accountants have an identifiable status in that they are new members of the profession who are engaged in the well-established process of apprenticeship. In the course of their training they will gain experience in a variety of functions and come under the supervision of a succession of managers. Although they do constitute important members of teams they are not really identifiable as either accountants or technicians and they will at different times have the competences of both. Given that one undertakes training with a view to becoming a qualified accountant it seems appropriate to include bona fide trainees along with accountants. The category of part-qualified accountant is bound up with bodies such as the AAT. Traditionally there have been two groups of part-qualifieds, those who were still on the way to qualification as accountants (trainees) and those who had run out of time or energy or both and were not likely to qualify. One of the reasons that the ACCA, ICAEW, CIMA, CIPFA and later ICAS have given their support to the AAT is that it offers such individuals the opportunity to obtain a recognised qualification with which they may begin to rebuild a career. In the future the part-qualified status should disappear as those who attract the designation proceed to one or another of the levels of qualification. If the number of people attracted to the profession continues to hold up, there will inevitably be a steady flow of part-qualifieds into the ranks of the technicians. Here they will join the rapidly growing ranks of direct recruits, individuals who have decided to pursue a career in accountancy from the bottom, a phenomenon which leads the AAT to describe itself as the fastest growing accounting body in the world today (Cropper,1990).

This brief discussion of trainee accountants and part-qualifieds/technicians reiterates the significance of *technical* competence as a means of differentiating between those involved in accounting labour. In the same way as technicians are differentiated from professional accountants by virtue of the latter's greater competence in technical accounting matters, a trainee accountant becomes a qualified accountant and not a technician by demonstrating a similar competence in the examination hall. Leaving aside difficult questions regarding the reliability of formal examinations, this all seems very rational and generally logical. One is left with the impression that accountants are busily involved with challenging problems which serve to constantly call upon their experience and expertise while their technician colleagues are engaged in, and stretched by much lesser work.

By now the perceptive reader might well be feeling a little uneasy since the view which was presented in the context of the extended discussion of corporate accounting was one of qualified accountants employed in the performance of highly formalised tasks, much of which was characterised as simply applying accounting formulae. In discussing public practice the point was made that most of those employed in the large firms were effectively specialists from an early stage in their careers and as a result were engaged in routine auditing activity, the preparation of accounts or taxation work. The point was also made that in the public sector the same formalisation exists with defined routines and procedures, the whole scenario being subjected to persistent political intervention. If the nature of much of the qualified accountant's work is so routinised and un-challenging, how does it differ from that of the technician? A recent article on the changing fortunes of accounting technicians reveals some interesting thinking on this issue (Brandenberg, 1987). A recruiter from one Big 6 firm is quoted as saying that technicians are now employed in work which has been changed by the advent of the computer, something which promises to allow his firm to use its graduate trainees more economically. Later it is stated that the employment of more technicians has resulted in forty fewer graduates being employed in 1988. Technician accountants are described as being cost-effective, their training schedules allowing more 'chargeable time'. On the other hand only 'top quality graduates' will be sought in future recruitment drives.

Two interpretations may be placed on these comments. On the positive side it may be that an increasing number of employers recognise that they owe their graduates only the most challenging work and the promise of exciting careers. Since these are firmly expected to be in shorter supply in the future then it is essential to employ them in the most effective way and clearly rather better than in the past. By implication there is a difference between the work which account-ants and technicians should be employed to do although there are now more jobs for the latter category. Alternatively there is a more negative view: more account-ing work can be performed by less qualified and thus financially more attractive technicians. As a result there will be a reduced demand for highly qualified, costly professional accountants while technicians find themselves the subject of great competition to secure their services. Whichever interpretation is correct two elements seem common to both: the future will see relatively fewer qualified accountants employed and secondly, the nature of much of their work appears to be changing in an unfavourable way. Neither of these can be good news for the profession and its members. Nor are many of the observations advanced in this chapter.

Chapter 3

Accountants' work experiences

Throughout the previous chapter the impression has been given that in a number of ways the work situations of many qualified accountants are less attractive than is imagined to be the case for professional employees. Public practitioners employed in large firms were described as being forced to choose a specialism and to develop a career in their chosen branch of accountancy. Those employed in industry and commerce were characterised as performing a range of routine tasks and applying accounting formulae in the highly formalised business environment. In the case of the public sector accountant the main point was that of increased outside pressure which is resulting in a reduced freedom to act in a professional manner. Finally, the emergence of the accounting technician was argued to be in some degree indicative of a further deterioration in the situation of the qualified accountant with fewer of them being needed in the future as technicians move into some of their former work roles. The purpose of this chapter is to discuss the reasons why this gap between public perception and reality exists. It draws on the voluminous literature of industrial sociology in an attempt to explain why it is not too surprising that many accountants experience such unsatisfying work situations at the present time.

THE SOCIAL ORGANISATION OF WORK

Work does not occur in a vacuum. It is performed within organisations which are themselves situated within the broader social order. Industrial sociology as a sub-discipline of sociology is interested in how society shapes and determines the nature of industry and within industry the experience of work and employment. One particularly influential contribution to the analysis of the social organisation of work dates back almost a century and a half to the earliest days of industrialisation in Europe. Its author was Karl Marx, better known to most readers as the political philosopher who advocated communism as the ideal form of social and economic life. Before Marx had really begun to develop his political thought he penned a large number of essays on various aspects of social life including one published in 1844 entitled 'Alienated Labour' (Marx, 1956). In it he identifies four interrelated aspects of the contemporary factory worker's negative identification with the newly emergent organisation of work. Firstly work no longer allows the workers to identify with the product of their labour; as a result of the adoption of the division of labour principle by employers, workers are increasingly found to be employed in narrower tasks which make it difficult for them to identify with what it is they are involved in making. Marx passionately believed that in the creation of material objects the human species was involved in an important act of self-realisation and that any obstacle to this constituted a degradation of human well-being. Because the task of determining the structure of production was now removed from the worker Marx believed that it was no longer possible for them to identify with the entire act of production, something which served to further degrade them. The human species was for Marx a social species which sought to engage in acts of sociability. Traditionally work had provided many opportunities for social interaction but increasingly it set individual against individual as they competed for employment or as they were locked in conflict as workers and overseers. Finally Marx concluded that all of these features of work resulted in the human species being contorted into a state in which its humanity was increasingly difficult to recognise, a state he termed *alienation* which he saw as the product of the system of alienated labour.

There is a sense of romantic naivety in this analysis when it is offered in the present day. Surely workers are motivated by financial rewards rather than seeking to find themselves. They need to be organised and supervised since they lack the capacity to do this themselves. Without strong management there would be industrial anarchy. It has to be remembered, however, that at the time when Marx wrote his essay there were few established rules or guidelines about how to achieve the advances believed to be both necessary and desirable in the newly emergent industrial sector. He himself was also keenly aware of the positive side of the division of labour, specialisation and organisation, being anything but a Luddite. The point he sought to make was that there were costs as well as benefits in the new patterns of work organisation. The benefits fell to those who organised production and extended far beyond increased profitability. These arrangements offered the prospect of great wealth and power to all who adopted them and thereby consolidated the new and still vulnerable industrial base of the capitalist order. To contemplate any radical departure from them was much too risky and so as long as there were benefits to be had such practices would persist. Hence Marx's more general conclusion that in order to regain its integrity, the class which bore most of the costs of the emerging social order, the working class, needed to reject it and replace it with its own arrangements. As long as capitalism persisted, Marx believed that work could never be in the real interests of those who performed it.

The second contributor to understanding the social organisation of work should also be known to most readers, being the founder of management science, Frederick Winslow Taylor. He is best known for his essays and lectures offered over a twenty year period beginning in 1895, the most important of which were later published in the 1964 collection entitled *Scientific Management*. Whereas

Marx offered a critique of the development of the industrial order of capitalism, Taylor sought to provide it with a practical philosophy designed to ensure its perpetuation. Taylor was not so much a devotee of capitalism as a convert to the quest for a science of manufacture. In the course of his own career he had observed that much management was too undisciplined and thereby less effective than it might be, and that workers were motivated principally by monetary incentives. He sought to bring together the most promising elements of management practice and to develop a science of management which would prove appealing to both workers and management alike. The essence of his approach was to divorce *conception* from *execution*. Management were to be concerned with the design of work, by which Taylor meant its organisation and structuration. They were also responsible for the selection and training of their workforces together with the development and operation of fair, and thus attractive financial reward systems. For their part the workforce were simply expected to do the job they filled and to receive the appropriate rewards. The harder they worked, the higher their rewards and, assuming management were effective in their role, the more profitable the enterprise.

Taylor's prescriptions do not actually cast management in the role of supervisors. In his view if managers were doing their job properly they should find their workforces responding in the desired way. In later years many commentators have pointed out that in fact few of those who claimed to apply his approach offered the appropriate financial rewards and thus ensured unrest among their employees (Mouzelis, 1967). Conversely, much subsequent management theory has debated Taylor's founding assumption that it is money alone which motivates. Whether Taylor was wrong about this or those who claimed to follow him were faithful to the dictates of his philosophy are undoubtedly very important issues. Of more significance here is the fundamental division of labour he advocates between those who work and those who manage. For Taylor the two functions are to be split henceforth if one is seeking to practise good management. As a result those who execute are to do so in not only a narrowly defined way, but also in a one-dimensional way. In addition to a long-practised *technical division of labour* Taylor commends to management a *social division of labour* designed to concentrate all such work in their hands alone. By relieving workers of the need to think you allow them to do what they do best, engage in productive labour. Viewed in this way Taylor's work constitutes a major advance in the social organisation of work as this was to be practised by the generations of management who have succeeded him.

Moving on a further sixty years, 1974 saw the publication of a study which subsequently reshaped industrial sociology and has had repercussions far beyond. In his study of the degradation of work in the twentieth century Harry Braverman draws extensively on the writings of both Marx and Taylor. The former is not so much the young, romantic Marx disturbed by the consequences of the emergent factory system but Marx the scholar painstakingly analysing the spread of the capitalist *labour process*. Taylor is portrayed as the designer of the

means to perpetuate this labour process to the detriment of every subsequent generation of the working class throughout capitalist society. In his analysis of the labour process Marx was able to identify the development of the twin divisions later advocated by Taylor. For Marx these were evidence of the worsening social organisation of work experience with labour becoming an ever more formalised process rather than the satisfying activity he always held it to be. As time passed there was more reason for the working class to challenge their rulers, at work and beyond. Braverman was himself a Marxist and his study was intended as a further demonstration of the need for change as labour processes continue to spread causing their inevitable degradation. In his own account he draws attention to the ways in which the ubiquitous technical division of labour has resulted in the progressive deskilling of workers leaving them unsatisfied, demoralised and able to gain only minimal pleasure from their employments. Critics have argued that Braverman overstates the extent of deskilling which has occurred, understates the success which workers' organisations have had in countering the degradation strategies of management and that he fails to appreciate the constantly changing identity of skill (Wood, 1982; Thompson, 1989). Nevertheless few would claim that much evidence exists to conclude that deskilling has not affected many work roles.

Braverman argues that Taylor's scientific management was intended to produce deskilling. More importantly it aimed to simultaneously concentrate control in the hands of those involved in the work of conception, management. The two were simply the different sides of the same coin. Where workforces possessed skills they were in a position of potential control over their supervisors. In this sense skill becomes equated with discretion to perform a task in a way determined by the worker. By taking away the skill, the discretion is also removed and the problem of control resolved. Managers are invested with this discretion and thus are in control of the workforce. They do the thinking and the employees carry out their narrow tasks within a highly organised set of arrangements. This neat thesis has also been widely criticised, the main objection being that Braverman greatly overestimated the influence of Taylorism. If scientific management was not widely adopted, evidence for which was forthcoming from a variety of sources, then perhaps workforces were not really so subject to the intensification of management control as was being suggested. Almost immediately further insight was provided by writers influenced by Braverman. Scientific management was described by Edwards (1979) as only one of a number of strategies which were being experimented with by management in their attempts to consolidate their position of control over their workforces. In later periods different strategies were deployed as necessary, not always successfully. Friedman (1977) argued that on occasion it was not possible for management to exercise *direct control* in the sense of Taylorism and they may have to extend a measure of autonomy to their workforces. But even in this situation the objective is to ensure effective control in the longer term. Again the balance of opinion is that while Braverman is certainly misguided in believing that Taylorism has been universally and successfully employed, a good deal of management theory and practice since his day has contributed to a greater degree of worker subordination. Control of the workforce by management is not total, no more than deskilling is absolute. The point being made by Braverman and his more sympathetic critics is the existence of a trend towards limited skill tasks and low discretion roles. Or stated in another way, the fashioning of an extensive technical division of labour together with a pronounced social division of labour, both of which result in limited employee involvement and satisfaction. This is the reality of the contemporary social organisation of work (cf. Thompson, 1989).

LABOUR PROCESSES AND ACCOUNTANTS' WORK EXPERIENCES

For Braverman the social organisation of work is marked by the existence of labour processes and is a situation to be repaired if the mass of the workforce are to experience any degree of self-realisation. Conversely, the position of Taylor and those who follow him is that labour processes are the necessary form which work must take given the objectives of management and the interests of workers. Whichever view one embraces, it seems clear that for many factory and kindred blue-collar workers, work is and promises to remain very unsatisfying. At this point the following question should be forming in readers' minds: what has this to do with the everyday work experiences of professional accountants? In Braverman's view it was perfectly logical that the twin divisions of labour would become established in non-manual work situations and much of the later part of his book is concerned with the spread of labour processes to other types of work. According to Marx's fundamentalist analysis, to the extent that any type of work is performed in a capitalist society it will be dissatisfying to most of those who engage in it. Turning to Taylor, it seems pertinent to ask whether it is only the lowest orders of worker who will benefit from a strategy of scientific management. What is it about manual workers that singles them out as being in need of such organisation? However sincere Taylor may have been in seeking to improve the conditions of employees who experienced scientific management, the outcome was that those concerned with the conception function were in control of those who merely executed the work. For Braverman it was the promise of control that endeared such theories to management.

Taking this view, the issue of control becomes relevant to the case of any group of workers who might be expected to experience a similar organisation of their work over time. In the literature on clerical work there has long been a realisation that specialisation has been widely practised and to the detriment of many of those concerned. Two of the seminal studies of the 1950s drew attention to the way in which much clerical work could now be described as routine (Mills, 1951; Lockwood, 1958). Both saw that the great growth in the scale of such work in the twentieth century had been accompanied by the emergence of routines and procedures with specialist clerical functions replacing the concept of the general clerk. The development of office technology also served to further structure the division of clerical labour with some staff such as comptometer operators being in the envied role of skilled worker if also highly specialised in function. Both writers were also aware of the parallel development of systems for the management of these staffs. However, at that time it was of more interest to characterise their control in terms of the spread of the bureaucratic phenomenon, the negative process which had earlier occupied the thoughts of Max Weber. The emphasis was very much changed in a more recent study of clerical work produced by Crompton & Jones (1984). Their research demonstrated a continuing process of specialisation in the field of clerical labour with the emergence of narrower job specifications, more routines and a spread of procedures. New technologies had resulted in more and more clerical staff becoming information operatives increasingly indistinguishable from their manual counterparts in the factory. Some clerks were still able to find intellectual challenge in their work and these individuals often had important-sounding job titles. But in reality they were not part of the management of the clerical function but simply a small, ageing echelon of skilled workers who typified what clerical work was once like. Management was something quite different, a specialist task performed by managerial employees many of whom had little experience of clerical work itself. For Crompton & Jones (1984) and de Kadt (1979), much contemporary clerical work has all the characteristics of a labour process, especially the technical and social divisions of labour.

Clerical work is not comparable to professional accounting work in a great many ways, not least because unlike clerical work it is 'professional' in nature. The reason for discussing it is to indicate that there is some evidence of the spread of the social organisation of work beyond the factory or the production line. There is a growing amount of evidence that other lower level white-collar employees have experienced similar changes in their work situations (Abercrombie & Urry, 1983). This suggests that nowadays more than manual workers need to be organised in the conventional way and thereby involved in labour processes. Turning to professional work, and more particularly to the most common form it takes in the advanced societies, *corporate professionalism*, there is again growing evidence of the emergence of similar work arrangements. Long before the publication of Braverman's study, a series of studies of professional scientists and engineers had identified dissatisfaction with the fragmentation and routinisation of such work (Prandy, 1965; Barnes, 1971; Cotgrove and Box, 1970). The writer's earlier research on the work situations of scientists, engineers and technologists supports the view that for many of those in the non-managerial grades there is much to cause dissatisfaction and demoralisation (Roslender, 1983a). Since the early 1970s Cooley has documented the progressive 'Taylorisation' of much engineering design work, singling out the diffusion of computer-aided design technology as the mechanism by which management have secured control of their growing labour force (Cooley, 1976, 1981). In a fascinating account of the work of ICI's process engineers, Hales (1980) discusses the ways in which those charged with designing other people's labour processes increasingly find themselves subject to management controls. Kraft (1977) has identified the development of a technical division of labour in the computing industry. The emergence of specialist functions such as programming, systems analysis and coding is seen as the first phase of the process. In the case of programming, the second phase was the emergence of further specialisation with individuals developing their expertise in sub-routine writing or working in higher-level languages. Kraft also identifies the emergence of programming managers whose task it is to organise the work routines of the highly specialised but narrowly skilled programmers, while Greenbaum has drawn attention to the increasing pressure on management in the computer industry to exert greater control over their workforces in the face of increasing competition (Greenbaum, 1976, 1979).

The emergence of managerial roles and perhaps more significantly management control within the context of professional work is consistent with the view that labour processes are increasingly a feature of the work experiences of many professionals. In a paper on recent developments in hospital medicine in Britain Mike Dent (1986) argues that the growing concern with financial control in the hospitals has given rise to the emergence of a damaging labour process within medical labour. Because junior doctors are being subjected to persistent calls for financial stringency they are not able to practise in an autonomous way, a change which constitutes a serious attack on their professional integrity. Although they are not being subjected to the discipline of the factory, the imposition of such financial controls is their particular experience of a divorce of conception and execution. Whether it is senior medical staff or, as is increasingly the case, professional administrators who exercise control, the situation of the junior doctor is one of less integrity than has traditionally been the case. The claim that managerial work itself is usefully understood as a labour process has also been made (Teulings, 1986; Hopper, 1988). As Thompson notes, this involves more than simply stating the obvious that different groups of managers are responsible for different things. The argument is that there are significant distinctions between those who are involved in managing managers and higher level decision-making, and those who supply information and implement decisions. The idea that there may be a social division of labour within management is difficult for some to accept of course, for it

> can legitimise theoretical incorporation of any non-productive activity, such as some of those connected to accounting, which are solely mechanisms of control associated with the realisation and enlargement of capital.
>
> (Thompson, 1989, p.239)

The ideal point at which to return to the experiences of the accounting profession perhaps.

When discussing the roles which accountants presently fill, one of the key observations was that many are involved in highly organised task structures with evidence of extensive formalisation. The point was made that this is the result of the introduction of management control strategies within the accounting and finance function. At that stage the pursuit of enhanced management control was portrayed as being a development with self-evident value. Given the arguments of the intervening pages, it now seems fairly reasonable to conclude that many professional accountants may in fact be involved in some form of technical division of labour. As a result they may experience the same sort of specialisation of function which characterises employees who are subject to labour processes. In this way they are in the same situation as other groups of professional workers as well as the great majority of manual and lower grade white-collar workers. A major objection which might be raised against this highly provocative conclusion is that in concrete accounting roles the individual actually performs a varied set of necessarily formalised tasks and not the same one again and again. In this way there is a very real difference between an assembly line worker who is required to perform an identical task every thirty-six seconds and an accountant who works through a set of routines some of which are to be completed daily, others weekly and others perhaps less frequently. Conversely, one of the most telling points that the Dent paper makes is that all labour processes will assume their own form. The implication of this is that while it is true that there is no direct identity between assembly line work and the performance of a range of routine tasks in an accounting role, in terms of the intrinsic satisfaction that either can provide there may be a high degree of similarity. The routine performance of a narrow range of audit tasks by highly qualified and well-motivated accountants to them is every bit as demoralising as assembly line work is to those who perform it. The related objection that these latter workers could not readily carry out the audit function should also be recognised as irrelevant. Assembly line workers would no doubt find the routines of auditing hard to master (as do many accountants if examination results are to be believed!) and most accountants would not last long on the line. But both are unimportant observations, the more significant issue being how any employee experiences the particular job they are required and contracted to do.

A second objection that might be raised against the suggestion that much contemporary accounting work takes the form of a labour process is that in terms of their respective *market situations* there are major differences between account-ants and clerks or assembly line workers. The financial rewards for accountants are much better; they earn more, they are salaried employees and invariably have some pension provision as part of their financial package. While it is hard to argue with these points, in themselves they are not evidence that accountants do not experience the negative effects of labour processes. One major reason why accountants are well rewarded is that they have been in relatively short supply at the same time as the demand for their services has increased. If the professional accountancy associations were to adopt the policy of, say, their engineering counterparts then there would be an immediate increase in this supply which would certainly have repercussions on salary levels. In the case of engineering, a graduate engineer in the UK normally becomes a chartered engineer without the need to complete any examination programme. Imagine this in the case of the accounting associations and the effect it would have on salaries. Another of the recurrent themes in the comparison of the market situations of the professions and the mass of wage-earners is that the former are secure against unemployment and thus able to plan their lives with some certainty while the latter have never had that pleasure. Again the facts speak for themselves but they are essentially historical. In contemporary Britain there are presently unemployed professionals including scientists, engineers and teachers and even some lawyers and doctors. True many might be able to find employment if they were willing to move to different parts of the country or accept lower level positions and possibly rewards. But these are new qualifications in the argument that professionals are far better placed in the labour market, and they are indicative of the future rather than the past. In the particular case of accountants, the Big 6 spokesman referred to when discussing accounting technicians was making the point that the emergence of the latter in recent years did offer the opportunity to employ fewer graduates (Brandenberg, 1987). The thin end of the wedge perhaps? Market situation also involves career considerations with professionals being in a position of great advantage over the mass of the labour force. Again the historical facts are difficult to argue with but significant changes may be occurring. The question of careers for professional accountants will be considered separately and in some detail in the final section since their existence, or otherwise, is of particular relevance to understanding the broader nature of contemporary accountants' work experiences.

Having disposed of some of the more obvious objections to the claim that many professional accountants, in common with much of the workforce, are subject to the operation of labour processes in their employments it is now necessary to explore further the precise form of their particular experiences. An accountant employed in a large undertaking will normally be involved in carrying out a specified part of the broad programme of work which is assigned to the group or team of which they are a member. In the case of an auditor the individual will be part of an audit team which will be charged with the task of satisfactorily performing a particular audit assignment. In industry, commerce, or the public sector the individual will normally be a member of a department or of a section within a department which is responsible for performing the accounting and finance function. Carrying out the work involves following routines and procedures as described in the previous chapter. Perhaps the most interesting and important feature of these routines and procedures is their *dual* nature. By analysing this dual nature it is possible to identify a social division of labour within the performance of accounting and finance work.

The most obvious reason to formalise the accounting and finance function of a large organisation, and to introduce routines and procedures, is to ensure that the financial control which is being sought is achieved in an orderly, dependable and predictable way. In order to be in a position of control it is necessary to design and implement the appropriate systems, routines and procedures. These must be operated, monitored, evaluated and, when necessary, amended. This is the essence of management control. Thus a standard costing system is designed to help control costs in order to achieve desired corporate objectives. The costs in question are incurred by the company in the course of its operations. In reality these costs are incurred by members of the company and it is these members whose actions the routines and procedures of standard costing are designed to control. Using standard costing as an example clearly illustrates how a typical management accountant is implicated in the management control structure in two senses. It is the management accountant who is seen by those who incur costs as the individual who exercises control. For this reason it is often concluded that such individuals are exercising control and are thus imposing labour processes on others. However, such accountants are simply carrying out their designated tasks. They are instructed by their own superiors what to do and more significantly the precise routines and procedures they must follow in doing it. The individual management accountant does not determine the detailed routines and procedures which constitute standard costing in a company. These are determined by the senior management accountants to whom they report both literally and in the organisation structure. To achieve the objective of cost control these junior accountants are required to operate the designated routines and procedures. At any point in time senior staff are in the position of knowing what their various subordinates are doing. Any departure, if discovered, can result in disciplinary action particularly if there are failures on the cost control side. Departures which do not prove problematic may not be commented upon by management although normally they are noted and may be raised when things do go wrong.

The social division of labour within the management accounting function is that which exists between those accountants who are responsible for the development of a standard costing system and its subsequent implementation, and those accountants who are actually involved in its operation. Using Braverman's terminology, the former are involved in the task of conception, the latter in the task of execution. Although these accountants are not subject to the control imposed by a standard costing system itself, they are in a very real sense subject to management control, the control sought by their own superiors. A financial accountant charged with the task of preparing periodic financial statements is in precisely the same situation. The form and content of what they are required to do is set out by their superiors as is the time when they have to be available. The routines and procedures followed to achieve the desired financial control are similarly the prerogative of senior accountants. All the financial accountant has to do is to carry out the work as planned. Decisions regarding the treatment of particular items are increasingly restricted by the existence of accounting standards. And there is always the possibility that the statements will be amended by senior management. So what might resemble challenging and high discretion work is invariably quite the opposite as the individual accountant simply follows the rules and applies the appropriate formulae. In the case of auditors, they are also required to follow the prescribed routines and procedures of their firms.

While they do not control the activities of their clients in any direct way, they invariably find themselves subject to the control imperatives of their own management. Their hourly or daily position is carefully determined by senior management who expect their junior staff to follow the guidelines which they devise and impose upon them.

It might be objected that in the last analysis there are very many benefits to be gained from practising effective management control. In much the same way, Taylor and those who subsequently embraced his philosophy claimed there are benefits for all in adopting scientific management. However, wherever there are benefits there are also always costs. In the case of any form of management control it is senior management who seem to gain the most benefits and those who experience their control who bear the greatest costs in the form of un-fulfilling, low discretion, alienating jobs. Like manual workers, many lower grade white-collar workers and several other groups of professional workers before them, many well-rewarded, highly motivated accountants employed in increasingly formalised work situations appear to be experiencing their own forms of labour process with all the negative consequences such conditions produce (cf. Cherns, 1978).

THE PROMISE OF INFORMATION TECHNOLOGY

So far little has been said about the effects which information technology has had and promises to have on the work of professional accountants. Given the lack of literature currently available on accountants' work experiences this is not surprising. However, in the earlier section on the emergence of accounting technicians it was suggested that the advent of the computer has had a positive influence on both their situations and those of their professionally qualified counterparts (Brandenberg, 1987). The ACCA were certainly enthusiastic about the general consequences of information technology for professional accountants in a wide-ranging study carried out in conjunction with the Department of Industry (Carr, 1985). For their part CIMA have urged members to embrace and employ information technology wherever possible, believing it to be a development which can only extend the contribution of management accountancy in the 1990s. What are the lessons which may be learned from the experiences of other groups of workers?

Industrial sociology has a considerable literature on the consequences of technological advance for the improvement of work experiences. For the most part it concludes that all parties should be cautious about the benefits to be gained from new technologies and should consider any changes in a broad way. Not surprisingly most of this literature is comparatively recent in origin and follows in the wake of Robert Blauner's seminal monograph *Alienation and Freedom* (1964). At the time industrial sociologists were in the process of integrating the thoughts of the classical sociologists, including Marx, Weber and Durkheim, with their own empirical and historical research. Blauner was attracted to Marx's account of alienated labour and the idea that the capitalist social organisation of work had produced a general situation of worker 'unfreedom'. For his part Blauner believed that contemporary developments in technology promised to reverse the trend of increasing alienation and to 'free' workers from their negative work experiences. His view was formed as a result of studies which he and others had carried out in the US chemical industry which at the time was undergoing a transformation due to the rapid diffusion of computer-based continuous-flow or process technology systems. The extreme forms of alienation which were associated with assembly line technology were simply not evident in these new technology settings. Workers were challenged by the demands which these developments brought with them. They were now called upon to learn new skills, exercise discretion, take responsibility, etc. As a result their alienation which had increased with successive forms of technology was now in decline. To the extent that these were the technologies of the future, Blauner argued that workers could look forward to less alienation and more 'freedom'. It was not capitalism which enslaved them so much as the technologies which had developed in the previous century. All of this was now to change without the need for the extreme measures previously advocated by Marx.

At the same time as Blauner was publicising the virtues of the new technology, an equally influential British researcher was discussing the same changes in a slightly different way. For Joan Woodward (1965) the coming of these new technologies signalled a need for management to rethink their views on supervision. In order to gain the most benefit from such developments it would be necessary to design jobs which integrated conception and execution, jobs which encouraged workers to play a fuller part in the production process than was commonly the case. Using her own research she argued that the more successful firms using these new technologies were those which had adopted consistent organisation structures and management strategies. This research was subsequently to inform the development of the *contingency perspective* on organisation and management theory. In the context of the debate over the effects of new technologies on work experiences, the key difference between Woodward's and Blauner's views is that the latter does not recognise management as a crucial intervening force. Blauner adopts the over-simplistic and flawed technological determinist position which was common in American sociology at the time (Kerr, Dunlop, Harbison & Myers, 1962). Woodward's position is much more insightful in that it identifies the role which management inevitably play in these or any similar developments.

Two British studies published in the early 1970s offer further insight on the consequences of technological change for the workforce. The chemical industry research of Wedderburn & Crompton (1972) concluded that the new technologies which were increasingly evident undoubtedly did offer the chance of greater job satisfaction and enhanced work experiences. But these were not shared by everyone in a plant, only those who operated the technology and who usually were in the minority. The passage of time might of course see the wider application but for the moment the promise of technology was less than universal and its beneficial consequences confined to the minority of employees. In a study of the introduction of a new extrusion technology in a man-made fibres plant, Cotgrove and his associates reported that the workforce were initially more satisfied with their enriched work roles with their greater decision-making content and enhanced control (Cotgrove, Dunham & Vamplew, 1971). However, in their concluding comments they remark that as they left the plant a year into the new operations they detected that the novelty was beginning to wear off as the workforce mastered the new technology. This suggests the obvious – the existence of what might be termed honeymoon periods following any change, technological or otherwise, a theme which was to be taken up in perhaps the most comprehensive critique to date of the positive consequences of technology for work experience, Nichols & Beynon's study *Living With Capitalism* (1977). Their research was again in the chemical industry and involved them in intensive observation over several years. This allowed them to live with a workforce who in their words were living with capitalism. The general conclusion of the study is that the 'new working arrangements' which were so acclaimed by the company did little or nothing to improve the conditions of the workforce and in a number of respects had resulted in a further deterioration for most. Among the new negative features identified were the physiological consequences of working the so-called continental shifts system, the extent to which individuals were required to work in isolation from their fellow workers and the ever present fear of disaster over which in practice there was very little control. Nichols and Beynon also discuss the anti-social nature of such working practices and the way in which the company used financial incentives to further degrade their employees (see also Nichols & Armstrong, 1976).

One of the most interesting features of the study, and one of particular relevance to the present text, is the account which they offer of the work experiences of the professional chemical engineers at the plant. In the early days, before the plant was commissioned and later as it began to build up to full capacity, a series of challenges was evident, the work was exciting and the chemical engineers were in their view fully employed. Trouble-shooting, design modification, working all day and night to keep on schedule had satisfied them. Now the plant was operating and very little went wrong. They had done their job so well in the early days that in effect there was no real engineering to do. Like their counterparts in the plant most of the chemical engineers were experiencing the routines of life with high-tech capitalism.

Earlier reference was made to Cooley's critique of the spread of computer-aided design technologies. He would never deny that many engineers have found working with these technologies exciting and in many respects he sees them as being potentially beneficial to society. His objection is to the way in which in many cases they have been used to deskill design engineers, to control them or to replace them with less expensive technician staff (Cooley, 1976, 1981). This is entirely consistent with Woodward's view that management play a major role in deciding how any technology is to be used. Some would go a little further and say that not only are management in a position to determine the specific way in which any particular technology is to be employed, they are actually in the situation of being able to design technologies to match their own interests and objectives (Mackenzie & Wajcman, 1985). Crompton & Jones's (1984) account of the introduction of computerisation into clerical work also suggests that many within management have been quick to recognise the benefits it could have for them. The computer has been used to deskill and control many types of clerical work. For example, computerised batch systems have been introduced into payroll and accounts departments with the result that much clerical labour now consists of simply preparing information to be input to the computer. This in turn has increased the demand for cheaper, less confident, female labour, thereby reducing the wage bill and increasing management's control of the workforce. In this way gender and technology are presented as being two interrelated labour process strategies.

The general tenor of the literature is that developments such as process technology, automation, CAD, computerisation and by implication the current information technologies should be viewed sceptically from a job satisfaction viewpoint. At best only short-term benefits are likely, for comparatively few workers and normally only with management's support. At the least optimistic end of the spectrum, all advances of this sort are in the interests of management. It must be conceded that in recent years there has been growing support for the view that there is a serious danger in adopting an over-jaundiced view of technological advance. On the factory floor there is evidence of extensive reskilling as workers develop a portfolio of 'flexible' skills to complement new flexible manufacturing technologies while in the office the rapid diffusion of information technology has perhaps not been so destructive as was predicted in the late 1970s. In a sense it is a return to an optimistic Blauneresque vision of a technologically infused future after a generation of overstated Bravermania (cf. Thompson, 1989).

What significance does this have for the professional accountant? If the arguments assembled in the previous section are accepted, then most accountants not involved in a managerial role are already experiencing deteriorating work situations. Salaries may be holding up very well at the moment and the status of the profession is still quite high. The cynical use of information technology could change all of this quite rapidly if that is the wish of management. Clearly the professional accountancy associations are attracted to the promise of information technology and it is difficult to see them changing this view. To do so would leave them open to the criticism that they are being conservative and do not wish to contribute to progress. This in turn could lead to other occupational groups (accounting technicians perhaps?) taking on the challenges of the new technologies, raising their status and earnings, improving their career prospects, etc. More generally there is the popular belief that the use of such technologies contributes to improvements in control, efficiency, profit or some similar outcome. The logic for making as much use of them as possible is inescapable, especially to an accountant. The problem is that those commending such advances, be they manufacturers, management, the associations or even the government, are not in the business of highlighting any of the drawbacks of embracing information technology. In such a situation it is hardly surprising that many accountants are themselves enthusiastic about embracing it. Their enthusiasm is likely to be heightened if they are already engaged in highly formalised work. The technology might promise to free them from tiresome routines or to let them do things they presently have no time to. Software packages which allow the performance of broader, fuller analyses and provide more information will be extremely seductive. And as has been remarked so many times before, a change is often as good as a rest. Once in place, the technology will create its own work experiences in the short, medium and long terms.

Another way of approaching the issue is to consider the mechanisms for introducing information technology into professional accounting work. For those involved in small-scale operations there will probably be the chance to participate in choosing the systems and packages to be adopted. In some cases accountants will be the only members of the management team who have any detailed knowledge of the technology available. As a result they are in a strong position to determine policy on information technology and more generally. This situation is not, however, typical of the contemporary profession which sees the majority of professionally qualified accountants employed in large undertakings. Here technology policy is determined by senior management and then relayed to the rest of the workforce. Only senior accounting staff will participate in the policy process on a regular basis. On occasion they may consult with their subordinates and while in theory the latter might exercise some influence, in the end they will not make any decisions. The outcome is that in most instances information technology is imposed on those who will experience its effects. In this way there is no significant difference between introducing information or indeed any new technology into a manual labour process or a professional one. The prevailing social organisation of work ensures this.

ACCOUNTANTS AND MANAGEMENT

The point has now been reached where it is necessary to debate at some length the question of whether accountants are management. In the previous paragraph the clear implication was that many accountants cannot be considered as management as long as they have such things as technological change imposed on them. On the other hand those senior accountants who participate in the policy or decision-making process are properly viewed as management. Throughout the present and the previous chapter the idea that there is a significant division between accountants and 'managing' accountants has been implied. The latter are engaged in the task of organising and managing the work of their subordinate accountant colleagues in the same way as office managers organise and manage the work of office workers or production managers organise and manage factory floor workers. This is the fundamental reality of the social organisation of work as it presently exists. Although it is possible to differentiate analytically between the task of organisation and that of management, in practice the two are entirely complementary. This was clearly established in Fayol's seminal account of managerial activities, first published in 1916, in which he identified five elements of managerial work: planning, organising, commanding, coordinating and control (Fayol, 1949).

In order to begin to resolve the question whether accountants are properly categorised as management it is necessary to understand the relationship which exists between the elements of managerial work or *functions of the manager* and what are commonly termed the *management functions*. In the previous chapter accounting and finance was described as one of the contemporary management functions, along with others including research, design and development, marketing, personnel, etc. At the present time the range of management functions in any sizeable organisation is undertaken by an army of employees. When the scale of operations was much smaller it was possible for the owner to carry out this sort of work with assistance from a few clerks. As the scale of operations and the need to devote more attention to the successful performance of this work increased, the numbers involved in it grew. Over time there has also been the emergence of the specialised functions, which in some part has contributed to the growth in the scale of the management functions. The received wisdom of contemporary organisation and management is that it is necessary to employ a large number of employees in these functions. This workforce is made up of both professional and non-professional elements and usually includes accountants in its numbers, together with clerks, technicians and various other professional groups. It also includes the various supervisory staffs who are engaged to oversee operations: for example, shift foremen and production superintendents in manufacturing industry, or in the case of commercial enterprises, office managers. In a technical sense all of these employees could be designated 'management' and it was in this sense that Goldthorpe & Lockwood (1963) drew attention to the long-established view that such workers were not part of 'us', the working class of manual workers, but were more appropriately viewed as part of 'them', the opposing class, i.e. management. As the authors pointed out at the time, this was an unhelpful dichotomy which was rapidly being overtaken by events. For them the growing ranks of 'affluent workers' were becoming increasingly indistinguishable from the majority of clerical workers on a range of indicators. Today very few people would seriously argue that there are any significant differences between the mass of manual and clerical workers but most would still balk at the idea that many of the professionally qualified accountants employed in large organisations should not be categorised as management.

While operations management is certainly one of the management functions along with accounting and finance or marketing, it is quite different to the others in a crucial way. This difference is captured in the literature of management science by the distinction between *staff* and *line* functions (Stewart, 1967). Those production foremen, superintendents and managers who are employed to organise and manage production are line managers as are their counterparts in insurance companies or government departments who are responsible for organising and managing the day-to-day work of their undertakings. They are directly involved in achieving the principal objectives of their respective organisations. By contrast the accountants who may be employed in the accounting and finance function, perhaps on the same site, are engaged in a staff function whose primary purpose is to provide a range of services to those responsible for line management. In this way it is possible to talk in terms of there being a *line management function* where the emphasis is on the performance of the functions of management properly conceived. This is quite different to the case of the *staff management functions* where the emphasis is on the performance of some specific part of the non-operational tasks of the organisation. This should not be interpreted as meaning that the former is the more important of the two. It is simply a different type of function. The two types of function involve entirely complementary activities and the effective performance of both is a prerequisite for successful operations. It is one of the challenges of executive management that it is able to bring together the line and staff management functions in successfully achieving the objectives which it has set for the organisation.

Within the line management function the existence of a chain of command is a widely recognised fact. Indeed it is this arrangement which gives rise to the term itself: the line of command. The result is that there are a series of levels of management which range from foreman and similar lower level supervisory positions through shift management positions to the higher level production manager or works manager positions, and in larger undertakings, on to the production or operations director who has the ultimate responsibility for ensuring the successful performance of the principal purpose of the organisation. In previous pages the term social division of labour has been used to draw attention to the way in which conception and execution have been separated from each other and invested in managerial and non-managerial roles respectively. Since line management is now recognised to involve a series of sub-divisions within the managerial function itself it is logical that the social division of labour concept be applied to the whole chain of command and not simply the fundamental division between managers and workers. In this way it is possible to conceptualise more senior management positions as entailing a portfolio which is skewed towards conception while the lowest level of supervisory posts are much more closely oriented to the tasks of execution. Most commentators acknowledge the existence of similar arrangements within the ranks of the staff management functions with the most senior managers at the head of their own chains or lines of command. Few, however, seem to recognise the significance of these arrangements, being content to draw attention to a similarity between line and staff functions. Distinguishing between different groups within the ranks of what might reasonably be termed management is of critical importance especially when it is recognised that the line principle applies not only to the lower ranks of clerks, technicians and kindred workers but also to professional staffs. The spread of the social division of labour to staff functions is evidence of the manner in which senior management have chosen to organise and manage the operations of their own functions. In this way the principles of operations management apply equally to management and non-management workers and have significant consequences for all who are subject to them. This of course includes the many professionally qualified accountants who find themselves employed in organisations.

The logic of this argument is unlikely to have immediate appeal to many of those on the factory floor, in offices, or indeed in Britain's schools and hospitals who feel themselves increasingly controlled by the activities of accountants. How is it possible that these management functionaries are not part of management? Again it is interesting to look to management science for some insight on this matter. Puxty (1986) draws attention to the *functional relationship* which exists between two departments in an organisation whereby members of one have *functional authority* over members of the other. He offers as an example the case of the management accountant in a manufacturing company who requests that line managers keep costing records for cost analysis purposes. Although production is the principal purpose of the organisation, line management will normally accept such a request in the interests of greater effectiveness in achieving the organisation's goals. The basis of this acceptance is two-fold. Normally it will have been initiated as a result of a decision at the executive level where the most senior managers are responsible for taking a broader, more holistic view. The production director will have discussed with the finance director the value of the procedure and will in turn instruct the middle ranks of line managers on the need to cooperate. Secondly as long as the arrangement is successful, i.e. cost analysis produces greater profitability, the middle ranks of line managers will continue to concede some extent of their authority and responsibility to their colleagues in the accounting and finance function. If things start to go wrong then it will be necessary to review the situation, to perhaps amend it in some way or even abandon it in the last analysis.

In the case of the individuals whose job it is to maintain such records the origin of the requirement is largely irrelevant. Whether they are directed by and report to their own managers or to an accountant from the accounting and finance function they are in effect subject to management control of some sort. Refusing to cooperate with an accountant is only likely to give rise to a repeat of the request from line management accompanied by a threat of the exercise of negative sanctions. This situation reflects the prevailing social organisation of work and the existence of a social division of labour within the operational structure of the organisation. However, it does not take into account the existence of a parallel social division of labour within the accounting and finance function of the organisation, and is resultantly an oversimplified view of the actual situation. The accountant exercising functional authority over the clerk in the production function is not doing this as a manager but as an employee who is invested with this authority by virtue of the fact of being part of the accounting and finance function. The request is made on behalf of those who manage the accounting and finance function. Being subject to management and the existence of a social division of labour, the accountant in question has no freedom to make such requests at will. If the request is not made then the accountant will inevitably run the risk of equally negative sanctions and in the knowledge of this will comply with the demands of the job. In this way it is not accountants as an un-differentiated occupational group who should be viewed as assuming an increasingly important role in the management of large organisations, to the supposed detriment of all concerned. Many of them are simply another group of employees in the position of having to implement policies which have been determined by their own senior managers in consultation with their counterparts in the other management functions. As Argyris recognised many years ago, those who fill accounting roles in large organisations routinely find themselves in the position of facing criticism which by rights should be directed at their own superiors and at senior management in general (Argyris, 1952). This is yet another destructive consequence of the prevailing social organisation of work.

In the passing reference to the work of Goldthorpe & Lockwood above, mention was made of the 'us' and 'them' dichotomy between the working class of manual workers and the opposing class loosely identified as management. The concept of class has been almost totally absent in this and previous chapters. The point has now been reached where it can be deployed to finally resolve the specific question of whether or not accountants are management, as well as to underpin a more general conclusion as to the nature of accountants' work experiences. Goldthorpe & Lockwood followed up their paper with a major empirical research project which became known as the Affluent Worker studies; in these the term *embourgeoisement* figured prominently (Goldthorpe *et al.*, 1968a, 1968b, 1969). By this they meant 'becoming middle class', the argument being that on a range of economic indicators at least there was very little difference between a growing number of manual workers and their clerical counterparts. The old dichotomy between clerical workers and manual workers was becoming more blurred with the latter moving up the economic class ladder to join an occupational group which had always been viewed as having some identity with the middle class and with management. The researchers were unwilling to commit themselves to full embourgeoisement conceptualised in the original 1963 paper as:

the large-scale assimilation of manual workers and their families to middle-class life-styles and middle-class society in general.

(Goldthorpe & Lockwood, 1963, p.155)

but they did feel that the unquestionable growth in working class affluence was having a significant effect on the British class structure.

Following the logic of this argument, if these manual workers were subsequently to improve their economic situation so that it became comparable with the more clearly middle class occupational groups such as the professions then economic embourgeoisement would have progressed even further. And if these same affluent workers were to begin to buy their own homes, invest their savings in stocks and shares, take out private health care and personal pension plans, etc. then their fuller middle class assimilation would have occurred. In many ways this was the reality for a privileged fraction of the working class, the C1s, who have supported the Conservative party at recent elections. To some extent they have succeeded in displacing many clerical workers and some professional workers as part of the contemporary middle class. At the moment, however, very few are able to compare with the accountancy profession on economic or indeed any indicators, the profession remaining very well placed in the upper reaches of the middle class, well rewarded, in secure employment, able to look forward to attractive pensions, etc. If this were to change as a result of further economic embourgeoisement, then few would surely doubt that the British class structure was a thing of the past. Or would they?

The principal difficulty with viewing the class structure in this particular way is that it portrays classes and class structures in an essentially *distributional* way (Crompton & Gubbay, 1977). In its simplest formulation the working class is characterised by its low level of income and indeed by the insecurity associated with this, the lower middle class by its greater earnings and economic security and so on through to the very richest elements in society. The manner in which this scarce but highly desired commodity is distributed forms the basis of the class structure. Contemporary sociological thinking on the class structure conceived of in this way draws attention to a set of interrelated class characteristics: rewards, life-styles, educational attainments, occupations, careers, life-chances, etc. Much has been made of the redistributional trends evident in the post-war period, with the Affluent Worker studies being only one example. The structure itself has been portrayed as diamond-shaped rather than the traditional pyramid, much flatter without the massive divisions between top and bottom. Greater opportunity for movement up (and down) the class structure is also widely documented by researchers. All of this, however, fails to recognise that while the class structure may have changed substantially in its form, its content remains the same. Simply redistributing people between the classes, however this is achieved, does not remove the fact that there are divisions between the classes which in the last analysis are difficult to come to terms with. In order to understand the divisions between classes it is necessary to think of classes and class structures in a *relational* way.

Whereas viewing classes as distributional groupings is derived from Weber, the relational perspective originates in the work of Marx. For Marx classes were distinguished according to their relationship to the means of production. In the classical formulation the capitalist class owned the means of production while the working class did not; the petit-bourgeoisie, the middle class of Marx's day, owned only modest amounts of the means of production. Because the working class owned no means of production, they were obliged to sell their labour to the capitalist class (or to the petit-bourgeoisie) to subsist. Once they did this they found themselves locked into contractual relationships with their employers further emphasising the relational nature of class structuration. This analysis served Marxist writers and militants well for over a century but was rapidly becoming outdated as post-war affluence extended to sections of the working class. Confronted with this, changing patterns of ownership and non-ownership and the growth of professional, technical and managerial workforces, a new generation of Marxist theorists including Poulantzas, Carchedi and Wright began refashioning the relational perspective to explain the class structure of contemporary capitalism (Cottrell & Roslender, 1986). Despite many differences in the positions adopted by these and other contributors to the new class analysis, all were intent on demonstrating that despite appearances to the contrary, the patterns of relationship between the classes in contemporary capitalism were essentially the same as they ever were. A class divided society is still very much with us.

Much of the debate inevitably centred on the professional, technical and managerial workforces and in particular on their place within large organisations relative to the two traditional classes: the working class and the capitalist class. Because many of these workers were found in the position of being exploited by their employers while simultaneously being required to exploit their own subordinates, they could not be identified as either working class nor capitalist class. This term *new middle class* is used by Carchedi (1975, 1977) in his analysis of the economic identities of the contemporary classes. In his schema the new middle class is like the working class when it is performing work of *coordination and unification* or alternatively, some technically skilled work, e.g. chemical analysis. Conversely it is like the capitalist class when it is performing work of *control and surveillance*. He continues by drawing attention to the way in which the new middle class is internally differentiated. Those at the head perform significant extents of work of control and surveillance in tandem with very limited extents of work of coordination and unification or technically skilled work. Those at the foot perform mainly work of coordination and unification or technically skilled work in a symmetrical manner. The former group are almost identifiable as the capitalist class, the latter the working class while in between there is a range of middle class identities. Described in this way it is immediately apparent that the new middle class are the class who staff the various chains of command, i.e. social divisions of labour, which characterise organisations.

Despite the insightfulness of Carchedi's position it contains a serious limitation which was soon recognised by critics. As Hindess and Hirst pointed out, control and surveillance and coordination and unification are only analytically separable (in Cutler *et al.*, 1977). Carchedi himself acknowledges as much when he uses the term *supervision and management* to describe them. Once this is taken on board, however, it is possible to use Carchedi's position to even greater effect (Roslender, 1983a, 1990a). Those who perform significant extents of work of supervision and management in tandem with very limited extents of technically skilled work are at the head of the new middle class. To be at the tail of the new middle class it is necessary to have only a minor supervision and management content in a position which is essentially one of technically skilled work. The crucial difference between this and Carchedi's own formulation is that in the case of the latter positions it is the extent of technically skilled work which gives rise to the similarity with the working class class identity. Again to be identified as new middle class it is necessary to exhibit a dual character but in this formulation the complementary nature of both aspects of the work of supervision and management is acknowledged in a way which enhances the original analysis.

To be categorised as 'management' it seems only logical that an individual is performing some work of supervision and management content in their work on a regular basis. If no such work is being regularly undertaken then it is not possible to apply the label management. In this way the lowest grades of foremen or office management are identifiable as management irrespective of their earnings, educational attainments, life-styles, etc., while many well-rewarded, highly qualified and technically able professional scientists, engineers, computer programmers, doctors, and of course accountants, who enjoy comfortable life-styles and are able to offer their children the best of life-chances are not. If they do not manage others they cannot be categorised as managers, being among the ranks of the managed and more specifically the managed working class. This is a highly contentious conclusion. The idea that many professionally qualified accountants are identifiable as working class is entirely at odds with commonsense thinking. However, it is a conclusion which has been implied throughout this and the previous chapter. Subjection to the technical and social divisions of labour, to labour processes, the growing experience of formalisation, the need to specialise in early career, the potential threats posed by the emergence of accounting technicians and information technology all point in the same direction. The seemingly attractive situation of the professionally qualified accountant may belie its underlying reality.

If this analysis is correct, the claimed economic embourgeoisement of growing sections of the working class seems wholly misconceived. Instead it would appear that sections of the middle class have come 'down' to join them, at least in terms of the way they experience their work. In the lexicon of the new class analysis this is termed *economic proletarianisation* which might be translated as 'becoming working class'. One of the implications of the economic proletarianisation thesis when applied to professional workers is that at some previous time their work was not as it is presently structured. Significant changes have occurred in the recent past, changes which have resulted in a deterioration of the situation of those who have experienced them either personally or *post facto*. These include the emergence of labour processes, the technical and social divisions of labour, the diffusion of routines and procedures, etc. (Kelly & Roslender, 1988; Roslender, 1990a). On the issue of careers for professional workers the thesis is particularly insightful. The introduction of a social division of labour with a multi-level chain of command obviously provides a much more formalised career structure than previously existed. Once on the ladder it is possible to move up toward senior management and indeed across to other managerial roles. The problem is to get onto the ladder bearing in mind the underlying argument that there are great numbers of professional workers in subordinate positions. While previously it might well have been possible for everyone interested in such a career to move to a junior managerial position and then onwards and upwards, the sheer numbers involved nowadays precludes this. In other words, once part of the professional worker fraction of the working class it is increasingly difficult to move out of it. Whether this particular aspect of economic proletarianisation applies to professionally qualified accountants at the present time is a fascinating empirical question. Judging by the number of appointments pages in the accounting press and the impressive sounding job titles they advertise all is well. But appearances can be deceiving not least for those who are seeking to secure these positions.

Chapter 4

Accountancy and ideology

The fact that many accountants do not experience the most attractive working conditions, nor are part of management, does little to refute the underlying thesis that accounting as a set of practices, like the broader institution of accountancy itself, is heavily infused with ideology. Some accountants are responsible for constructing ideology although the majority are only concerned with its implementation. In either respect it is very much a part of the dominant ideas-set which characterises contemporary capitalist societies. Accountancy is invoked to legitimate decisions about expanding or contracting operations, committing or withdrawing funds, introducing more stringent financial controls, paying out dividends or retaining earnings, etc. In many cases it appears to be the only basis for selecting particular courses of action and as such it is the target for much criticism. In this chapter a number of aspects of the relationship which exists between accountancy and ideology are examined. The first section provides an anatomy of the concept of ideology. This is followed by a section which considers some of the arguments developed by the critical accounting tradition on the ideological qualities of modern accountancy. In the third section a number of alternative ways of accounting proposed during the past twenty years are outlined and discussed. Finally, human resource accounting is subjected to more detailed scrutiny, both as it has been developed in the past and as it might be reconstituted in the near future as a complement to recent changes in outlook evident in management theory and practice.

IDEOLOGY: THE ANATOMY OF A CONCEPT

Ideology has been one of the most important concepts in the history of sociology, a situation which seems unlikely to change in the future. It is also one of the richest concepts in the history of the discipline, which entails that it is not possible to define it with any ease. The concept of ideology has been developed and employed by many writers whose interests and objectives have varied. As with concepts such as value or profit in accounting, it is possible to discuss its meaning and significance *ad infinitum* and still not be any nearer its definition, only more convinced of its importance. The purpose of this section is not to produce a definition of ideology but to outline some of the more important sociological thinking on it. The starting point, however, is not with the discipline itself but with the oldest and possibly the most commonly used connotation of the term, the accusation of political bias.

In the early nineteenth century the recently coined term was appropriated by Napoleon Bonaparte who used it against the democrats whose political philosophy he sought to discredit (Williams, 1983). Since then there has always been a derogatory use of the term in the political arena. To take a contemporary example, successive Conservative administrations have persistently been accused of seeking to destroy the National Health Service for ideological reasons. Those who voice this criticism believe the outcome will be disastrous for large sections of the population who are not in a position to afford private health care. The government's belief that it is the responsibility of individuals to provide for their own health care is at the heart of the matter. Their opponents do not accept this belief. They view it as posing a serious threat to the future of society as we know it hence their criticism of any moves which seem to be part of the process of destruction, e.g. allowing hospitals to become self-governing trusts outside of the NHS. Because they do not share the belief in individualism, they accuse those who do so of acting in an ideological way. This inevitably results in counter-accusations of behaving ideologically. The critics of reform are simply seeking to perpetuate the existence of the 'nanny state' without any concern for the resources which this may squander. In this way it is they who are the real threat to society as we know it. In due course the electorate will be allowed to decide which ideas they favour, the victorious party claiming a mandate to act on their beliefs. Committed to the democratic system, whoever loses can only respond with further accusations of ideology, thereby demonstrating the futility of party politics perhaps.

For the young Marx the political arena was only one place in which the ruling ideas of any epoch were evident. In his view ideology was the whole range of beliefs which the most powerful sections of society advanced as constituting the order of things or how things are and should be. Because they were in the position of being able to control the means of mental production, the ruling class were able to formulate ideology (Abercrombie, 1980). When consumed by the masses this ideology would secure the former class's dominance. Thus for Marx ideology was of necessity illusory, designed to effect the reproduction of a prevailing social order and so protect the interests of those who presently rule. Ideology was false, a misrepresentation of reality served up in the interests of the ruling class for consumption by the subordinate classes. These ideas were first advanced by Marx (and Engels) in *The German Ideology* in 1846. At that time the ruling class were the bourgeoisie who needed ideology to retain their dominance of a social order, i.e. capitalism, which in Marx's view was rapidly becoming an untenable basis for civilised life on the part of the mass, the working class. The thesis that it was inevitable that the working class would become aware or conscious of their situation and act appropriately follows neatly from this analysis and soon passed into the realms of Marxist theory. In practice the formation of working class consciousness was far more problematic as Marx and those who embraced his political philosophy soon discovered. This in turn gave rise to a substantial body of Marxist theory including Georg Lukacs' seminal 1923 study *History and Class Consciousness*. Like the young Marx, Lukacs relied heavily on the notion of false or illusory ideology. In his view the way in which the working class understood the world was determined by the bourgeoisie. However, in his view it was the ruling class's consciousness which was a false consciousness, i.e. ideology. Inevitably the consciousness of the working class was similarly ideology as a consequence of its being a received consciousness. Lukacs continued by arguing that in time the working class would come to its own consciousness and at that point it would be in a position to overthrow the bourgeoisie, their false consciousness and, of course, their ideology. Working class consciousness would be the true consciousness, devoid of ideology, a line of reasoning designed to motivate the faithful in their struggle to create socialism.

By the time of his death in 1883 Marx had begun to entertain a rather different notion of ideology. Now the idea that ideology should be viewed as false or illusory is replaced by the more persuasive notion of ideologies being the systems of ideas appropriate to different classes. Thus bourgeois ideology is the manner in which the ruling class/bourgeoisie would have the world understood while proletarian ideology is the construction of the working class/proletariat. Of necessity both are designed to secure the position of the class which has devised them but in this sense of the term neither is to be viewed as false nor true. Every class devises ideology in line with its own interests, the different ideologies being sets of ideas arising from a given set of material, ie class, interests (Williams,1983). Taking this view, the position of writers such as Lukacs seems naive on two major counts. The idea that a true consciousness is possible must be rejected on the grounds that all consciousness is necessarily partial because the interests of the different classes are themselves partial. Secondly, the inevitability of the triumph of a proletarian consciousness has to be seen as an act of faith since one of the conditions of its emergence is that there is a free market in ideas, something which the dominant bourgeois ideology will recognise and seek to guard against. As a result much Marxist thought in the post-war period has been concerned with the question of the content of the dominant ideology and perhaps more significantly its transmission and acceptance by the masses. It is in this sense that the sociological study of ideology has tended to develop in recent times (Abercrombie, Hill & Turner, 1980).

The Marxist tradition is not the only source of insight on ideology within sociology. The work of Karl Mannheim and in particular his introduction to the sociology of knowledge entitled *Ideology and Utopia* (1954) has also been widely influential. Mannheim was not a Marxist, but writing in Germany in the late 1920s meant that Mannheim's thinking inevitably reflected some of the concerns of Marxist theory. His own contribution begins with a distinction between the *particular* and *total* conceptions of ideology much in the analytical tradition of Weber or Simmel (Mannheim, 1954, p.49). The particular conception is likened to a 'lie' of some importance, one which would normally serve an 'opponent' rather than ourselves. The total conception is described as the 'total structure' of the mind of an age or a concrete historico-social group, e.g. a class. It is in a second distinction between *ideology* and *utopia* that Mannheim's distance from Marxism is evident. Only dominant groups have ideology, belief-systems which despite being ill-informed in important ways still serve to ensure their dominance. Dominated groups have utopia, belief-systems which besides being heavily infused with prevailing ideology also tend to be so bound up with opposition to the present order that they fail to recognise what really exists. Both systems of belief are in Mannheim's view 'situationally transcendent' (p.175). In this way it is possible for the dominated group to become dominant as its brand of utopia becomes caught up by a changing society. However, due to the persistence of the utopian mentality, a new utopia will inevitably emerge. The tension between ideology and utopia is thus posited as the driving force of history. What interested Mannheim as a sociologist of knowledge was explaining the formation of ideologies or utopias and the dynamic relationship which exists between them. Class for him is little more than an explanatory variable and the contemporary political struggle an example of the dynamic tension between (bourgeois) ideology and (proletarian) utopia. The resolution of this particular struggle is no more significant than any other.

Two writers in particular are responsible for the modern notion of ideology, Antonio Gramsci and Louis Althusser. Both were interested in the idea that we live ideology in the sense that ideologies are everywhere around us and are thus more than simply ideas or belief-systems. Gramsci's thoughts on ideology were contained in the notes that he made during his long imprisonment in the 1930s, the result of his political activities in earlier years. The main elements of his work were only published in English in 1971, over thirty years after his untimely death in 1937 (Boggs, 1976). Although Gramsci never offered a theory of ideology, he addresses the subject throughout his writings. This reflects the principal point of Gramsci's view of ideology, its omnipresence. It is present in the family as much as in political parties, in work organisation as much as in constitutional arrangements. As a result at all times everyone lives ideology, which is the reason for Gramsci it is a *lived relation*. Another important insight is that we should not think of the different class ideologies as being distinct. In the case of the working class, its ideology is not so much the received ideology of the bourgeoisie as a complementary ideology fashioned in response to it. However, its potential to replace the latter is reduced to the extent that it is built around critical received wisdoms. For this reason Gramsci, like many before and since, recognised the ultimate futility of the wage struggle embraced by the trade unions and their members on the basis that it poses no threat to the control which capital has in the workplace. Only by seizing control will it be possible to replace the tyranny of the factory. But in a capitalist society workers' control cannot guarantee to pay the rent whereas increased earnings have usually done so. To create a genuinely oppositional consciousness the mass need to understand fully the incorporated nature of their present ideology. Their masters, however, are in a strong position to ensure their supremacy over time by taking on board the main criticisms of the masses, a tactic which can readily be represented as a mutually beneficial state of affairs. In the terminology of Gramsci, they possess ideological dominance or *hegemony*, a dominance which necessarily extends far beyond the realm of political ideas.

In contrast to Gramsci, Althusser produced a great volume of thought on ideology during the 1960s and 1970s. As a philosopher he was always rethinking his ideas in the attempt to provide greater insight and naturally enough managing to contradict himself at every turn. Perhaps his most enduring thesis on ideology characterises it as a representation of the imaginary relationship of individuals to their real conditions of existence (Althusser, 1969). Here he seeks to reject any notions of false consciousness by characterising ideology not as some representation of real conditions (which could be a false representation) but as a representation of an imaginary relationship of individuals to these real conditions. Again the emphasis is on the lived relation aspect as in Gramsci, and the way in which this is constituted in class society returns to the point made by Marx about the material basis of any ideology. Althusser shares with Gramsci the position that in every realm of existence individuals experience ideology. In his essay on the *ideological state apparatuses* (ISAs) he provides a list of the institutions in civil society which he believes contribute to the ideological dominance of the ruling class. Education is singled out as the dominant ISA as a result of its critical contribution to the reproduction of ruling class ideology (Althusser, 1971). This essay also sees Althusser moving the concept ideology on another important step. Put simply he asks his readers to conceive of ideology in a material way, as a practice, rather than in an ideational way. It is not only the ideas of the ruling class which are experienced but the material forms of these ideas. For example, a workforce experiences both exploitation in their employment (in the interests of capital accumulation) and work structured in ways designed to invest control in supervisory positions as discussed in the last chapter. As a result they experience ideology in two ways which in the normal course of events they believe to be the most appropriate mode of operation. They may have alternative schemes of their own but at best these will be accommodatory in content as opposed to revolutionary. In Althusser's view the material forms of ideology constitute the greater part of everyday social life. And it is their very familiarity to us, as individuals, which contributes greatly to their continued acceptance.

Summarising these thoughts on ideology serves to highlight a powerful concept with which to analyse modern accountancy. Five important points are evident in the development of the concept. Firstly, while it is inescapable that the derogatory connotation is in common currency at the present time and is well understood, it is not a major feature of sociological analysis. Talking about ideology solely in a derogatory way is to score points rather than to increase understanding. Secondly, ideology is not restricted to political ideas unless by political is meant any consideration of the phenomenon of power in society (Weber, 1948). All of the institutions of civil society are underpinned by ideology. Equally, ideology is not simply ideas. It is experienced in its many material forms with far greater frequency and is thereby entirely familiar to us in the elements of the social structure. Fourthly, ideology is not a lie nor a set of fabricated truths. It is the manner in which groups or classes seek to characterise, structure and reproduce social reality. It is intended to serve their particular interests rather than those of other groups or classes although the latter are free to devise and promote their own ideology. At any point in time there will be a dominant ideology and a series of subordinate ideologies. Finally, this latter point may be taken to mean that there is a steady succession of ideologies (i.e. utopias) with the passage of time. In class societies, however, there is little real challenge to the dominant ideology as long as that ideology is sufficiently acceptable to the mass. One means of ensuring this is for ideologues to listen to criticism from below and to be willing to promote a measure of change, i.e. to be responsive to the wishes of other constituencies in society.

THE IDEOLOGICAL NATURE OF ACCOUNTANCY

A general conclusion which can be drawn from reviewing previous chapters is that there is very little in the way of a literature on the sociology of accountancy. Therefore to expect much in the way of a sociological analysis of the ideological nature of accountancy would be a little optimistic, despite the fact that both Marx (1974) and Weber (1968) did refer to it. For once subsequent generations of sociologists seem to have passed up the opportunity to build on their insights, preferring to focus on the role of ideology elsewhere in society.

In order to consider the ideological nature of accountancy it is necessary to turn to the literature of what has been termed *critical accounting* which began to emerge a decade or so ago (Cooper & Hopper, 1990). The most valuable starting point is the enormously influential paper published in *Accounting, Organisations and Society* in 1980 by Burchell, Clubb, Hopwood, Hughes & Nahapiet entitled 'The roles of accounting in organisations and society'. As the writers themselves say

> Our discussion of the organisational and social roles of accounting has tried to identify an area of enormous and largely uncharted complexity.
>
> (Burchell *et al.*, 1980, p.22)

Nevertheless they succeeded in conveying to many accounting researchers the pressing need to begin to think about accounting and to do so in a critical way. Among the many issues which they raised was the necessity of considering the relationship between the stated roles of accounting and those which it actually plays in practice. Accounting is presented as having established itself on the basis that it provides a means to achieve much needed accountability, promotes

efficiency within the organisation, furnishes information which is useful to shareholders in making investment decisions and makes a significant contribution to management control. Burchell *et al.* pose two complementary questions: are these the actual roles which accounting plays and are there other roles which accounting plays? For them there is only one way to find out. It is necessary to carry out a programme of case studies of actual accounting systems employing perspectives and methodologies drawn from beyond the boundaries of 'the behavioural in accounting' (p.23). In the context of future research in management accounting this call soon gave rise to the emergence of a strong sociological tradition which is discussed further in Chapter 6 below and in Roslender (1990b).

Understandably Burchell *et al.* were generally reluctant about extending their critical approach to actually asking more radical questions about the espoused or any additional roles which accounting plays either in organisations or society. Their desire to be seen as being objective can be judged from their designation of Marx's view of accounting as 'dogmatic'. But insightful criticism can be gleaned at several points. Burchell *et al.* argue that when used as *ammunition machines* accounting systems often promote and articulate particular interested positions and values while as *rationalisation machines* they may be used to justify, legitimise and rationalise earlier decisions. No attempt is made to reject Braverman's view that accounting has contributed to the process of separating conception and execution in the labour process as discussed in the last chapter. Perhaps most insightful of all is a short sentence tucked away in the middle of the paper which announces that it would appear that accounting is 'made to be purposive rather than being inherently purposeful' (p.13). Lacking any sort of theoretical perspective on ideology Burchell *et al.* could not be expected to follow these points through to their conclusion. When Burchell, Clubb & Hopwood turned their attention to value added accounting (1985) the same diffidence to adopting a thoroughly critical perspective is evident, leading Richardson (1987) to describe the paper as perhaps the best example of a social constructionist analysis of accounting. This designation certainly accords with the perspective which their earlier paper seemed to commend to accounting researchers.

Richardson's comment is advanced in the context of a useful review of the literature which has sought to reconceptualise accounting as a legitimating institution. The paper is heavily informed by a range of sociological thinking which explains why Richardson chooses to make extensive use of the concept *legitimation* rather than ideology. In his view the three sociological perspectives of structural-functionalism, social constructionism and the hegemonic (i.e. Marxist) perspective are all intimately concerned with legitimation. For structural-functionalist sociology legitimation is the creation and validation of the normative order. To the extent that accounting contributes to this function it is a legitimating institution. Research based in this perspective portrays accountants and accounting systems as playing a purely technical role. It is not concerned with the values which accountants implement, suggesting that the use of accounting adapts to reflect the dominant functional values of the organisation. In this way such work is totally uncritical. Unfortunately it has also tended to be the perspective which dominates much accounting research. By contrast the social constructionist perspective problematises social reality and its constituent elements, including legitimation and thus accounting. The emphasis is on the ways in which accounting is actually used to constitute reality and the effect on individuals of the legitimation of a particular version of reality. The relationship between this perspective and the one which appealed to Burchell *et al.* several years earlier is immediately apparent. The inherent limitations of such a perspective are also equally clear. Although social constructionism recognises the existence of diverse interests, it does not seek to prejudge these. In other words, although concerned with how society is, as opposed to how it is said to be, this perspective remains essentially unconcerned with offering any comment on it. This is left to sociologists who embrace a more radical stance such as the hegemonic perspective.

The account which Richardson offers of the hegemonic perspective is rather selective, relying more on a specific reading of Gramsci than on Marx or indeed on Lukacs or Althusser. Work based on this perspective takes as axiomatic the fact that the source of social values is elite ideology rather than being the result of some form of predetermined or, alternatively, a negotiated consensus. As a result the range of conceivable actions is defined by elite self-interest while the nature of the link between action and values is false but (crucially) it is believed by subordinate groups. In this way the link between accounting, legitimation and elite ideology is made. As a legitimating institution accounting and accounting systems are bound up with the processes of creating, distributing and mystifying power in the interests of elites. Accounting is therefore not simply a set of techniques which somehow adapts to the dominant values of organisations and society. Nor is it a set of techniques which can be 'captured' by particular interest groups and used to their advantage in some way. It functions as an element of elite ideology, legitimating the actions of that elite and thereby amplifying their already considerable power in society. For Richardson the role of accounting research based on this perspective is to 'demystify this use of accounting, exploring the means by which it achieves it effect and, thereby, emancipating those affected' (p.351). Clearly it is not sufficient to know what accounting is and how it functions in concrete organisations and in the society. The presumption has already been made that it must be changed in important respects, a position which accords with the tradition of critical theory, another variant of Marxist sociology which has attracted a number of accounting researchers.

I turn now to some of the more substantive literature on the ideological nature of accountancy which has emerged from the critical accounting tradition in the past decade. Two of the most influential writers, Tony Tinker and David Cooper, have both employed a broader political economy of accounting perspective rather than some form of Marxist sociology. For Tony Tinker the ideological nature of accounting is a consequence of its unquestioning reliance on the principles of marginalist economic theory (Tinker, 1980; 1985; Tinker, Merino & Neimark,

1982). Marginalism was the form of individualistic value theory upon which capitalist economics was built in the mid-nineteenth century. Its emphasis is on the individual and the critical role which the market plays in resolving all conflicts which might occur in society. It is not concerned with issues of social development which it posits should also be left to the market. In this way it is in contrast with the views of the social value theorists such as Smith, Ricardo and Marx (Tinker, 1985). Drawing on the literature of the Cambridge Controversies, Tinker makes the telling point that 'markets are not "free" but structured' (1980, p.158). It is in this way that marginalism is clearly ideology and must be recognised as such. On the specific question of the continuity between marginalism and accounting theory two observations are offered. It shares the emphasis on individualism, thereby pre-empting questions on the role accountants play in class conflicts. It has attempted to preserve an image of objectivity and independence by shunning 'subjective' questions of value and in this way has allowed the accountant to avoid taking any responsibility for questions of social distribution (Tinker et al., 1982). In later empirical studies Tinker has gone on to explore other aspects of the relationship between ideology and accountancy. With Neimark (1987) he has demonstrated how the annual reports of General Motors serve as coercive, ideological weapons in manipulating the social imagination regarding the role of women in the workforce (see also Macintosh, 1990). With Lehman (1987) he has argued that the literature of accounting serves an ideological purpose in helping to shape social con- sciousness in a more general way (see also Lehman & Tinker, 1985, 1986).

It is in the context of a discussion of Tinker's 1980 paper that Cooper (1980) claims that accounting is overwhelmed by the assumptions of capitalism and that accountants accept the socio-economic institutional structure which is capitalism. As a result accounting may be viewed as 'a means of sustaining and legitimizing the current social, economic and political arrangements', i.e. as an ideology (p.164). He then goes on to list some of the numerous ideological characteristics of contemporary accounting: it regards market transactions as objective and free from bias; it does not question property rights; it measures only those aspects of performance that are regarded as crucial; and it does so only in terms of profitability or cash flows to investors. He concludes by arguing that unless accounting researchers begin to consider issues such as these and do so in a critical way, accounting theories will inevitably remain ideology. In a later paper with Sherer (1984) Cooper argues that accounting and accounting research presently serves only a very narrow set of interests, those of the 'shareholder and financial class' and that it is now necessary to entertain alternative conceptualisations of social welfare and the form of accounting which may be appropriate to these. The political economy approach to accounting research favoured by Cooper & Sherer is viewed as having three key attributes which are commended to colleagues: make your value judgements explicit, i.e. be *normative*; describe and interpret accounting in action, i.e. be *descriptive*; and recognise the contested nature of the accounting problematic, particularly the concept of the public interest, i.e. be *critical* (p.225). The value of these exhortations was soon demonstrated as Cooper and his fellow researchers began to publish the results of their study of the accounting practices employed by the National Coal Board which revealed their powerful but complex ideological role (Berry *et al.*, 1985; Hopper *et al.*, 1986). More recently Cooper has turned his attention to the regulation of the UK accountancy profession which has involved a critical analysis of the ways in which it has been successful in representing itself to business, to the state and to the broader society (Cooper *et al.*, 1989; Cooper & Robson, 1990).

The accountancy profession and its role in ideology has also attracted the interest of sociologists who have become involved in the development of critical accounting. In a study of the reasons for the accountancy profession's high profile in British management hierarchies and the emphasis on financial modes of control within British companies, Armstrong (1987a) draws attention to the way in which the profession has been in the position to provide a succession of acceptable solutions to the problems faced by British capitalist enterprises. The financial modes of control which presently characterise the management of British companies are not simply the result of the pre-eminence of accountants in senior management positions. Armstrong argues that for the past 150 years the profession has been successful in having its own particular solutions accepted by shareholders, the banks and other financial institutions, successive governments, etc. Much of its early influence was built on the perceived contribution of a professional audit function, from which time the profession has gone from strength to strength. By implication it is conceivable that the profession's power could wane but nowadays there is no sign, in the British context at least, that any other profession with its own solutions threatens to challenge it (cf. Armstrong, 1985, 1986, 1987b).

Willmott (1990) approaches the issue from a different direction, electing to scrutinise the claim that the profession serves the public interest. This claim has long been made for the profession and for the most part it has gone unchallenged by either the public or the profession. Willmott argues that the profession's perception of serving the public interest is that it is able to successfully provide the users of accounting information with the sort of information they require in order to monitor past performance and to enhance decision-making about the future employment of resources. In this way the public interest is best served by the pursuit of technical excellence in accounting theory and practice. The public's perception of the profession serving its interest is restricted to the expectation that it will be effective in regulating the activities of accounting practitioners who might find themselves 'influenced or even corrupted by those whose self-interest is affected by the content of accounts' (p.316). In this way neither the public nor the profession problematises the public interest since both accept that the prevailing social order with its characteristic social relations embody a universal, public interest. In the case of the accountancy profession Willmott is unequivocal that it continues to play an ideological role by 'assuming and upholding the legitimacy of the private interests of investors and business' (p.324). In this way it has been successful in portraying accounting to the public as a neutral activity and thereby to *naturalise* the status quo, i.e. the value and rationality of capitalism as a provider and allocator of wealth. Willmott concludes with a couple of sentences which perfectly capture the purpose of critical accounting:

> If it is accepted that an important role of the academic is to enrich and extend public debate, this must include the scrutiny of the claims of powerful groups, including the professions. A primary objective of such research is to deconstruct the authority of accounting in order to facilitate alternative contexts of accounting in which existing means of producing and allocating scarce and valued resources are superseded by more democratic, publicly accountable forms of practice.
>
> (Willmott, 1990, p.327)

SOCIAL REPORTING

Social reporting or *corporate social reporting* is the term used to identify a range of ways of accounting different to those associated with conventional financial reporting. The impetus for the development of social reporting was the growing recognition in the 1960s that the top management of business organisations had a responsibility to account to the broader society for the various courses of action which they followed. Moreover, they could not fully discharge this accountability by providing information in the form of periodic financial statements. These were designed for and directed at the owners of the business, i.e., the shareholders, although they were often of equal value to those who provided other forms of finance including bankers and various creditor groups. They were of little or no significance to other *stakeholders* including employees, the local community, local and central government, the wider public, i.e. society in general. Businesses could no longer be conceived of as simply enterprises designed to make money for their shareholders (cf. Friedman, 1962). They were now to be seen as accountable for the ways in which they might make this money. A growing catalogue of socially unacceptable business practices was becoming evident. Among these were pollution, resource misutilisation, waste; overpricing and profiteering; the production of poor quality and dangerous products; inadequate provision for and treatment of employees in different labour markets; restrictive trade practices and the negative consequences of the growth of multinational corporations. As many of these practices applied with equal force to non-business organisations, from the outset social reporting sought to ensure that as far as possible those who managed all organisations did so in a socially responsible manner. By requiring them to report on their actions in some form of social report they would be held to account by society in the same way as the owners of a business had traditionally been able to hold their agents to account. Social reporting is thus the process of providing information designed to discharge social accountability, the responsibility to account for actions for which one has social responsibility (Gray *et al.*, 1987, p.4).

The pressure for social reporting has tended to come from sections of the professions, academics, the intelligentsia and various interest groups rather than society itself. In this way it is not a development which is of a purely accounting nature. As Gray *et al.* argue, no one group could hope to report on the social impact of organisations without the benefit of the experience and insight of many other experts. Within the accountancy profession it has been mainly academic accountants who have been interested in the issues involved, in persuance of their prescribed research function (cf. Arnold, 1989). And although the average person has to date shown little interest in the issues involved, it has been supported by many of their trade unions and political representatives. At the time of writing there seems to be renewed interest in the UK for social reporting particularly in the context of environmental or 'green' matters. This has recently given rise to some developments in *environmental accounting* which will be considered later. In general, however, the 1980s were not a good time for social reporting. Like so many other positive legacies of the progressive 1960s it was the subject of great attention and endeavour in the following decade before rapidly falling from favour. In the first instance this occurred in the wake of the worldwide economic recession and then subsequently, in the UK at least, as a result of the successful promotion of a culture of individualism and enterprise in which little or no credence was given to the idea of society, far less notions of social responsibility or social accountability. It is for this reason that a major part of the literature on social reporting is of 1970s vintage (cf. Parker, 1986).

A useful starting point for considering examples of social reporting is *The Corporate Report* published in July 1975 by the UK Accounting Standards Steering Committee (ASSC). The document was produced by a working party set up by the ASSC in the autumn of 1974 under the chairmanship of Derek Boothman to re-examine the scope and aims of published financial statements in the light of modern needs and conditions. Although the committee and its report were specifically concerned with the future nature of financial reporting by business enterprises, what it had to say set the agenda for much of the subsequent debate on social reporting in the UK. The report took the view that it was the implicit responsibility of every economic entity of significant size or format to report publicly without being obliged to by law or regulation. Public account-ability, the basic philosophy underlying the report, was viewed as an ethical matter and not something that should be done simply because it was required by law or some regulatory body. Understandably such a bold, progressive stance attracted criticism from sections of both the accountancy profession and the business community. Much of this was voiced in response to a Department of Trade discussion document 'Aims and Scope of Company Reports' which broadly endorsed the ASSC report, published almost a year later. Undeterred by the lack of enthusiasm for implementing the report, the Labour government published a Green Paper on 'The Future of Company Reports' in July 1977. It signalled an intention to introduce legislation requiring the publication of a value added statement in the annual report together with an employment statement of some description. Additional disclosures were also mentioned together with a call for further study intended to inform the development of a comprehensive framework for future financial reporting and one which reflected the wider public responsibilities of business enterprises and those who directed them. These proposals were never enacted and with the return of the first Thatcher government in 1979 they were soon to become largely of historical (and academic) interest. Nevertheless, the findings of the working party are still on the table.

In essence *The Corporate Report* takes the view that the set of financial statements which a company is required to produce, i.e. a balance sheet, a profit and loss account and a statement of source and application of funds, does not serve the information needs of the various *user groups* adequately. Therefore it is a matter of necessity that a series of additional financial statements be produced thereby expanding the size of a company's corporate report, and more significantly, its value to the many user groups identified by the ASSC as having a legitimate right to financial information. In addition to the *equity investor group*, i.e. shareholders, the report identifies a further six user groups believed to have a reasonable right to an entity's financial information. The first of these is the *loan creditor group* and includes both existing and potential holders of debentures and loan stock together with the various providers of short term funds. Next are the *employee group* which is taken to include prospective employees as well as existing employees, all of whom have a right to information about their security of employment, future prospects and the basis for any collective bargaining activity they may envisage. The *analyst-advisor* group is the third user group to be identified and it is taken to include a number of financial specialists together with researchers, trade union officials and journalists. Their needs are for information in order to provide sound financial advice for their various clients. A number of *business contacts* including both customers and suppliers, together with competitors and potential rivals constitute the fourth and in some ways the most contentious grouping. The *government* are the next group to be identified as being entitled to a fuller corporate report package; this includes both central and local government agencies. Finally there is the *public* which in the view of the ASSC includes consumers, tax and rate payers, political parties and the many pressure and interest groups. Such is the scope of the various stakeholders identified by the ASSC, it is reasonable to conclude that it had adopted the view that in some sense everybody in society has a reasonable right to some level of financial information.

Six additional statements were proposed by the ASSC as a means to promote a better understanding of corporate financial statements. Four have subsequently more or less disappeared from the debate in the intervening period: a statement of *money exchanges with government*, a statement of *transactions in foreign currency*, a statement of *future prospects* and a statement of *corporate objectives*. By contrast *value added statements* were already becoming increasingly popular in the early 1970s as an additional way to report the performance of a business entity in terms of value added and the manner in which this was subsequently allocated to the various parties to the process: employees, providers of capital, government and the business as an entity in itself. Value added statements have the merits of being concise and relatively easy to understand. Despite the general response to *The Corporate Report* their popularity continued to increase throughout the 1970s with around one third of the largest UK companies including such a statement in their corporate reports at that time (Morley, 1981). Subsequently they have become less fashionable, due in some part to the fact that there has never been either an exposure draft or accounting standard published on such statements.

The call for *employment reports* reflected the working party's belief that enterprises have a responsibility to report a range of information on employment matters to both their employees and to the wider society. Among these are information on numbers employed, age distributions, employment functions, expenditure on training, details of health and safety provision and selected ratios relating to employment. In the words of the committee such a report

> will make available information of use not only in judging efficiency and productivity but will also provide significant information concerning the workforce of the reporting entity, its personnel policies and industrial relations record.
>
> (para 6.21, quoted in Gray *et al.* 1987, p.159)

Employment reports have never been popular with employers although they have continued to attract the attention of researchers (Thompson & Knell, 1979; Fanning, 1979; Maunders, 1984). However, since 1977 French companies with over 750 employees have been required to produce an annual social balance sheet or *bilan social* much like an employment report. This is quite separate from their financial report or *plan comptable* and must provide information of both a factual and a policy nature. The result is that companies are encouraged to carry out a critical appraisal of their employment activities thereby improving the situation of their workforces and thus enhancing their contribution to the broader society (Rey, 1978; Glautier and Roy, 1981). Rather than produce employment reports, British companies have elected to provide *employee reports*. These have taken a variety of forms but in general they are rather simplistic statements which present a collection of financial and employment information in ways designed to maximise communication. Among the techniques employed are pie charts and bar charts together with line graphs, photographs and multi-colour illustrations, all intended to promote readability. As for their real value, researchers are far from convinced (Hussey, 1979, 1981; Lyall, 1981, 1982).

Although *The Corporate Report* was received with horror by large sections of the accountancy profession, business and the Conservative party, in general it was hardly a radical proposal for the promotion of social reporting. It was essentially concerned with more socially-aware financial reporting rather than social reporting as it was defined earlier. This can be seen both in the additional statements which were proposed and the manner in which these were to be constructed. Unquestionably the most progressive of these six statements was the employment report. On the one hand it promised a means to promote a measure of accountability to workforces, on the other it was envisaged to involve a combination of financial and non-financial information. This might go some way to explaining why such reports are still not terribly popular in the UK and why organisations have shown much greater enthusiasm for reporting corporate financial information by way of the 'safer' employee report. However, despite the value of developing genuinely progressive forms of employment reporting, this would only be one example of social reporting and an obvious one at that. Social responsibility has long been recognised to extend to the ways in which all organisations and their managements come into contact with their environment, both local and global; make use of the world's energy supplies; provide their various products to different consumer groups; conduct their business in distant locations; provide equal opportunities for minority groups, women and other special interest groups, etc. These are equally the legitimate foci for social reporting.

To date it has been the USA which has tended to be in the vanguard of voluntary social reporting, reflecting the long established traditions of generous corporate involvement in the community. Corporations have traditionally taken great pride in, and receive much kudos from, their charitable and kindred activities and commonly encourage their young executives to make their mark in the community. For its part, the state in the form of the Internal Revenue Service is more kindly disposed to such activities than is the case in most of the other advanced societies (Gambling, 1984). In the 1960s it was the USA which led the way on environmental and ecological issues, championed equal rights and promoted the protection of the consumer, so it was not suprising that in the following decade it also provided a lead in social reporting. There was also a good deal of evidence of experimentation both with what to report and how to report it as business and not-for-profit organisations sought to communicate their social responsibility endeavours to the public. Narrative reports were an obvious medium having the merits of being comparatively inexpensive and easy to assemble while being readily understood by the public. Both the American Accounting Association and the American Institute of Certified Public Accountants have supported such an approach which has been employed for reporting on the whole range of issues including disclosure on environmental initiatives, conservation measures and employment practices in the Third World. Information has also been presented in a statistical rather than in a financial form while government agencies have employed social indicators to communicate non-financial information. Reporting on pollution or emission levels, accident rates, purchasing policies, etc., has often been couched in terms of compliance with external standards. In some cases organisations employed a combination of different approaches integrating relevant financial information where appropriate.

By comparison with *The Corporate Report* this looks much more progressive in form if not in content. However, there is a downside to the move away from an essentially financial approach to social reporting. It provides too great an opportunity for selectivity in reporting. What is not reported is often as important as what is reported which may in fact be trivial. There is no requirement to provide for continuity of information; indeed it will only be a tiny minority who will remember what was said in previous reports. Any attempt to make comparisons between the reports of different entities is unlikely to be successful. Some have gone as far as arguing that much of this sort of reporting is little more than a public relations exercise (Wiseman, 1982; Rockness, 1985). Not all researchers who were attracted to social reporting sought to abandon a conventional financial accounting based approach. As a result a number of financial models were developed in the 1970s alongside the above approaches. Some were conceptually simple such as Solomon's (1974) statement of social income which was intended to provide a financially quantified measure of corporate social performance. It entailed adjusting the value added in the productive process to take account of the additional costs and benefits which the corporation imposed upon or gifted to the broader society. The difficulty was in measuring the monetary value of such costs and benefits. At the opposite extreme were attempts to develop comprehensive social reports such as Estes' (1976) social impact statement. The difficulty in this case was the sheer sophistication of what was being proposed which resulted in its being impractical to implement. On the other hand such models highlighted the extent and complexity of the focus of social reporting. Linowes' (1972) socio-economic operating statement like Dilley & Weygandt's (1973) social responsibility annual report were by contrast less ambitious and thus in principle easier to operationalise. However, by adopting a cost outlay approach to reporting they fail to consider the cost borne by the environment, the community, the public, the broader society, etc. In this way they offer a corrupted form of cost-benefit analysis in which the corporation bears the costs as well as gaining many of the benefits. In the view of Gray *et al.* (1987) much of this interest in the development of *social accounts* has been misguided and by the end of the 1970s it was generally accepted that effective social reporting would require to carefully integrate both types of approach.

A different approach to social reporting was developed in the UK in the 1970s, one which complemented the above in a familiar way. This is the *social audit* approach. There is a sense in which social reporting itself might be termed social auditing. Organisations which elect to report in this way are offering some form of review of their own activities and in this way they are simply extending the boundaries of the internal audit function which has become increasingly important in the past twenty years. Not all social audit work has been of this sort however. Occasionally individuals have been invited to 'audit' the social reports of companies such as happened with the Atlantic Richfield Company in the 1970s, much in the manner of the statutory audit. A more common approach to the social audit has seen external agencies carrying out their own investigations, with or without the agreement of the 'client'. The early work of Social Audit Ltd exemplifies the potential of this approach. In just four years they carried out audits of the activities of several major companies and a government agency. The most widely known of these was their work with the Avon Rubber Company Ltd which ended in the company dissociating themselves from the the audit report which they claimed was inaccurate and biased. A second agency, Counter Information Services, also performed social audits but these were wholly uninvited and, unlike those produced by Social Audit Ltd, openly politically motivated. While their approach may have resembled that of journalists working for left-wing newspapers rather than accountants committed to the promotion of greater social accountability, their work had the merit of facing head on the hidden political agenda for social reporting (cf. Medawar, 1976). Once this begins to pose difficult questions and to provide answers which are commensurate with radical in the sense of revolutionary political theory, it is unlikely to have much success in persuading companies or democratically elected governments to change their outlooks or practices. There are clearly implicit limits on what is acceptable social reporting and what is to be promoted as such.

In the UK for almost the entirety of the 1980s it seemed as though there was very little that was remotely acceptable in this sense and, to borrow a phrase once used by the dominant political figure of the decade, social reporting almost 'withered on the vine'. This was also a period when a wider view of account-ability might have been successful in curbing some of the excesses of those who seemed to benefit most from the 'new realism' as it was termed at one time. At the end of the decade a new political 'opportunity' presented itself in the face of a renewed international concern with the environment. As a result the govern-ment has promoted concern with 'green' issues for the past eighteen months. Bearing in mind that the enterprise culture is still being promoted it was hardly suprising to learn that the Big 6 had gone green with Coopers & Lybrand Deloitte 'adding a new service to its standard financial audit to help companies develop a practical environment policy' (*Accountancy*, October 1990, p.10). And at the time of writing a major international conference is being planned designed to 'show how companies can increase their profits and profitability by introducing environmentally sound practices and policies' (*Management Accountancy*, March 1991, p.5). Environmental or *green accounting*, however, entails rather more than this and, presumably, as long as it remains within the limits of political acceptability, it will receive governmental support. This in turn may result in renewed interest in social reporting in general, a change in attitude which should please researchers such as Rob Gray who has championed its case throughout the 1980s. In the summer of 1990 Gray's report *The Greening of Accountancy* reviewed the various ways in which accounting can already contribute to the greening of organisations as well as indicating how it might develop this contri-bution in the future. In line with his general thinking he takes the view that environmental accounting should seek to develop more qualitative, environ-mentally sensitive approaches to social reporting rather than aim to provide harder information in the form of social accounts. Among the practical recommendations are the institution of systems for the regular monitoring, reporting and auditing of legal and quasi-legal compliance; the extension of the compliance audit to encompass the ethical audit; the development of a mechanism for conducting environment impact analyses and systems for appraising environmental options. Whether, after so many false starts, a genuinely radical social reporting ethic is about to emerge remains to be seen.

HUMAN RESOURCE ACCOUNTING

Human resource accounting (HRA) is an appropriate topic with which to draw to a close both the present chapter and the first part of the text. At first sight, it is a topic where it might reasonably be expected that the disciplines of sociology and accounting would have come together in a fruitful way. This has not happened to date. HRA is also a topic which is considered to be within the scope of social reporting, one which has an obvious potential for promoting accountability to the workforce as an element of an employment report (Gray et al., 1987). This too has not happened to any great extent since HRA is generally regarded as a means of providing management with the information it needs to manage human resources more effectively and efficiently and for reporting to shareholders the value of a firm's human assets (Flamholtz, 1974). In these various ways it is clear that the topic of accounting for human resources is heavily infused with ideological considerations. Indeed how could it be otherwise given the nature of the relationship which exists between management and their workforces, i.e. between capital and labour, in contemporary capitalist society? In this light it is perhaps not suprising to learn that after almost 25 years, HRA being another of the positive legacies of the 1960s, the topic is in need of more research, both basic and applied (Sackmann et al., 1989, p.260). And yet, like environmental accounting, there are signs that HRA could soon experience a major revival in its fortunes in the wake of a rediscovery of the worth of human resources by some sections of management. This in turn may well have significant implications for the continued dominance of labour by capital, something which raises the question of how successful this revival in HRA's fortunes will be, or be allowed to be? All the more reason, of course, to consider the topic at this juncture.

At its inception HRA was more concerned with human resources than it was with accounting. Although there were already researchers interested in accounting for human assets (Hermanson, 1964), it is generally acknowledged that the work of Rensis Likert (1961, 1967) sparked off the intense activity in HRA during the late 1960s and throughout the 1970s. Not an accountant himself, Likert's interest was in human resource management, i.e. the effective use of human resources by organisation managements. Like a number of his contemporaries including Argyris, Herzberg and McGregor he was particularly interested in developing the legacy of Human Relations thinking in the form of practical applications. He advocated the need to develop a participative approach

to human resource management which he termed *System 4*. This approach necessitated the adoption of both new organisational structures and styles of management behaviour which he argued would give rise to increased levels of productivity in the workforce, reductions in costs and in the levels of scrap, all of
which would result in increased earnings for the organisation and its shareholders. He termed the former *causal variables* and the latter *end-result* variables. Between them were what Likert termed *intervening variables* among
which he included the attitudes, motivations, perceptions, performance goals and
job satisfaction of the organisation's human resources. The link between these
three sets of variables was conceptualised by Likert in the following way.
Intervening variables change in response to any changes in causal variables, the
effects of these changes being seen in terms of end-result variables.

Measuring and reporting on the latter has long been recognised as one of the
functions of conventional accounting. Likert was conscious of the predominantly
short term emphasis of such accounting and contrasted it with the longer term
process of building up the value of the *human organisation* which he saw to be
the key determinant of the continuing health of any organisation. The objective
of HRA, or human asset accounting as Likert termed it, was to measure the causal
and intervening variables in some way in order to estimate the value of the human
organisation. Although he talked mainly in terms of measuring causal and intervening variables to establish the value of an organisation's stock of human
resources, he was also aware of the fact that some part of that value can be
established by taking into account what he termed the *original investment* in any
human organisation, i.e. the costs of hiring, training and developing personnel.
Once established, the value of the human organisation would be reported to
management on a regular basis in order that they were constantly aware of the
success, or otherwise, of their commitment to a System 4 approach to managing
human resources. Naturally any external financial reports should also include
appropriate estimates of the current value of the human organisation as this
would also be of interest to shareholders, such estimates being derived from the
new, comprehensive internal management reporting system devised to apprise
management. For Likert if HRA was to be developed within accounting rather
than human resource management, then it should be recognised in the first
instance as a challenge to management accountants to provide (enlightened)
management with the information which it required. This is an interesting point
of departure and not simply because HRA very quickly appeared to lose sight of
the progressive emphasis which Likert envisaged for it. Irrespective of the
emphasis which most writers place upon HRA's value for both management and
investors, to a very large extent its subsequent development has been as a
financial accounting topic, one which seemingly has little place in management
accounting thinking.

During the following decade HRA became one of the most researched areas
within accountancy. Interest reached its peak in the mid-1970s and then gradu-
ally tailed off during the 1980s (Sackmann *et al.*, 1989). Initially a number of

financial accounting based models for measuring the value of human resources were formulated. By common consent they were not very successful in advancing the widespread practical application of HRA. These various measurement models were either *cost-based* or *value-based*. In the case of cost-based models, the simplest measure of value is that of original or *historical acquisition cost*. This can be readily established and offers an objective measure, so by aggregating all of the various costs of recruitment, selection, hiring, placement, training, etc., a value can be placed on an organisation's human resources. This can then be capitalised and amortised over the expected life of the (human) asset and in this way be included in both an income statement and balance sheet. However, historic cost's general shortcomings were soon imputed to this model and in its place a *replacement cost* approach was canvassed. Here the value of an organisation's human resources is taken to be the current cost of recruitment, selection, hiring, etc. This has the merit of measuring their value in an up-to-date way and also serves to draw management's attention to the full value of their stock of human resources (Flamholtz, 1973). One of the difficulties of a replacement cost model is that, being reliant on actual costs, it may in fact undervalue some employees and overvalue others. For this reason an *opportunity cost* based approach was favoured by some writers. Here the value of human resources is determined by what management are willing to bid to secure the services of individual employees (Hekimian & Jones, 1967). This may also be conceptualised in terms of *realisable values*. If a third party were to come along and offer the value which a manager places upon a particular individual then the manager should be willing to 'transfer' the individual as in football. However, this sort of exercise is inherently subjective, a problem which highlights the strength of a historical cost approach. In this way cost-based models were soon recognised to offer little purchase on the problem of measuring human resource values.

The various value-based models were much more numerous and, over time, more sophisticated. But they were eventually to prove no more practical than the cost-based models. Many of them were reliant on what is termed an *economic income* approach to valuation, itself an alternative to the general problem of valuation in financial accounting theory. One of the earliest models began by forecasting the future earnings of the firm. These were discounted to determine the firm's present value and then a part of this was allocated to human resources on the basis of its contribution to the total valuation (Brummet *et al.*, 1968). Lev & Schwartz's approach also relied on discounting. In this model it was individual future salaries which were discounted and then aggregated to establish the value of the various occupational groups and thus the total human organisation (Lev & Schwartz, 1971). A more sophisticated model developed by Friedman & Lev (1974) used a measure of value based upon market wage and the firm's wage as a measure of the firm's investment in human resources. The difference was held to give rise to a stream of cost savings which can be discounted to present value and used to measure human resource value. Such models have many limitations. They commonly make use of surrogate measures of value. The difficulties of estimating future rewards, earnings, cost savings, etc. are not explicitly acknowledged. Determining an appropriate discount factor is always a major problem in economic income models. Finally the subjectivity which is inherent in human resource valuation is only avoided by advocating superficially scientific models which are themselves heavily reliant on subjective judgements.

Not all value-based models were reliant solely on monetary-economic measures. Sackmann *et al.* (1989) acknowledge that Likert's own model uses only non-monetary–behavioural measures although they are unable to provide any further examples of this approach. At best subsequent models combined the two emphases, the outcome tending to be an alternative form of economic model. Flamholtz (1971,1972) utilised both monetary and non-monetary models to develop a *service states* model. This was based on the premise that an employee is of value to an organisation in terms of the future role s/he is expected to occupy and the sevices rendered thereby. The model views the movement of employees between organisational roles over time as a probabilistic process with attendant service rewards. The value of an individual employee is the present worth of their potential services, on the assumption that s/he maintains organisational membership. This led to the development of similar models, e.g., Gambling (1974), Ogan (1976) and even Likert's later work evidences a more economic emphasis (Likert & Bowers, 1971).

Despite their increasing technical sophistication, such models were of little practical utility. A decade of intense research work and model building had seemingly failed to make much progress. At this point many researchers simply abandoned HRA while others switched their attention to studying the 'second generation' of HRA systems or the impact of HRA on decision-making. For the most part this has generated a rather bland, uninspiring literature. After 1976 the flow of new measurement models quickly turned to a trickle and then effectively dried up. Against this background it is hardly suprising that Sackmann *et al.* conclude their review of the literature of the rise and fall of HRA with a call for more research on the subject. In other words, after 25 years of research and development, accountancy has still not come to terms with accounting for human resources in a meaningful way.

While in the UK the 1980s were for the most part a decade during which labour suffered at the hands of a government seemingly committed to turn back the industrial relations clock a full century, taking a broader view there were encouraging signs that some sections of management were rediscovering the worth of human resources and the value of the human organisation. Twenty years on from Likert and the neo-Human Relations tradition, Peters & Waterman (1982) commended the thinking of Mayo and McGregor to management, along with that of Chester Barnard and the organisational sociologist Philip Selznick. Other writers highlighted some of the key lessons which might be learned from looking at the success of Japanese industry in the previous decade (Ouchi, 1981; Drucker, 1981; Schonberger, 1982; Pascale & Athos, 1983). The aphorism 'productivity through people' perfectly encapsulates this new philosophy and signals a recognition that it is the people in the organisation who make things happen and who produce results. In order to ensure that an organisation is successful it is necessary to manage its workforce in an appropriate way, stressing cooperation rather than conflict, integration rather than exploitation, respect rather than disdain. It is very easy to be cynical about these ideas and to view them as little more than enlightened self-interest on the part of those responsible for ensuring the success of business enterprises in the increasingly competitive global market place. Equally there are signs that all is far from well on the factory floor (and beyond) in Japan and that many of the 'excellent' corporations identified by Peters & Waterman have subsequently shown themselves willing to respond to market forces in entirely predictable ways.

One thing is clear about these new ways of thinking about and managing the human organisation. Where they have been embraced by management, there is little sign that they have had any use for the notion of accounting for human resources, hardly suprising given its general irrelevance for management. This is principally a consequence of its being developed as a financial accounting rather than a management accounting topic and a distinctly unprogressive one at that. However, the emergence of the 'productivity through people' perspective would seem to provide HRA with an opportunity to reconstitute itself as a valuable complement to it. This would have to be in the form of a management accounting development, something which has been conspicuously absent from its history to date. To be of use to management, a revitalised HRA would have to be able to provide them with the sort of information they require to manage their stock of human resources more effectively and efficiently, and for mutual benefit. This would involve providing relevant quantitative information about the cost and value of people as organisational resources, designed to perform two functions. Firstly, it would serve the conventional accounting function of informing management in their various planning, control, decision-making, performance measurement and evaluation activities. Secondly, it would serve to motivate management to recognise the worth of the human organisation.

In practical terms this would involve providing information on the actual level of investment in human resources over time, i.e. the costs of recruiting, selecting, hiring, training and placing existing employees. These *formation costs*, as they might usefully be termed, are not difficult to collect and if expressed in historical acquisition cost terms, are readily presented to management. The value component of the worth of an organisation's stock of human resources is a much more problematic issue for at least two reasons. Initially there is the question of what characteristics management see to be of value in a workforce? And having established these characteristics, how can they be translated into some form of quantitative measurement by accountants? Perhaps the key to answering both questions is the idea implicit in the new philosophy that it is imperative that successful organisations retain their present stock of human resources as far as possible. Logically management should know what it is about their present workforce that makes it desirable to retain it. At the same time the challenge to the accounting function is to translate this into some form of financial number which can then be presented to management. One possible means to achieve this is to employ an opportunity cost approach. If management were to be without a valued member of the workforce then clearly this situation would constitute a lost opportunity for the organisation as a whole. The cost of this lost opportunity will constitute the value component of the worth of this valued member of the workforce. Measuring these *retention costs* would involve accountants gaining a comprehensive knowledge of the various labour markets in which the organisation operates. Although this might not seem to be a conventional management accounting function it is no more radical a departure than Bromwich (1990) envisages in the case of strategic management accounting.

If HRA were to develop in this way, accountants who become involved with it may find themselves becoming interested in and informed by parts of the literature of industrial sociology. In this way they would simply be following in the footsteps of writers such as Peters & Waterman. The initial point of contact would be in respect of the characteristics of human resources which management see as being valuable. The attributes of human resources which Likert drew attention to, e.g. attitudes, perceptions, motivations, performance goals, satisfactions, etc., were understandably rather behavioural in nature. Nowadays a social and organisational emphasis such as sociology offers might prove more insightful. Among the possible sources of value are such things as expertise and experience, the potential for creativity and inventiveness, cohesiveness and workgroup integration, a capacity for adaptability and flexibility, possession of standards of excellence, etc. It is attributes such as these which accountants could well find themselves seeking to understand, quantify and report to management in a reconstituted HRA.

Since this new philosophy is inherently more open and consensual, progressive employment reporting which makes the fullest possible use of HRA should become a standard feature of any corporate reporting system. One of the possible consequences of this could be a significant development in terms of management's accountability: it could find itself having to explain to its workforce the relationship which exists between the figure placed upon their worth and the level of rewards which are currently being offered to them. Such a situation seems somehow too utopian of course, prompting the obvious question: at what point will ideology have to intervene?

Part II

Sociology for accountancy

Chapter 5

Financial accounting

When they think of accountancy, the great majority of people have in mind some conception of financial accounting. By 'accounts', the way in which most people conceptualise accountancy, they mean the maintenance of financial records, the collection of money and the periodic balancing of 'the books'. Many have some personal experience of these activities in the context of hire purchase agreements or using account cards in department stores. Fewer people would think of published accounts when thinking about accounts but by comparison with management accounting, finance or auditing, the other main branches of contemporary accountancy considered in this text, these too are a part of public knowledge. For this reason it seems logical that the second part of the text begins with an analysis of financial accounting. The principal focus of enquiry, however, is not public conceptions of financial accounting but the interest which this branch of accountancy has with theory construction. Because financial accounting shares with sociology the status of being a social rather than a physical science such as physics or chemistry, the chapter is written on the premise that there might be some valuable lessons which it can learn from theory construction in sociology rather than embracing the more popular physical science model.

THE NATURE OF FINANCIAL ACCOUNTING

Financial accounting can be divided into two complementary sub-branches which more or less correspond with the two public conceptions mentioned above: book-keeping and financial reporting. Book-keeping or 'accounts' is concerned with the function of measurement while reporting or 'accounting' is concerned with the function of communication. The study of book-keeping involves learning a set of accounting techniques: partnership accounts, branch accounts, royalty accounts, manufacturing accounts and the like. These are all associated with the recording aspect of measurement rather than with questions of valuation. They are all examples of a very practical form of accountancy, being tightly governed by a set of rules which are internalised during the course of training. Book-keeping is based on the principles of double entry which were developed by Pacioli in the fifteenth century and which have been used by the profession ever since. In theory every financial accountant is able to maintain the appropriate ledger accounts which constitute the system of books within the organisation and also is able to make the relevant journal entries as required. Even the widespread use of computerised financial accounting systems still necessitates a competence in the mysteries of double entry. The purpose of book-keeping is to ensure that there is an effective system of financial control operative within an organisation. Thus at any point in time it is possible to establish the financial state of the entity, e.g. the extent of stock, debtors, bad debts, trade creditors, dividends payable and their associated tax payments etc., all expressed in monetary terms. Knowing all of these in turn allows financial accountants to periodically draw up financial statements such as a profit and loss account or a balance sheet, thereby demonstrating the link with the other sub-branch of financial accounting, financial reporting.

Financial reporting is basically the preparation of a range of financial statements which are intended to communicate to their users an account of the financial reality of the reporting entity. In addition to the profit and loss and balance sheet statements, there are funds statements such as the sources and applications of funds, value added statements and the various forms of consolidated accounts. The greater part of the advanced study of financial accounting is geared towards training young accountants how to prepare these various statements in more or less the same way as apprentice electricians or plumbers are trained in the respective ways of their crafts. In the case of financial accounting this is sometimes termed becoming familiar with the 'regulatory framework of accounting'. As well as the standard formats for the various financial statements and a broader range of legal requirements, much of the framework consists of statements of standard accounting practice (SSAPs). Presently there are twenty-one UK SSAPs issued by the Accounting Standards Committee, dating back to 1971 when they replaced the 'recommendations' or 'opinions' on 'best practice' which the ICAEW had issued since 1942. In addition a number of exposure drafts are normally in existence, reflecting a dynamic process of SSAP extension and amendment. Since the mid-1980s a second form of UK accounting standard has emerged, those known as statements of recommended practice (SORPs). They differ from SSAPs either because they are not viewed as being of fundamental importance or because they are of limited applicability. Unlike SSAPs they are not mandatory. Many UK standards incorporate the provisions of a series of International Accounting Standards which have been issued over the past fifteen years by the International Accounting Standards Committee as do the stock of Generally Accepted Accounting Principles (GAAPs) in the USA.

The twenty-one SSAPs can be categorised in a variety of ways reflecting the different factors and cicumstances which have called them into existence (Underdown & Taylor, 1985, pp.41–42). Some are concerned with issues of disclosure, e.g. SSAP 3, 17, 18; presentation, e.g. SSAP 6, 10, 24; preparing consolidated accounts, e.g. SSAP 1, 14, 22, 23; and accounting policies, e.g. SSAP 9, 12, 13, 19. Trainee accountants are required to know and to learn what these standards contain and the guidance they provide for financial reporting. Examination questions which require the preparation of financial statements and their accompanying notes are simply attempting to replicate as far as is possible the work that the trainee might reasonably be expected to perform as a practising accountant. It is for this reason that in studying financial accounting a willingness to devote significant amounts of time to doing examples rather than reading about it is a strategy likely to bring about success, at least in the qualification stakes if not in career terms. This said, it should never be imagined that there is nothing to be read about in the context of learning financial accounting. Quite the opposite in fact, because in many ways thinking about financial accounting and reporting is much more exciting than actually doing much of it, a state of affairs which reflects the enigmatic status of theory in this particular branch of accountancy.

Anyone who has studied financial accounting beyond the most elementary level, and particularly students on accountancy degree programmes, must have noticed that matters of a theoretical nature seem to take up much of their teachers' attention, many pages of more advanced accounting texts and a sizeable proportion of most examination papers. Equally the vast majority never seem to be sure about where all of this theory fits into the broader scheme of things. So much is known about the various bases for valuation in financial statement preparation yet the debate continues to focus on comparing the advantages and disadvantages of the historical cost convention, replacement values, current purchasing power, economic values, etc. Regardless of the need that any business entity has for positive cash flow, accruals accounting still underpins most financial statement preparation. Moving to a more abstract level, the debate about what to report to whom and in which form seems to be well enough explored but with few signs of having given rise to much change in conventional reporting practice. Alternatively the search for a *conceptual framework* for financial accounting and reporting has resulted in a more extensive literature on the validity of such a project than content for the framework itself. All of these issues are commonly part of the syllabi of financial accounting courses, constituting some kind of necessary evil which all should know something of and even be able to tackle examination questions on – if only to pick up the 'easy' marks on offer. But their link with the mainstream of practical financial accounting remains at best tenuous, one of the seeming mysteries that even with the best will in the world few can fathom. However much teachers give classes on theory or academics produce texts on it or examiners offer suggested solutions for their theory questions it still doesn't seem to get much clearer. This potentially damaging situation is largely diffused by the fact that most of the unenlightened move on to other, more concrete issues and matters leaving their teachers, academics and theorists to ponder their own esoteric concerns.

In every discipline theory is always more difficult to come to terms with than learning techniques or substantive content. Being abstract and conceptual in nature makes it more difficult to learn by rote or master with practice. Getting to grips with a theory requires an understanding of what it is that the theory itself is seeking to understand and explain. In the case of a great deal of financial accounting theory a major problem exists in this respect which has the consequence of making the study of theoretical issues much more difficult than it needs to be. Many financial accounting theorists together with those who write texts on theory and those who teach and examine theoretical materials are themselves far from clear about the task of theory construction which they seek to contribute to. As a result the whole body of financial accounting theory is far less well understood and developed than it might be, something which is reflected in the enigmatic status which theory has in this branch of accountancy. At the root of the problem is a belief that there is only one model for theory construction available, that which is exemplified in the physical sciences and in physics in particular. As long as this belief remains dominant then theory will remain the proverbial black hole of financial accounting teaching, research and scholarship.

THE ANATOMY OF FINANCIAL ACCOUNTING THEORY

Almost without exception discussions of financial accounting theory, whether in texts dedicated to the subject such as Belkaoui (1985), Underdown & Taylor (1985) or Watts & Zimmerman (1986), or in briefer accounts such as those offered by Lee (1986), Glautier & Underdown (1989) or Samuels, Rickwood & Piper (1989) take on the same form. They begin with a brief review of some of the general parameters of theory before moving rather quickly to a much fuller discussion of the field of contemporary accounting theories and theoretical perspectives. Although these are slavishly linked back to the parameters of theory, any reader is left with the impression that there may be rather more that could usefully be said about theory in an abstract sense. It is as if these authors feel compelled to address the basics before they move on to matters with which they are seemingly more at home. In short, the normal treatment is less than satisfactory. The aim of this section is two-fold: to say a little more about theory in the abstract in the hope of impressing its importance fully, and to add several further points about theorisation which are relevant to the on-going development of financial accounting theory. The usual treatment of theory in the abstract sense is to identify a series of what are perhaps best described as *oppositions* and then very briefly discuss these in the context of financial accounting theory. Perhaps a better description is to say that these oppositions are rehearsed since normally there is little by way of conclusion reached at the end of such discussions. This seriously limits the value of the exercise. The approach adopted here is to consider these same oppositions more fully and hopefully in a more conclusive way, not least by collapsing them whenever appropriate.

Initially, however, it is necessary to have some understanding of the purpose of theory and more generally of the role it plays in scientific endeavour. The rationale of scientific endeavour is to produce knowledge about some aspect of the world which surrounds us, both the natural and the social worlds which have given rise to natural and social scientific knowledge respectively. This knowledge exists in the form of understanding and explanation which in turn serve to provide the basis for improving the quality of life for those who inhabit the world. Science, theories and the knowledge which they generate are not pursued for their own sake. They are problem-driven since if the world which surrounds us were not problematic then we would not need to understand how these 'problems' have arisen, explain the ways in which they function or persist and suggest how we may begin to tackle them. Take, for example, current concern with the earth's damaged ozone layer; scientists have recently become aware of the existence of holes in the ozone layer in the Antarctic and now in the Arctic. As a result they are seeking to understand how this damage has come about and the ways in which it is presently increasing, not for its own sake but because existing scientific understanding suggests that such developments seriously threaten the quality of life for the whole planet. If it is possible to understand and explain this change the next step is to begin to counter it in some way. At the moment the rapid growth in the use of chlorofluorcarbons or CFCs in aerosols in recent years is viewed as a major contributory factor hence attempts to replace them with 'ozone-friendly' alternatives. But this is all still very speculative. It may be that the explanations which presently exist are mis-conceived and that CFCs have nothing to do with the problem. Ozone-friendly products may pose their own problems in the longer term, as some experts have already suggested. It may indeed be the case that there is no real danger from the ecological changes now in process. As long as the problem of ozone depletion persists scientists will continue to theorise about it.

Theories are the currency of scientific understanding and explanation: in the case of damage to the ozone layer there is the underlying theory that such a change poses a catastrophic threat to life as we know it. This is an example of what is sometimes termed a meta-theory – one which has a very general but a fundamental character – being in some ways more in the nature of a set of premises than a typical theory, which is one with a modest focus of interest. What this particular theory is saying is that given existing knowledge, a change of this sort threatens the long term survival of the planet. It could be a completely misguided belief but seems unlikely to be so. Providing an understanding of and explaining why these chemicals are damaging the ozone layer is a complementary theoretical activity, one more typical of a modestly focused middle-range theory. In its turn it generates ideas and proposals which may serve to resolve or at least reduce the problem. Thinking through the consequences of such proposals is equally necessary and is again a theoretical activity involving understanding and explanation. In all these forms theory is an inherently speculative activity not too different to someone thinking that they know why this or that has happened. The principal difference between a scientific theory and an instance of personal speculation is the intellectual rigour normally associated with the former activity. This necessarily brief account of science and theorising may seem to portray them in a way which conflicts with the impression which most of society has of them. It must be emphasised that it does not pretend to be a description of the institution of science nor the professional practice of scientific workers both of which have been extensively studied from a variety of vantage points, not least the sociology of science (Merton, 1973; Kuhn, 1962; Barnes & Edge, 1982; Boyle *et al.*, 1984).

The first opposition which is usually encountered in discussing financial accounting theory is between *normative* and *descriptive* theories. The former are characterised as theories which prescribe what ought to be done and in the context of financial accounting this type of theory is identified with prescriptive valuation principles or more commonly an integrated body of accounting standards which set out clear treatments for financial reporting purposes. By contrast, descriptive theories are concerned with the way in which something is done, and in the case of financial accounting how accountants normally treat particular items. Some writers, most notably Watts & Zimmerman, refer to descriptive theories of this sort as *positive theory*. Opinion is keenly divided between those who favour a normative approach and for this reason support the development of a *conceptual framework* for financial reporting and those who believe that such a framework would be to the detriment of the accountancy profession. The conceptual framework debate has been in progress for some years now (Peasnell, 1982) and focuses on the desirability of developing a framework which would provide a theoretical basis for financial accounting and reporting. In the view of the US Financial Accounting Standards Board, the body which to date has been responsible for much of the work towards such a framework, a conceptual framework is:

> a constitution, a coherent system of interrelated objectives and fundamentals that can lead to consistent standards and that prescribe the nature, function and limits of financial accounting and financial statements.

> (FASB, 1976)

On the basis of this and similar descriptions of a conceptual framework it is easy to understand its appeal to many academic accountants, particularly those who are attracted to theory and theorisation. It is also understandable that others will raise the objection that in practice such a framework could prove a serious constraint to accounting. In this way the battle lines have long been and continue to be drawn: normative/prescriptive versus positive/descriptive. But is this a useful opposition?

To use the term normative in the context of most theories would appear to be misleading. Theories are intended to provide insight in the form of understanding and explanation and to suggest (beneficial) ways of moving forward. To describe them as being prescriptive in the sense of setting out what must be done is disingenuous. It may be acceptable to use the term theory to refer to, say, a totalitarian political philosophy such as Marxist-Leninism or National Socialism. In such cases, however, it is necessary to remember that these are in fact examples of a meta-theoretical nature, theories deeply infused with beliefs and assumptions rather than understanding and explanation. Viewed in this way, the development of a conceptual framework would seem to be an exercise in meta-theory. In its own terms it is a constitution, a coherent system of objectives and fundamentals which is intended to give rise to a comprehensive set of pre-scriptions. However, the reality of the FASB project during the past twenty years or so has been that its essentially liberal approach to building such a constitution has resulted in rather less in the way of prescription and more speculative knowledge of a middle-range theoretical nature. Thus what begins as a normative exercise in meta-theory has given way to an inconclusive voluminous literature of a thoroughly speculative kind. One conclusion might be that if financial accounting really desires a normative conceptual framework it only needs to establish a small coterie of thinkers and an administration charged with ensuring univeral compliance, much in the manner of any totalitarian regime. The issue of whether this will resolve the many problems associated with financial accounting and reporting would be of little importance.

Turning to the notion of descriptive theories, it would seem that all theories in the form of understanding and explanation are descriptive since when something is being explained it is necessarily being described, and in a conceptual and an analytical way. This truism is not what those who advocate descriptive theories mean however. Their notion of a descriptive theory only makes sense in opposi-tion to the designation normative theory, and is better characterised as positive theory. While normative theories set out how things ought to be done, positive theories literally describe how they are done. In this sense positive or descriptive theories are not theories at all. In the case of financial accounting they are little more than the identification of how accountants carry out their work, being relatively unconcerned with the question of why they carry it out in particular ways. This question in turn has given rise to a body of theory, most particularly in the hands of the arch-advocates of positive theory, Watts & Zimmerman. Whether or not this is legitimately a form of accounting theory is discussed at length in the final section of this chapter. For the moment it is sufficient to conclude that in their different ways both normative and descriptive conceptions of accounting theory are of little direct use in understanding its nature. In essence the opposition is between two polar opposite modes of financial accounting that have very little to do with the modest activity of middle-range theorising.

A second opposition also makes reference to the conceptual framework pro-ject as an illustrative device. The interest here is with the two different ways of building theories and the two types of theory they give rise to. *Inductive* theoris-ing involves building theories by means of collecting evidence and then pain-stakingly establishing common patterns or trends in it. At its simplest it is moving from the specific to the general, from the particular to the universal. This approach gives rise to an inductive theory. In the case of financial accounting an inductive theory is presented as one which involves establishing a set of generally accepted accounting principles or standards from the critical mass of accounting practice. This, of course, is in essence the principle which underpins positive theory discussed above and not surprisingly the inductive mode of theorising is favoured by writers who reject the conceptual framework project as the means to develop financial accounting theory. The *deductive* mode of theorising and the conceptual framework are closely interrelated in that a deductive approach is one which moves from the general to the specific with the latter being derived from and consistent with the former. Thus if accounting standards are to form a fully coherent set of desirable accounting practices they need to be deduced from a higher order theoretical entity, the constitution or conceptual framework proper. In both instances it is interesting to note that it is effectively the actual standards which constitute the theory in question. In the case of inductive theory it is those practices which commend themselves for universal application which form the theory for positive financial accounting while in the case of deductive theory it is the standards which are deduced from the meta-theory which assume this role.

As with the normative/descriptive opposition, closer scrutiny of this opposition indicates that it may be unhelpful. By far the most serious problem with it lies in the fact that while the distinction between inductive and deductive theorising is entirely valid, this does not mean that there are resultantly two different types of theory. Inductive and deductive theorising are the two complementary stages of building any theory with induction preceding deduction. When developing theories, scientists normally work in an inductive way. They make the necessary observations, collect the evidence and sift through it in order to provide understanding and explanation. Others interested in the same topic might offer counter-explanations based on the same evidence which in turn will inevitably give rise to debate, more research, amended explanations and so on. At all times the objective is a more consensual understanding and explanation of the issues involved. The principal means by which advance is made is to engage in hypothesis testing which is where deduction comes into the picture. Being in possession of a possible explanation allows testable hypotheses to be advanced on the basis that if the existing theory is sound, then under specified conditions particular outcomes can be expected. These outcomes are derived from the theory in question by way of the deduction process. The results of such hypothesis testing can be related back to the founding explanation and serve either to provide support for it or perhaps cast doubt upon it. In time a consensual theory will, it is hoped, emerge but equally, further evidence may give rise to an entirely new explanation which will again be subjected to enquiry and so on. Viewed in this way, it makes no sense to talk in terms of an inductive theory or a deductive theory since all theories inevitably rely on both processes for their formulation and continued existence.

The term methodology has not as yet been mentioned in connection with this particular opposition but it is crucial in understanding it. Harvey & Keer (1983) refer to Lipsey's methodology of theory construction while Watts & Zimmerman make clear at the outset of their text that they are concerned with both theory and methodology. By methodology they mean the principles of theory building, testing, modification, etc., the same activities as those discussed in the previous paragraph. The distinction between induction and deduction is fundamental here as are the descriptions of the processes of research involved. It would seem more relevant to restate this particular opposition as being between an inductive methodology and a deductive methodology with both being stages in the development of any mature theory. The implication of restating the opposition in this way is that it provides a clear instruction to any writers seeking to develop meaningful accounting theory of any sort that they will need to begin in an inductive mode and as their understanding and explanation develops switch to a more deductive approach to strengthen their theory.

This conclusion has implications for the status of both a conceptual framework or any alternative to it such as that proposed by Watts & Zimmerman. In the case of any conceptual framework there will inevitably be a major element of induction involved in establishing the proposed constitution. It cannot possibly be an exercise entirely abstract in nature. However, once in place such a broad philosophy can be employed to develop a coherent set of standards, at least in principle. But this is not a deductive process in the sense discussed above and its products, prescriptive accounting standards, are not theoretical entities of any sort. They are guides for action, proposed by a body constituted to establish such. If they are similar in nature to anything, it is to the legal prescriptions introduced by ruling political administrations. Moving to the counter-proposal of Watts & Zimmerman for some form of self-selected set of useful standards, even the suggestion that there is an inductive mode operative here is difficult to accept. In an important sense the operation of a market mechanism of some sort is simultaneously an unscientific notion but suggestive of a powerful meta-theory. These points will be discussed in the final section of this chapter. For the moment it is sufficient to conclude that the set of standards embraced by Watts & Zimmerman as legitimate guides to accounting practice share with those developed within the context of any conceptual framework the quality of not being theoretical entities. Both are simply useful guides to action.

The third opposition commonly identified is possibly the most critical and as a result the most problematic. It is between theories which *explain* and theories which *predict*. In some instances the opposition is left implicit as in the case of Belkaoui who sees that an accounting theory

should explain and predict accounting phenomena, and when such phenomena occur, they verify the theory.

(Belkaoui, 1985, p.3)

or Watts & Zimmerman who take the view that the objective of accounting theory is

to explain and predict accounting practice . . . . Explanation means providing reasons for observed practice . . . . Prediction of accounting practice means that the theory predicts unobserved accounting phenomena.

(Watts & Zimmerman, 1986, p.2)

In both of these cases the clear impression is given that theories which predict are more desirable than those which simply explain, a view shared by Underdown &

Taylor who explicitly state the opposition in their characterisation of 'good theory'. Good theories

> explain or predict phenomena . . . . Theories are tested to determine their ability to explain or predict observable phenomena.
>
> (Underdown & Taylor, 1985, p.2)

Advocacy of a strong predictive capacity in a theory is an understandable position to adopt. It is a consequence of the dominance which the received model of a physical science methodology has in the minds of the public and the scholarly community alike. Only by understanding the nature of the relationship between prediction and explanation is it possible to properly appreciate how the physical sciences actually function and the utility of this particular opposition.

The key to understanding the relationship between explanation and prediction lies in the concept of a *scientific law*. Few people are not familiar with several such laws from their knowledge of physics: Boyle's law, Charles' law or Hooke's law perhaps. Alternatively there are Newton's three laws of motion or the three laws of thermodynamics. All are examples of scientific generalisations which are known to apply whenever particular, specified conditions apply. Much of the time spent in physics practical classes in schools is taken up testing these laws as a means to develop the experimental skills of would-be scientists. These laws are not intended to explain the scientific generalisations they are concerned with. This is the task of theory. The precise relationship between a law and a theory is that the latter is a higher order intellectual artefact designed to supply an answer, however speculative, to the question why? In this way theories do not predict – that is the function of laws. It is this fact that most people fail to recognise about laws and mistakenly attribute to theories. Part of the problem is the lack of clarity which surrounds the relationship between a scientific prediction and a scientific hypothesis. The former is associated with a law and is expected to occur with great, even absolute certainty. The latter is expected to occur if a particular speculation is well-founded, i.e. if a theory is correctly framed. In practice only a modest part of scientific endeavour is taken up with hypothesis testing proper. Most is essentially work of a predictive nature, reflecting the routine nature of science and, of course, serving to convey the impression that science is mainly concerned with predictive activities. In a widely influential text Thomas Kuhn (1962) misleadingly termed this 'normal science', compounding the problem. His own view was that the most exciting and progressive side of scientific work was when prediction and certainty broke down giving rise to revolutions in scientific activity, the exception not the rule. If theories do serve a predictive function they do so only through the medium of laws and in this form they are no longer speculative theories, being part of the received, established body of scientific knowledge.

All of this can be expressed in a simple maxim: theories explain while laws predict. Therefore any talk of explanatory theories and predictive theories is wholly misguided. Any science must have its body of explanatory theories, however speculative, together with a capacity to predict particular outcomes. It is impossible to have a true science which is lacking in either element. This admitted, it should not be imagined that all sciences will assume the same form, a conclusion which takes the argument back to the physical sciences and their influence on questions of scientific methodology. Physics undoubtedly boasts a great number of laws, a characteristic which reflects both its maturity and its subject matter. As a long established discipline it is likely to have a substantial body of established knowledge which might take on a law-like form. Its specific subject matter also makes the likelihood of developing a mass of laws highly probable. It has a significant theoretical content too, in parts highly speculative, e.g. in the case of black holes, but in general it is a science in which laws and a predictive ethos appear to flourish. Chemistry, another of the physical sciences, is much more theoretical and features a large body of analytical knowledge. It also embraces a highly predictive branch, sometimes known as physical chemistry. Astronomy does not have the experimental character of either physics or chemistry yet it is recognised as a physical science along with them, all of which serves to demonstrate the dangers of employing particular disciplines as paragons.

Moving to the opposite end of the spectrum, social sciences such as sociology are short on laws but seemingly well-endowed with theories of all sorts. It might be tempting to say that in time they too will develop their own established bodies of knowledge in which laws will figure strongly, but this neglects the fact that these disciplines have also existed for many years. The reality is that these are sciences in which laws are of much less value than theories, and where a predictive capacity is of much less significance than the ability to explain, offer understanding and suggest ways to resolve pressing social problems. It is not that many sociologists are unable to make predictions. They are quite capable of doing so. The fact is that most of these predictions are in fact extremely trivial in nature, contributing little to society's self-knowledge. For example, what value is there in the prediction that drunken football fans will be arrested for fighting at most matches this coming season? Better to explain what makes them demonstrate their support for their clubs in this particular way. Trying to force every science to replicate the form characteristic of physics reflects a failure to recognise that each must develop its own characteristic form. The lesson for financial accounting theory should be clear: what are the relative merits of a capacity to predict and the ability to explain accounting practice?

The fourth opposition which crops up with some regularity is between the *empirical* and *a priori* approaches to scientific research. The former again tends to be closely identified with the experimental methodology of the physical sciences while the latter are often characterised as the speculative, rational endeavours of armchair theorists who normally appear unwilling or even unable to subject their ideas to substantive testing. It is hardly suprising to find that the advocates of an empirical approach also favour a predictive, inductive and an essentially positive approach to financial accounting theory. They contrast this with the essentially *a priori*, prescriptive, deductive conceptual framework type of approach. Conversely those who are attracted to such a framework find that the self-evident appeal of an empirical approach is difficult to counter and so remain silent on the matter. They find it hard to deny that a conceptual framework is by definition a highly *a priori* device being intended to form the underpinning constitution of financial accounting. It cannot be tested in the same simple empirical way as a physical science law because it is of a fundamentally different order. The test of such a framework is its usefulness in guiding financial accounting practice over time, and to the extent that it is judged to do this it will be deemed to be a useful framework, an inescapable tautology. To represent the empirical approach as another paragon of scientific practice is to be closed minded about the variety of forms which even a science-based pursuit of an improved quality of life may entail. It provides further substance for the view of many social scientists that the advocacy of unhelpful physical science models has hampered those concerned with human affairs for far too long.

To leave the argument at this point would result in overlooking what is probably the key criticism of the empiricist view of science, either physical or social science. Earlier the opposition between an inductive and a deductive methodology was rejected on the grounds that science is reliant on both at all times. The same is the case for the opposition between *a priori* and empirical approaches to theorising. Thinking about problems, attempting to devise explanations and seeking to extend understanding in an insightful way is the other side of the coin of hypothesis testing, collecting empirical evidence and providing support or casting doubt upon a scientific theory. They are entirely complementary in that *a priori* activity is only of any scientific value if it is subsequently subjected to some form of empirical testing. On the other hand collecting empirical evidence is a meaningless activity unless some theoretical framework exists to guide the process. Underdown & Taylor (1985, p.5) state the case succinctly when they say:

> A priori theorising is a necessary complement to empirical research since it provides a framework of definitions, concepts and hypotheses to guide empirical researchers. Without such a framework it is difficult to interpret the results of empirical research.

All scientific work involves both empirical and *a priori* activities in the same way that it is always both inductive and deductive. Both are necessary if science is to progress effectively.

The fifth and final opposition is also one which is not always explicitly stated. One writer who does refer to the opposition between *general* and *middle-range* theories is Belkaoui. His conception of a middle-range theory is the one advanced by Robert Merton, the American sociologist, in his seminal essay 'On the strengths and limitations of theories of the middle-range' (Merton, 1967). Merton's thesis is that sociology, and by implication the social sciences in general, should seek to develop theories of more modest proportions rather than the comprehensive, all-embracing, general theories which were in his opinion hampering his own discipline. He favours the fashioning of theories which are logical, rigorous and soundly grounded in empirical evidence but theories which are not derived from a single general theory. In his view it is more appropriate to work up from the middle to the more general level of theory, but always in the knowledge that there can never be one single, all-embracing general theory which would serve to explain all. Indeed he expressly states that these middle-range theories could be consistent with a variety of higher level theories such as Marxism or Parsonian system theory in the case of contemporary sociology. The purpose of mature sociological analysis is not to establish a totalising theory of society but to generate a mass of theories applicable to a limited range of phenomena. In Merton's view the former is not possible since all middle-range theories involve a 'specification of ignorance' (Merton, 1967, p.68). It should come as no surprise that in the context of financial accounting theory the conceptual framework project is normally presented as an example of an attempt to develop a general theory. Given Merton's critique, financial accounting theorists will be better employed devising more modest middle-range theories than pursuing some form of conceptual framework.

Should this be taken to mean that the enormous amount of effort and resources which have been expended in the attempt to develop a conceptual framework have all been wasted and that there is nothing of real value that can be had from it? It really all depends on what is recognised as a middle-range financial accounting theory. During the past two decades there are grounds for concluding that the conceptual framework project, or more correctly projects, has given rise to some very valuable middle-range theorising. A good example of this is the identification of the various users of financial reports and their differing needs in *The Corporate Report* (1975). Equally the identification of a set of additional accounting statements is an inherently theoretical activity. This work was concerned with providing both understanding and explanation in the context of financial accounting and reporting, being inherently speculative in nature. While none of these are predictive in some narrow empirical sense, the object of all of these exercises was to contribute to making financial reporting more generally useful. Their value is to be judged by their usefulness not by the accuracy of their predictive capacity. In principle they would be commensurate with a range of meta-theories – something which is equally true of another example of middle-range theorising in connection with the conceptual framework, the FASB's identification of the desirable characteristics of financial information. Not every aspect of the FASB's work to date is theoretical in this way. The identification of the three 'objectives' of financial reporting is a much more philosophical exercise (FASB, 1978) while the consideration of the 'elements' of financial reporting is an explicitly definitional exercise (FASB, 1980).

The conclusion that a major part of financial accounting theory is properly concerned with identifying a range of users of financial reports and their various needs, additional financial statements which might contribute to meeting these needs, the qualities desirable in financial accounting information, etc., might seem to be some distance from the image of theory which many have. Yet they are very similar in nature to a body of thinking which would immediately be recognised as accounting theory but which has not been considered in any detailed way in this section: the various bases for accounting such as the historical cost convention, current value accounting, current cost accounting, current purchasing power accounting, etc. Each of these has been also developed in an attempt to enhance accounting practice. Each offers its own understanding and explanation of the merits of a particular way of accounting and in this way each is inevitably partial and speculative. Each is characteristically analytical, being a combination of empirical observation and *a priori* reasoning. Each is commensurate with a range of possible meta-theories. And none is predictive in the sense of a physical science 'theory'.

This conclusion needs to be much more fully and positively supported. The objective of the next section is to demonstrate the value of employing a social rather than a physical scientific model as the basis for advancing financial accounting theory.

THEORY CONSTRUCTION IN THE SOCIAL SCIENCES

While many of those interested in developing theory in accounting seem intent on employing a physical science approach in their work, few would disagree with the fact that accounting is a social science of some description. Being a social science means that it should employ a social scientific approach to theory construction. Part of the difficulty is that many accounting theoreticians do not appreciate that there are major differences between the two approaches. Invariably the social science with which they are the most familiar is economics, arguably the least methodologically self-conscious of the social science disciplines. In contrast sociology is a discipline which sometimes seems more interested in how it is possible to understand and explain the social world than it is in doing so. From the earliest writings of the founding forefathers such as Durkheim and Weber to the introductory chapters of foundation level texts such as Lee & Newby (1983), Bilton *et al.* (1987) and Giddens (1986, 1989) there is a continuous concern with the ways in which sociology can legitimately be viewed as a science but is not to be identified with the like of physics or chemistry. There have been sociologists who have argued for a sociology which adopted a distinctly physical scientific approach. One was Auguste Comte, the savant who coined the term sociology in the early nineteenth century for what he conceived of as a physics of society. In the 1930s George Lundberg advocated the idea of a *positive sociology* modelled on the physical sciences, although with little success. By the late 1960s 'positivism' had become a term of abuse in sociology, often being used to label anyone whose perspective you disagreed with. Twenty years on, few sociologists would ever advocate a sociology which merely aped the physical sciences however empirical their work might be.

The work of Robert Merton spans over half a century and includes some of the very best sociological analysis carried out during that time. Although never explicitly concerned with debating the difference between the physical and social sciences, Merton has made a major contribution to the development of social science methodology. His advocacy of a middle-range approach to theorisation as the most appropriate means to theory construction in the social sciences was discussed in the concluding paragraphs of the previous section. Attention is now switched to his own substantive work where it is possible to identify a model which may be employed in the social sciences in general. The specific lessons for financial accounting theory will be discussed after considering Merton's seminal account of the relationship between anomie and the social structure of American society.

The original essay entitled 'Social Structure and Anomie' was written in the late 1930s and is included together with a second 'Continuities' essay in his *Social Theory and Social Structure* volume first published in 1957. Merton's focus for enquiry, his 'problem', was the levels of deviance and criminal behaviour in particular which certain ethnic groups were exhibiting in contemporary America. Behaviour of this sort was recognised as a major social problem which required to be resolved in order to maintain if not improve the quality of social life for the mass of the population. The earlier psychologistic explanation that a particular type of person was responsible for such problems had given way to a much more sociological explanation that it was essentially a case of malsocialisation. The perpetrators of deviance were those who had not been properly brought up by their parents, who had not learned to respect the rights of others, who lacked the necessary self-discipline to control their actions, etc. The solution to the problem of deviance was to ensure that as far as possible all in society were properly socialised in their early life and of course that for those who erred, appropriate correctional institutions were in existence. Merton believed that this sort of explanation was as simplistic as the psychologistic one it had replaced. *Socialisation* was a key factor without a doubt but the existing explanation had failed to go beyond the obvious. To begin with it had not distinguished between *means* and *ends*. By ends he meant the culturally approved goals which all societies have as part of their central value system. In the case of America he identified financial success, comfort and security as of crucial importance. Means are the ways of achieving ends and again in any society there are particular ways of achieving which are culturally approved. Hard work, perseverance, dedication and so on are identified by Merton as the normal means to achievement in American society. Proper socialisation requires that the young are made aware of both means and ends. A failure to promote either would constitute the basis for malsocialisation.

In a perfect society everyone would internalise both means and ends. Equally, in a perfectly functioning society everyone would have the same right of access to the means and the same expectations that their successful performance in the prescribed ways to achieve would give rise to appropriate rewards. The point which Merton was seeking to make was that in an actual society there are all manner of constraints at work and it is for this reason that deviance occurs. In the context of the means prescribed by society, to the extent that it is not possible to gain access to good schooling then it is extremely difficult to demonstrate academic worth. Even where good schooling is available, if the home environment is not conducive to study it is difficult to perform adequately. And if there is a shortage of employment opportunities then it is difficult to work hard and thereby earn the right to live comfortably. In Merton's view American society did not provide equal access to the means to achieve its culturally approved goals. Its opportunity structure severely disadvantaged large sections of the population, precisely the same groups who were most commonly to be found involved in criminal activity. His explanation does not end at this point however. He continues by making the observation that there is much evidence that these same people are no less committed to the realisation of goals which society has set out for them. They have internalised the desire to become financially secure, to have a house, a car, a family at college, but are resultantly the more frustrated by the lack of opportunity to make this dream a reality. These frustrations are for Merton the evidence that sections of American society are in a situation of *anomie*. The lack of consistency between the prescribed means and those actually available gives rise to a distressing state of normlessness. They seek the ends but lack the means. Is it any suprise that some choose to devise their own means to achieve the desired ends, with the all too familiar consequence of escalating criminal deviance?

This simple but compelling explanation of the increased propensity to criminal activity among the socially disadvantaged forms only one part of Merton's broader explanation of deviant activity. Although he was particularly interested to provide an explanation of urban and minority group crime he provided the basis for an explanation of deviance of several different kinds. This is found in his typology of modes of individual adaptation to the disjunction between cultural goals and institutionalised means. Four adaptations are identified and contrasted with *conformity*, the simple acceptance of both goals and means. *Innovation* is the situation where there is an acceptance of the goals but where the prescribed means are not accepted. This is the basis of much criminality in that the individual is forced to innovate by devising alternative means to compensate for the lack of opportunity on offer. In this way criminal deviance is presented as a rational response to what might be described as an irrational situation, the inconsistency of means and ends.

The second adaptation which Merton identifies is that brought about in situations where an individual fails to identify with the goals of society but nevertheless continues to stick by the rules. This is termed *ritualism* to draw attention to the way in which some groups make a near ritual out of following the rules. As a student of the dysfunctions of bureaucracy, Merton cites the petty official as an example of the ritualist who cares little for anything other than following the procedures of the office. Although few would have believed that such a person was a deviant, Merton's argument is highly compelling.

Retreatism is the adaptation evidenced by those who come to identify with neither goals nor means for some reason. They retreat from society and live their lives on its margins. At the time of writing the following groups were identified by Merton as retreatists: psychotics, artists, pariahs, outcasts, vagabonds, tramps, chronic drunkards and drug addicts all of whom are viewed as asocial groups. Subsequent research has suggested that some of these groups, such as artists, tramps and drug addicts in particular, are more meaningfully categorised as exhibiting the fourth adaptation termed *rebellion*. In this case the deviant group rejects both the prevailing means and ends while substituting their own alternatives in their place as part of what was in later times to be termed a counter-culture (Roszak, 1970). Here Merton returned to emphasising the constructive aspects of deviant behaviour in the face of a social structure which was not serving its participants in a way which they could easily accept. This typology was to have a significant influence on the sociological study of crime and deviance and continues to do so. The main reason for this lies in the insight and understanding it generates about the parameters of deviance.

Returning to Merton's main interest, the explanation of criminal deviance among the most disadvantaged sections of society, it is possible to identify the main features of this powerful example of sociological analysis. Firstly, it is clearly problem-driven, the essays being an attempt to contribute to society's understanding of a pressing social issue, one which persists to this day. It is an attempt to offer an explanation of the problem which in turn will suggest ways in which to begin to resolve it. Merton is not concerned with predicting criminal deviance. While it would be possible to set up predictions for testing and in the process collect a mass of empirical data this would be trivial by comparison with attempts to develop programmes designed to reduce the levels of social disadvantage and thereby increase access to opportunity structures presently denied to many sections of society. Although Merton is a consistent advocate of an empirical approach to sociological analysis this should not be confused with simply collecting evidence in the light of prediction. Merton is advocating an approach which integrates *a priori* and empirical elements with the latter serving to substantiate the former in an inductive way. If this is not a prescriptive theory it most certainly is not a descriptive theory. What it does exemplify is the desirability of developing an analytical approach to theory-building. Merton's analysis is built around the distinction between ends and means as a basis for both his explanation of criminal deviance and his typology of individual adaptations. This example of a social science theory clearly demonstrates the important role which an analytic schema can have in theory construction. One final observation about Merton's theory is that like very many sociological theories it has a 'political' quality in the sense that it draws attention to the failings of the present social order as the cause of social disorder. This has led to the criticism that sociologists are simply using the discipline to advance their own political beliefs and that it is imperative that the rest of society is aware of this. There is a simple answer to this charge but one which has repercussions across the entirety of social science and perhaps beyond. If there were no problems with the social structure or the broader social order, then there would be no need for social scientists to understand, explain and hopefully improve upon it.

This summary of the main features of Merton's theory of anomie, deviance and the social structure can be fruitfully compared with the main features of the sort of theory which needs to be developed as part of the corpus of financial accounting theory and as a constituent of any broader conceptual framework. Both are middle-range theories which should be commensurate with a number of different meta-theories. Both are problem-driven in the sense of having originated out of some form of social disorder. In the case of Merton's theory this disorder is evidenced by the persistence of criminal deviance while in the case of financial reporting, it is the perceived failure of financial statements to communicate effectively to those who make use of them which is the basis for concern. The search for explanatory theories which will provide some insight on how to tackle present problems characterises both types of theory, rather than the development of a series of predictions which will be used to establish their value. Value is to be judged on the basis of utility in reducing the problems which have given rise to the need for understanding. Conversely neither theory offers a guarantee that it will produce this result, since any theory is inherently speculative in nature. The adoption of an analytical approach to theory construction is also common to both exercises, as distinct from either a normative or a descriptive approach. In financial accounting, the identification of different user groups, their different needs, the desirable qualities of information, etc., are evidence that the need for an analytical approach is already recognised by some theorists as the appropriate way to proceed. Finally, both are inherently political enquiries. While Merton was raising the question of equality of opportunity, some financial accounting theorists have raised the equally contentious question of the very purpose of financial reporting. Both have pointed the way to changes in their respective social orders, changes which would undoubtedly result in a redistribution of power between the different parties involved. The general conclusion of much sociological research has been that such changes have always been fiercely resisted by those who benefit most from the present order of things. This seems as good a reason as any to continue with work of this sort.

WATTS & ZIMMERMAN AND THE SOCIOLOGY OF ACCOUNTING

In reviewing the anatomy of financial accounting theory the work of Watts & Zimmerman was mentioned on a number of occasions, particularly in support of the development of positive accounting theory. These writers advocate a distinctly non-normative approach to the development of accounting theory. They seek to replicate the physical science model of theory construction and testing within accounting, with great emphasis upon predictive capacity and the opportunity for empirical enquiry as the indicators of good theories. Their approach has been highly influential in the USA for the past decade, with their 1986 text building on work begun in the mid-1970s (Whittington, 1987). It was a pair of provocative essays published in *The Accounting Review* in the late 1970s which established them among the leading accounting theorists of the 1980s: 'Towards a positive theory of the determination of accounting standards' (1978) and 'The demand for and supply of accounting theories: the market for excuses' (1979). And it was these same essays which led one of their most celebrated critics to describe their work as not so much a contribution to accounting theory as to the sociology of accounting (Christenson, 1983). A brief discussion of their work would therefore seem to be an interesting way to conclude this chapter.

In the 1978 essay they were seeking to provide an explanation of the motivations and machinations of senior managements in their support for or opposition to the development of particular financial accounting standards. They argue that senior management normally take account of a number of possible consequences before deciding whether to support or oppose a proposed change in standard. These include the probable tax consequences of change, the possibility of greater government intervention, the internal 'costs' of change and the effects which change would have on their own compensation plans. Watts & Zimmerman hypothesise that senior management have a greater incentive to support accounting standards which result in reporting lower earnings in the short term, particularly in the context of larger enterprises. In short they are driven by self-interest to lobby for accounting standards which result in reporting lower earnings:

> As long as financial accounting standards have potential effects on the firm's future cashflow, standard setting bodies . . . will be met by corporate lobbying.
>
> (Watts & Zimmerman, 1978, p.132)

After examining written submissions by major corporations to the FASB's proposal to require General Price Level Accounting, as a means to test their self-interest thesis, they conclude that, other things being equal, larger firms are more likely to favour GPLA if earnings decline, adding that this finding is supportive of their broader belief that political factors are highly influential in determining the way in which the practice of accounting is shaped in contemporary society.

Although a highly provocative conclusion, the essay itself is far less strident than the one which followed it. The self-interest thesis is again at the centre of the argument which in this case is directed against those accounting theorists who would support the development and application of normative theory. If senior management are in the market for theories which will serve their own interests then any theory which finds favour does so not because of its 'public interest' qualities but because of its sectional value. However well-intentioned accounting theorists committed to the development of normative accounting theories may be, Watts & Zimmerman characterise them as supplying the 'excuses' which are in great demand from self-interested parties. Appeals to the public interest which emanate from industry or commerce must be recognised as attempts to cover up sectional interests. As a result, any theory which promises benefits to a particular party will always gain its support.

As positive theorists, the writers embrace the position of not passing judgement on the market for excuses. Their motivation is to observe, analyse and then explain what is in place and not to offer any judgement about what might exist as an alternative. Or at least this is the impression they would wish to convey. By arguing that there is no such entity as a socially beneficial accounting framework, since such a framework would always be in the interests of particular parties and against those of others, they are arguing for the status quo. Their opposition to the development of normative theory is not on the grounds of its impossibility but of its desirability. They object to it on the basis that in the course of its realisation, fundamental restrictions would be imposed on the actions of senior managers with power being transferred to other parties. In this way they too are in the business of prescription: there should be no restrictions on the activities of those entrusted with the task of stewardship, with the market for excuses being maintained as a free market. In the terminology of social theory, they believe that what is the case ought to remain the case.

The 1986 text has as its objective the task of explaining why accounting and auditing practice is as it is. For example, why do some firms use accelerated depreciation and others straight line depreciation? Why do some firms use Big 6 auditors and others not? Also is it possible to predict the choice which senior managements will make in these respects? The level of analysis has shifted from lobbying for particular accounting standards to that of explaining and predicting (i.e. a 'good' theory of) accounting choice. But the basic argument remains the same, that it is the self-interest of senior managers which determines the nature of accounting practice. In the course of the text they identify three 'hypotheses' which they test empirically: the bonus plan hypothesis; the debt/equity hypothesis and the size hypothesis. Their general conclusion is that in the main the objective of senior management is to reduce current earnings for reasons of self-interest. The rejection of normative theories in the first chapter and the inclusion in the text of the 1979 essay (as chapter 14) indicate Watts & Zimmerman's continued commitment to a free market in accounting practice. What is new about the text, however, is the writers' desire to develop a theory which embraces financial reporting, auditing and finance, a general theory of accounting and finance perhaps? This is intended to restore to finance the theoretical basis which it began to lose in the early 1970s, while at the same time integrating it with the new positive theory in financial reporting and auditing. The structure of the text itself supposedly demonstrates the continuity of finance and accounting research but in key places contains little more than assertion. The same can be said about the arguments for adopting a distinctly physical science methodology in the case of positive accounting theory construction. As the writers themselves concede even after a decade or more of intense activity their project is still in its preliminary stages, a view reaffirmed in their recent review paper on the progress of positive theorising (Watts & Zimmerman, 1989).

The suggestion that their work is best understood as a contribution to the sociology of accounting or, more specifically, accounting choice has not been exploited by Watts & Zimmerman. The most likely explanation of this is that they find the suggestion embarrassing, particularly so given their implicit intention of constructing a general theory of accounting and finance. This should not be allowed to rule out of court the question of whether their work is in fact a contribution to the sociology of accounting choice, however. It is an entirely legitimate question, not least because they draw attention to what is an interesting and potentially fruitful focus for sociological enquiry and theory construction (cf. Whittington, 1987, p.334). Their work is certainly an attempt to understand and explain why accountants act in the way that they do when it comes to financial reporting. The self-interest thesis is a provocative if simplistic explanation of the widely recognised practice of manipulating accounting numbers. That it is senior managers who instruct accountants to devise ways of manipulation which will best serve the former's interests only serves to confirm the validity of sociological enquiry in this arena. Turning to the question of whether such enquiries are at base problem-driven, Watts & Zimmerman are understandably a little ambivalent. They clearly recognise that these activities are often likely to be to the disadvantage of other parties but in the last analysis they seem happy to accept that senior management and their accounting functionaries ought not to be fettered by a set of normative prescriptions devised to serve the interests of the other parties. A more socially aware or concerned approach, i.e. the motivation of most sociologists, would clearly recognise the problems which result from the free market in accounting practice and would approach the issues involved in this way.

The fact that this work has provided a body of evidence on the extent of self-interested accounting choice certainly commends it as a contribution to a sociology of accounting. It is an area of enquiry which those sociologists interested in the dynamics of accounting and finance should perhaps pursue in preference to other issues. But they must be careful not to overstate their case in the manner of Watts & Zimmerman who clearly wish to see their particular theoretical endeavours as the most important ones, and ultimately the only basis for positive theorising. As things stand the study of accounting choice could well give rise to much incisive middle-range theory to complement other theories on users, user needs, financial statements, qualitative matters, etc. To cast it in the role of the central theoretical issue is a very real danger which could have many damaging consequences. Equally the tendency to empirical prediction and hypothesis testing, as advocated by Watts & Zimmerman, must always be subordinated to the need to develop strategies designed to improve accounting practice in a socially beneficial way. This of course raises the question of the political dimensions of any sociology of accounting choice and the possibility of controversy and conflict. If such enquiries succeed in promoting these, as they seem likely to do, they will simply serve to reaffirm the point which was made earlier: if there were no problems with the social there would be no need for social scientists to understand, explain and hopefully improve it.

Chapter 6

Management accounting

If sociology has had little significance for financial accounting to date the same certainly cannot be said for management accounting. During the past decade a growing body of management accounting writers, if not practitioners, has demonstrated a far-reaching and enthusiastic interest in the variety of theoretical perspectives which characterise post-functionalist sociology. Because of this interest, it seems inevitable that management accounting research, teaching and practice in the 1990s will assume a form quite different from that which it has had for much of the past half century. This should not be taken to mean that sociology is transforming management accounting on its own. From within the mainstream of management accounting research a powerful critique has recently emerged, one which pays no attention to what the discipline of sociology has to offer. However, the significance of some of the issues which this critique has raised may be better understood if they are viewed in a more sociologically informed way. The present chapter is perhaps best described as an attempt to substantiate these rather extravagant claims regarding the value of sociological modes of thinking for the future development of management accounting.

THE NATURE OF MANAGEMENT ACCOUNTING

Most modern textbooks begin their discussion of management accounting by distinguishing it from financial accounting. The basis of the distinction is that while financial accounting is principally concerned with the reporting of information to parties outside the organisation, particularly shareholders, management accounting is concerned with the provision of information to management, a party inside the organisation. Thus management accounting is described as *internal* accounting while financial accounting is *external* accounting (e.g., Drury, 1988, p.4; Horngren & Foster, 1987, p.2). In practice these two sets of information are not distinct, constituting the different aspects of an integrated accounting information system developed by and thus under the control of senior management. Information reported to external users may be for such purposes as investor decision-making, tax assessment and collection, etc., while internal accounting information is utilised by management in planning and controlling routine operations, in making non-routine decisions and in formulating major policies and plans (Horngren & Foster, p.2). For Drury, the purpose of internal or management accounting is the provision of information for management activities such as decision-making, planning and control (p.20).

Normally the next task is to distinguish management accounting from cost accounting. Again the focus is on the issues of planning, control and decision-making and the managerial nexus. In his survey of the literature of management accounting, Scapens (1984) makes the point that general use of the term, together with its North American equivalent *managerial accounting*, only dates back to the 1950s. He approvingly cites Shillinglaw's thesis that the development of cost accounting was a response to the emergence of scientific management at the turn of the century while management accounting proper developed as a response to the identification of the management control problematic in the 1950s (Shillinglaw, 1980). Recent research has suggested that some of the information nowadays associated with management accounting had long been produced by accountants working in the most successful business enterprises (Johnson & Kaplan, 1987). However, the conventional wisdom remains that cost accounting was the primary focus of internal accounting before the Second World War with its emphasis on product costing and a concern with cost accumulation for stock valuation and external reporting purposes. By contrast the scope of contemporary management accounting is much wider, encompassing a growing body of techniques which have been developed in the light of the needs which management have to plan, control and make decisions. Management accounting is presented as a far superior entity to cost accounting which is best understood as only one aspect of management accounting. It must be recognised for that which it is best suited, the requirements of external reporting, hardly a substantial enough basis upon which to develop an important management service. In the professional sphere there has also been evidence of a desire to distinguish between the two. In 1958 the National Association of Cost Accountants, the principal US managerial accounting association, changed its name to the National Association of Accountants in an attempt to keep abreast of the development of management accounting. In 1965 the UK Institute of Cost and Works Accountants retitled its journal *Management Accounting* (formerly *Cost Accountant*), a title it retains to this day. In 1972 it changed its name to the Institute of Cost and Management Accountants and subsequently in 1987 to the Chartered Institute of Management Accountants as part of a strategic review of the organisation's future development.

The identification of management accounting with the management control problematic is the basis upon which its value is claimed, both for management and more generally. It is therefore necessary to understand what the problematic entails and in order to do so attention needs to be focused on the body of knowledge known as management science. From the late 1940s onwards there had been a growing interest in the development of a science of management which would build upon the legacy of Fayol rather than Taylor the erstwhile father of scientific management. Fayol's prescription that the functions of management were to plan, organise, coordinate, command and control were expanded and reworked by a succession of management scientists including Simon and Drucker and later Argenti, Ansoff, Ackoff, etc. Although disagreeing in matters of detail, their collective labour gave rise to the ubiquitous managerial decision-making, planning and control process (alternatively known as the *strategic management process*) which features in almost all texts on corporate strategy, business strategy, business policy and in many management accounting texts (e.g. Arnold & Hope, 1990, p.12; Drury, 1988, p.10). Among the various contributions to the science of management was one specifically related to accounting in general and management accounting in particular, the seminal work of Robert Anthony. In his analysis of managerial activity, Anthony (1965) integrated two already well understood ideas. Managerial decision-making could be differentiated into long term, broad or strategic decisions; medium term, implementation or administrative decisions and short term, narrowly focused or operational decisions. Planning was concerned with the *a priori* structuring of programmes and the setting up of systems as opposed to control which was concerned with ensuring that what was intended to be actually comes to be. The points of contact between strategic decision-making and planning and operational decision-making and control were obvious but equally there was an overlap between the implementation of plans and devising the means of their effective control. Anthony proposed a tripartite typology of managerial activity: strategic planning; management control and operational control.

Strategic planning is concerned with the setting of broad corporate objectives, searching for possible strategies to achieve these, comparing those strategies which are available in order to identify the most desirable course of action and making the decision to implement it. This process involves mainly the most senior levels of management and takes place in the highest echelons of the organisation. By contrast, *operational control* is concerned with the day-to-day management of the organisation and is performed by a large number of persons in the lower reaches of the management hierarchy. This type of activity is highly varied with individuals normally being responsible for a narrow range of tasks. *Management control* is the type of managerial activity which is intermediate between the two and as such it forms the vital link in turning objectives into results. For many managers, particularly middle management, it is synonymous with the activity of management itself (Otley, 1989). Management control is concerned with translating long term objectives into short term activity in some way and with providing the mechanism for effective medium term control. Characterised in this way it is clearly the most critical level of managerial activity. Anthony took the view that accounting information was the major tool for achieving management control, especially the sort of information on offer from management accountants. The essence of management accounting's contribution lay in its interest in budgetary control. In Anthony's view, management control involves monitoring the courses of action chosen for implementation by senior management, and where necessary, taking action to correct any departure from plan. Plans, performance and corrective action need to be expressed in some common, quantitative form, the most obvious one being financial in nature. A financial budget provides the means to set out the parameters of a chosen course of action, the guidelines against which to compare actual (i.e. monitored) performance and the basis upon which to modify the initial plan if necessary. A budget thus provides the means to report on the performance of all aspects of an organisation's activity on a regular basis which in turn allows the systematic review of all areas of activity (Emmanuel & Otley, 1985, p.75). The information which it provides allows line management to make the decisions which are necessary to realise the objectives set for them by their senior management. It is in this way that management accounting provides the necessary financial information for managers faced with the task of decision-making, planning and control.

The identification of management accounting with the development and operation of effective budgetary control systems may initially appear to portray only one, albeit a major, aspect of this branch of accounting. In most texts equal attention is paid to product and variable costing and invariably the study of budgeting is shared with standard costing and variance analysis. Then there are the more advanced topics: opportunity costing, performance measurement, transfer pricing and those associated with the information economics approach to decision-making. Research too has traditionally covered a much wider range of topics. But in the last analysis most texts begin by stressing the significance of management accounting for decision-making, planning and control, thereby emphasising the management control/budgetary control linkage, explicitly or otherwise. In the sphere of practice, management accountancy and the development, implementation and operation of budgetary control systems have traditionally been synonymous for many of those involved. The connection cannot be overstated despite appearances to the contrary. It is also the connection which provides part of the explanation of why a growing number of management accounting researchers have become increasingly interested in sociological ideas during the past decade.

BUDGETS AND THE 'BEHAVIOUR IN ORGANISATIONS' PERSPECTIVE

In 1952 Argyris, then a young industrial psychologist in the Human Relations tradition, wrote an essay whose title makes the connection between budgets and behaviour in a succinct way: 'The Impact of Budgets on People'. Like all forms of managerial activity, budgets affect people. They are the reality of what is termed 'labour' in any costing schedule in the same way that they are the human factor in a production schedule. While it is possible to represent them in this seemingly objective manner, in the context of strategic planning and management and operational control, it is always necessary to remember that they are quite different to the other costs or factors. Argyris' main concern was to point out some of the dysfunctions of budgets, drawing attention to four in particular.

In general they are viewed by workforces to be another means to exploit them and as a result they often serve only to harden the resistance of employees. Because they are seen to be the work of accountants, budgetary systems portray accountants as the enemy of workforces. Equally they may serve to direct criticism away from senior management who in Argyris' view are responsible for creating the underlying climate of worker–management relations. Finally, the setting of budgets and their subsequent realisation by middle management can often become a technical ritual. Self-interest, empire building, interdepartmental politics and the like are all bound up in the formal budgetary system, to the detriment of the organisation and the majority of its members.

Despite its obvious importance to management accounting, research into the behavioural aspects of budgeting did not really begin until the later 1960s by which time industrial psychology had been moved on by writers such as McGregor, Herzberg, Likert, Blake & Mouton, all of whom in their different ways advocated forms of participative management. When research did begin it was focused on the effects of budgets on managers rather than the broader interactions charted by Argyris. In 1968 Hofstede compared the use of budgetary systems in the USA and in Europe, concluding that in the American context they were taken very seriously by management and as a result often engendered negative feelings. By contrast in Europe budgets were not widely used as a means of managerial performance evaluation and so did not produce the negative feelings among managers. Hofstede's conclusion was that managers should perhaps treat budgetary control as a game, a view which on reflection seems a trifle misguided. The work of Lowe & Shaw published in the same year outlined some of the ways in which the lower levels of managerial employee accommodated to the need for budgetary control imposed from above, in other words the ways in which they were playing the game. In 1970 Schiff & Lewin were to entitle their own essay on the behavioural aspects of budgeting 'The Impact of People on Budgets', demonstrating the interactional nature of the relationship between them. It is interesting to recall that the concept of *zero-based budgeting* was also introduced at this time (Pyrhh, 1970). One of the advantages claimed for this technique of 'bottom up' budgeting is that it incorporates a measure of participation. The lower and middle levels of management, those whose performance would be measured and evaluated by means of budgets, are now to be consulted at the development stage in an attempt to produce better budgetary packages and, of course, enhanced management control. The rules of the game needed to be modified to produce a more favourable result.

Into this fast emerging tradition of *behavioural accounting* stepped Anthony Hopwood, a British researcher who has had an unparalleled impact on academic accounting research and scholarship ever since. Not surprisingly he was interested in the interaction between people and budgets and in the early 1970s carried out empirical studies of managerial performance, spending some time at the University of Chicago. His first text shows all the signs of a natural scientific approach to the study of accounting systems and human behaviour (Hopwood,

1973). In it he identifies three styles of using accounting information to evaluate managerial performance: the *budget constrained* style; the *profit conscious* style and the *non-accounting* style (in which accounting information in fact plays a comparatively minor role in performance evaluation). The general finding of the study was that while both the budget constrained and profit conscious styles usually resulted in a high level of involvement with costs, the latter tended to be less dysfunctional in terms of (negative) management tension. Although clearly favouring the profit conscious style with its less parochial managerial behaviour, greater openness and perceived sense of fairness, he stops short of recommending it to senior management arguing that more research is needed to 'isolate the conditions, if any, under which the styles are appropriate' (Hopwood, 1973, p.195). In retrospect, this formulation is typical of a contingency perspective on organisations, at the time the dominant mode of organisational analysis (Lawrence & Lorsch, 1967; Woodward, 1965, 1970).

When recounting his findings in *Accounting and Human Behaviour* (1974) Hopwood advances an even more distinctly contingency-informed conclusion:

> the precise balance of costs and benefits associated with these three styles might well be different for the control of a stable technologically simple situation . . . than for an uncertain and highly complex situation.
>
> (Hopwood, 1974, pp.113–4)

The contingency perspective was to inform his thinking on participation in the budgetary process also discussed in the text. After reviewing the existing literature Hopwood concludes that only the most naive observer could feel safe in the view that participative approaches are always more effective than authoritarian styles of management. Participation may raise morale but this is not the same as raising efficiency and productivity. In other words, there are no panaceas, there is no 'one best way', the very essence of contingency thinking.

Hopwood was not alone among management accounting researchers in discovering the contingency perspective in the mid-1970s. The main reason for this was an intellectual appeal based on a number of desirable criteria. First there was the admission that there were no panaceas in the field of organisation and management theory, a position which distinguished it from the mass of previous theories and prescriptions from the most managerial to the most humanistic. In the form in which it was developed in the Aston studies it assumed the form of an eminently scientific mode of social analysis, comparable with any other social scientific work (Pugh & Hickson, 1976; Pugh & Hinings, 1976). It was inherently interdisciplinary, integrating a range of disciplines and techniques including both psychology and sociology. The fact that it was coming under some criticism from the latter discipline at the same time was irrelevant, at least in the short term. In 1976 Hopwood became the editor of a new accounting research journal *Accounting, Organisations and Society*, a post he has retained to date. Writing its founding editorial he identified the pressing need to accelerate the social, organisational and behavioural study of accounting. Behavioural accounting papers figured strongly in the early issues and have continued to do so since then. A commitment to the contingency perspective was also evident from the outset (Gordon & Miller, 1976). The need to look to organisation theory for insight was reiterated by Hopwood himself in an essay published in 1978. The systems perspective, which pre-dated and had itself strongly influenced contingency thinking, also became more evident in the journal's pages at this time.

Social theory was conspicuously absent until 1980 – something which had not gone unnoticed by the editor and some of his closest colleagues. In their seminal essay published in that year Burchell *et al.*. effectively presented the case for incorporating a broader range of insights from the social sciences and most particularly those of a critical nature. By far the most critical of the social sciences was sociology and, from this point on, the journal and many of those who have become associated with it have been engaged in integrating socio-logical perspectives and management accounting. Papers written from a con-tingency perspective still appeared although Otley's critique (1980) together with those of Wood (1979) and Cooper (1983) ensured a reduced influence. A more developed organisational emphasis still has a good deal to offer as the recent text by Ezzamel & Hart (1987) demonstrates. Nor does sociology have the monopoly on critical analysis in accounting research, and alongside it there has been a series of contributions from the political economy perspective: e.g. Cooper (1980); Cooper & Sherer (1984); Tinker (1980); Tinker, Merino & Neimark (1982); Neimark & Tinker (1986). The journal is no longer the only vehicle for publish-ing sociologically informed accounting research nor has it ever restricted itself to management accounting. However, a decade on, the three are still closely and productively interlinked.

SOCIOLOGICAL PERSPECTIVES AND MANAGEMENT ACCOUNTING RESEARCH

In this section four sociological perspectives evident in management accounting research are discussed. These are the interactionist perspective, the labour pro-cess perspective, critical theory and the Foucauldian perspective. They are con-sidered in this order both for ease of understanding and because they have more or less found their way into the literature in this order. At this point it is only possible to reiterate that these (and several other) perspectives fit together as parts of the theoretical framework of contemporary sociology. To understand how they do, the reader is advised to reread the relevant section of the introductory chapter of the text and perhaps refer to one of the many general sociology texts. Each perspective is considered in the same way: an overview of the perspective is followed by an account of the way in which writers on accounting have employed it. A brief critique completes each review. It must be stressed that much of the following discussion is inescapably partial and cannot avoid doing some damage to the intentions of many of those involved. It is offered in the interests of an increased awareness of the value of integrating the two disciplines of sociology and accounting.

The interactionist perspective

Interactionism is an attempt to understand the social order in terms of its being the result of the interactions of social actors. It is a perspective which is concerned with individuals and in particular with their meanings. What we see as the social order and the meanings which it has for us are seen as the product of social interaction. In this way interactionism sees that the social structure is the consequence of the existence and interaction of the meanings of many different social actors. Thus education is understood as a complex of meanings which are given to it by the various social actors who are participants in it, and who thereby invest it with its meaning: pupils, teachers, parents, employers, governments and in a more passive sense the broader society. Like all social entities it is a multi-meaning phenomenon with which all parties can identify to some degree or otherwise it could not be described as being genuinely social. As a way of seeing the social order which focuses on social actors and their meanings, interactionism is distinct from the more holistic or systems sociologies of the 1950s and early 1960s, many of its main elements being developed in opposition to these (Silverman, 1970; Burrell & Morgan, 1979).

Contemporary interactionism has progressed from being concerned essentially with structure and its relationship with meanings to consider the nature of the processes of structuration. Interest now focuses on the way in which any structure is in fact always in process with the result that we experience a social order which is always a *negotiated order* and as such is always changing as meanings change, and in turn serves to change meaning in a dialectical way. The processual orientation has also embraced the inescapable fact that in any process of negotiation the different actors usually possess different degrees of power to control the interaction. Consequently the social order which we experience is portrayed as one which inevitably reflects the meanings and serves the interests of some social actors rather than others. In this way the social construction of reality is viewed more critically than perhaps was the case in the work of the early interactionist writers such as Goffman (1959), Blumer (1969) and Glaser & Strauss (1967).

Within management accounting research the interactionist perspective provides a means whereby the design, development and operation of management information and control systems can be understood in a much broader and insightful way than would ever be possible employing the behavioural perspective which had attracted much attention during the 1970s. Thus it is of no surprise to find that interactionism was the first genuinely sociological perspective to establish itself in the management accounting research literature. In 1981 *AOS* published Ian Colville's essay 'Reconstructing "Behavioural Accounting"' as the first contribution to a literature which was to popularise the 'naturalistic' tradition (see also Tomkins & Groves, 1983). Interactionism's value for understanding the nature of accounting in action was soon evidenced by a series of case studies: Rosenberg *et al.* (1982); Covaleski & Dirsmith (1983, 1986); Tomkins & Colville (1984); Preston (1986). In recent years there has been a move away from interactionism to some of the other perspectives on offer although in a recent paper Birkett & Chua (1988) offer a powerful reformulation of some interactionist themes and concepts. There are also some grounds for interpreting Giddens' attempt to devise a general structuration theory as a form of interactionism, perhaps more oriented to structure than action. Thus the recent work of Macintosh & Scapens (1989) with its case study emphasis further evidences a move back to an interactionist perspective (see also Roberts & Scapens, 1985).

To date probably the most widely known example of interactionist management accounting research is Berry *et al.*'s NCB case study published in 1985. Describing their project as 'an attempt to understand management control systems in practice', they discovered that two such systems have traditionally existed, one operative at the local level of collieries and areas, the other at the national and regional levels. The former is based on a production or 'coal-getting' culture in which budgeting is based on output and production targets. Little or no account is taken of the level of capital investment in the individual collieries or the area as a whole. The absence of colliery or area balance sheets is symptomatic of the insignificance of the financial planning and control in the coalfields. Together they reflect the dominance of the coal-getting culture in the industry. At the national and regional levels, however, a sophisticated system of financial planning and control exists, at least in theory. It gives rise to the financial reports which the NCB has produced for successive governments, the industry's masters. The subordination of the finance function to production, and to mining engineers in the areas, was evident in the role the latter played in investment appraisal, a crucial aspect of the system of financial planning and control. Berry *et al.* conceptualise this negotiated order of management control in terms of the development and reproduction of a set of loosely coupled control mechanisms within the industry. These had served the interests of all parties to date but only at a cost. At the time at which the authors were writing, 1983, it was clear that the Conservative government with its commitment to the market would soon require the NCB to rethink its financial procedures. This would inevitably result in a radically changed agenda, something which the industry had been protected from so effectively by the existing arrangements. The passage of time has seen the defeat of the mineworkers in their fight against a programme of closures. One reason offered for their defeat in 1984 was the level of coalstocks at the beginning of their action which meant that it was always unlikely to succeed. It is somehow ironic that the dominance of the coal-getting culture was ultimately to undermine the position of those upon whose labour it was built.

The first point to make about interactionist case studies is that their appeal is arguably their greatest weakness. From the earliest studies by the Chicago sociologists to cases such as the NCB, interactionists have provided analyses rich in detail and insight about the relationships existing between structure and meaning. After reading a good case study you feel as though you now know a lot more about the subject under enquiry and the issues involved. The problem is that the focus of interest is very narrow and the analysis partial in the sense of being a particular account of reality construction. In short, the detail and analysis on offer can easily result in the reader forgetting the very limited advance which it offers to understanding. In the jargon of the philosophy of the social sciences, the idiographic emphasis of case studies can readily obscure the need for any science to adopt a nomothetic or theory-building methodology to some extent. The idea of grounded theory and the adoption of an inductive mode of theory building in the social sciences is, to use a cliche, all very well in theory. In practice, however, it is extremely difficult to move from the particular (case study) to a higher level of generalisation such as a middle-range theory. It would involve carrying out a series of parallel case studies as well as extensive replication over time, which itself is extremely problematic in the social sciences – all in a very narrow field which may in time prove to be relatively unimportant. This is not to deny the many positive qualities of interactionist or any form of case studies. It is simply a matter of identifying some of the costs as well as the benefits of this method-ology. And as a link into discussing the labour process perspective it is important to draw attention to another serious shortcoming which has been identified with the interactionist perspective. It has tended to produce an uncritical form of sociology, with rich descriptions often accompanied by equally bland analyses.

The labour process perspective

While the interactionist perspective embraces a wide variety of ways of under-standing the social world the opposite may be said of the labour process per-spective. It has only two key figures the (mature) Marx and Braverman. Unlike interactionism it is not concerned with epistemological issues, being focused on what in Chapter 3 was termed the social organisation of work. Both Marx and Braverman were committed to the task of radically reshaping work and society. This they believed was only possible in the wake of the transformation to an alternative socialist order. Their respective writings on the labour process, and in Marx's case much more besides, were conceived of as contributing to the development of the political consciousness of the oppressed working classes. In this sense it is arguably more correct to see the labour process perspective as an aspect of Marxist political economy rather than sociology. The reason why it is usually identified with sociology nowadays is because Braverman's seminal account of the development of the capitalist social organisation of work, *Labour & Monopoly Capital* (1974), first found favour with writers working in the field of industrial sociology who were themselves interested in a more radical approach to the study of work, e.g. Buroway, Edwards, Freidman, Nichols and Beynon. Braverman's influence quickly spread to the study of organisations and

industrial relations, then to the professions and gender before finding a new
audience among writers on management, which is one route by which it came to
the attention of management accounting researchers. The kernel of Braverman's
project was to identify how capital has been able to retain and reproduce its
control over labour in the twentieth century. In other words, he was seeking to
offer an account of the development of management control, one which was both
analytically sound and potentially useful for those engaged in the class struggle.
The same remains true of many of those who have subsequently adopted this
perspective. How many of them would happily see themselves as Marxists is
another matter.

The principal advocate of adopting a labour process perspective on management accounting is Trevor Hopper, one of the researchers involved in the NCB
study who soon recognised the potential limitations of the interactionist perspective (Hopper *et al.*, 1986, p.138). The appeal of a more radical approach to
management accounting research was evidenced in an earlier paper with Powell
(1985) and developed in a joint paper with Storey and Willmott presented at the
first Interdisciplinary Perpectives on Accounting conference, and subsequently
published in *AOS* in 1987. Among the insights which a labour process perspective is claimed to offer on management accounting are that it highlights how
it contributes to the institutional subordination of labour, how its language serves
and legitimates sectional interests, and the ways in which like other forms of
management control it has been fashioned largely to meet the perceived interests
of capital (Hopper *et al.*, 1987, p.446). One writer whose work informs Hopper's
is Peter Armstrong, an industrial sociologist who has been associated with labour
process thinking for over a decade (Nichols & Armstrong, 1976). In the early
1980s Armstrong had become interested in the competition between three professions – engineering, personnel and accounting – for recognition by senior
management (*qua* capital) as being able to control labour most effectively in the
twentieth century (Armstrong, 1985, 1986, 1987a). While Taylorism relied on a
combination of all three, the passage of time has seen the rise to dominance of
accounting controls and of the accountants who employ them (against the
interests of the working class). More recently Wardell & Weisenfeld (1988) have
provided evidence in the case of the USA that the emergence and practice of
management accounting must be seen as inextricably linked to the class struggle.

Among the themes which Hopper *et al.* address in their 1986 labour-
process-informed reinterpretation of the NCB case is the importance of class
relationships for an understanding of accounting and financial control within the
labour process. In their own words the control of the controllers is problematic
(p.111). Having previously demonstrated the existence of major divisions within
what are usually termed NCB management and the loose coupling of management control mechanisms, Hopper *et al.* go back into the data to see how the
NCB's (top) management use these arrangements to manage the lower echelons
of management. Attention is again drawn to the complexity of the control system

which has been constructed and the manner in which financial information also serves to manage the managerial labour process. This leads them to conclude that there is clearly an urgent need to carry out further research into the position of accountancy professionals in the contemporary class structure. At a theoretical level this work had already begun. Having discussed the emergence of labour processes amongst scientists and engineers in the post-war period and the attendant proletarianisation of this particular profession, the writer has sought to employ the same analysis in the case of accountants (Roslender, 1983a, 1990a; see also Glover et al., 1986; Kelly & Roslender, 1988). The main elements of the analysis have already been set out in Chapter 3 where the labour process perspective was integrated with neo-Marxist class analysis. While the accounting and finance function as a whole plays a major role in the control of the organisation, individual accountants are only controllers in other people's labour processes by fiat. They are also subject to labour processes which are designed and managed by senior accountants who also find themselves involved in the design of labour processes in other functions. It is necessary that this situation is fully appreciated by accountants, especially those confined in the lowest echelons of the profession. Their contradictory situation *vis-à-vis* control is further evidence of the contradictions which characterise contemporary social organisation of work.

Adopting a labour process perspective is a potentially fruitful approach particularly when it is articulated with a case study methodology. The labour process concept provides the 'theory' which the case material and analysis serve to inform. The theory doesn't develop from the study as in interactionism since it is already in place. This is also the principal problem of the labour process perspective. In the hands of its more committed advocates it is an unashamedly partial perspective on work and organisations. The labour process perspective sets out from the premise that in a capitalist society work and employment, the organisation and industrial relations are all shaped and structured to serve the interests of the capitalist class. The study of these aspects of the social order is intended to demonstrate the substance of the founding assumption of the perspective. Labour process researchers are not seeking to demonstrate that labour processes do not exist. Their objective is to reveal their variety of form and content, how they have been developed over time, how they have become seen as the normal form of work and employment, and so on. It would be difficult to deny that the labour process perspective has a conspiratorial quality, with researchers normally finding what they are seeking. But this is to say nothing about either the truth or falsity of the knowledge they have generated or the standards of scholarship which they demonstrate in their research. Any researcher seeking a radical viewpoint on management accounting in practice, one which will permit critical comment, will find the labour process perspective both appealing and insightful. It should not be embraced lightly however.

Critical theory

The third perspective which has attracted the interest of some writers is that known as critical theory. Like the labour process perspective, critical theory is based on the writings of Marx, although in this case it is the young Marx who informs those responsible for its development. Many of the key figures in critical theory are often known collectively as the Frankfurt School because of their association with the Institute for Social Research at Frankfurt. In the 1930s Horkheimer and Adorno were responsible for much of the early work of the School together with Benjamin, Neumann and the young Marcuse. After two decades of war, reconstruction and then increased affluence in the West, Marxist thinking was rediscovered in the mid-1960s. The work of the Frankfurt School was part of this, Marcuse's writing becoming particularly fashionable in the USA (Marcuse, 1954, 1964). At this time the writing of Gramsci and Lukacs was also categorised as critical theory due to the philosophical foundation and political intention of their work. The School itself had reformed in Germany soon after the war and was to survey a new social order as Europe moved towards political crisis in the late 1960s. Jurgen Habermas was the most prominent of the new generation of critical theorists supported by Offe and Lorenzer as well as the legacy of Horkheimer, Adorno *et al.*.

In contrast to the comparatively narrow focus of the labour process perspective, critical theory takes as its subject matter the broader social order of capitalist societies. Any aspect, issue or event is potentially a focus for critical enquiry and analysis. This explains why over the past sixty years or so the work of critical theorists has covered such a wide range of topics. Nevertheless, their work displays a distinct bias towards things of an ideational nature, being more concerned with the *superstructure* than the *base* as Marxist theory terms it (Williams, 1973). Thus critical theory has provided a wealth of insight on art and literature, science and knowledge systems, ideology and consciousness, culture and communication, etc., the sort of issues which are ideally suited to a more philosophically informed analysis, itself perhaps the distinctive feature of critical theory. If the labour process perspective offers insights of a concrete nature, critical theory complements these with its wealth of speculative and reflective critiques of the more intellectual aspects of society. But ultimately both exist for the same purpose: to contribute to the development of a critique of the prevailing social order intended to inform those engaged in class struggle. They seek to bring about the defeat of the capitalist class and the replacement of the existing capitalist order by a socialist order in which the mass of individuals would enjoy their life experiences to the fullest. The project of critical theorists has been succinctly described in the following terms:

> [They] seek to reveal society for what it is, to unmask its essence and mode of operation and to lay the foundations for human emancipation through deep-seated social change. It is an overtly political philosophy in that it stresses the

need to follow the logic of one's philosophic and sociological analysis with practical action of a radical kind.

(Burrell & Morgan, 1979, p.284)

In short, critical theorists seek to follow Marx's thesis that the purpose of philosophy is not simply to interpret the world but to change it (Marx, 1975).

In Britain the greatest interest in employing a critical theory perspective in accounting research has been shown by a group of writers who have at some time been associated with the University of Sheffield: Laughlin, Lowe,and Puxty. In the main it has been the work of Habermas which has interested them, especially his later work which has been viewed as less critical than most of the writing in this tradition (Power, 1985). In the context of a series of papers on financial accounting and the problem of regulation written in the early 1980s, Laughlin *et al.* use Habermas' work to draw attention to the role played by 'worldviews' or sectional interests as distinct from self interest (Laughlin, Lowe & Puxty, 1982; Laughlin & Puxty, 1983, 1984). For Habermas, all knowledge reflects sectional interest and in a capitalist society it is the interests of the capitalist class which are the dominant interests. It is the role of critical theory to expose the interests behind knowledge and indeed the knowledge which exists behind the interests. However, these were the ideas of the young Habermas, the more radical figure whose writings were embraced with such enthusiasm by critical sociology in the early 1970s. By the time that Laughlin and his colleagues were reading Habermas, he, and they, were into 'the possibilities of a "justified" or "grounded" consensus under certain defined conditions' (Laughlin & Puxty, 1984, p.594), a form of rational political incrementalism.

Puxty and Lowe were subsequently to pursue the issue of accounting regulation (see Puxty *et al.*, 1987) while Laughlin (1987, 1988) has employed critical theory to help understand accounting systems in their organisational contexts. In these papers critical theory becomes a methodological approach which can be used to understand and change accounting systems. The basis of the methodology is Habermas' theory of social evolution with its focus on the role of language. The distance travelled from the project that inspired the founders of the Frankfurt School can be judged from the following description:

> Critical theory is a vehicle through which understanding about reality can be achieved and transformation of concrete institutions occur . . . . It is the view that the present is not satisfactory, that reality could be better than it is, and that . . . critical theory can create this improvement which marks out this thinking as essentially critical.

(Laughlin, 1987, p.482)

Although Laughlin mentions the work of Horkheimer, Adorno and Marcuse no attempt is made to consider the potential their approach may have for understanding accounting in contemporary society. In fact there seems to be a general lack of interest in using either their work to construct a radical critique of

accounting or the related work of Lukacs. Richardson (1987) has drawn attention to the use which several writers including Tinker have made of Gramsci's hegemonic perspective and the concept of ideology. The passage of time may, however, see a rediscovery of the richness of a more genuinely critical approach to accounting theory and practice.

There are a number of difficulties evident which might counter this. First, there is the political legacy of critical theory. Like the labour process perspective, critical theory is at base a Marxist mode of analysis. Those who developed these and other perspectives, e.g. Althusser and Colletti, were quite open about their commitment to socialist revolution and the need to provide the working class with an understanding of the totality of modern capitalism. Critical theory is not an impartial methodological tool, nor should it be presented as such. Secondly, there is the problem of the language of the texts of critical theory, the Frankfurt School in particular (Connerton, 1976). They are written in a different tradition, often poorly translated, seemingly rambling and open-ended. It takes time and patience to appreciate the approach to cultural critique on offer in critical theory. Next there is the problem of whether there is justification for employing a critical theory perspective for carrying out micro-level case studies. Since these are presently viewed as the most appropriate means to perform management accounting research the two need to be commensurate to some extent. The general focus for critical theory has been on societal level issues as a consequence of its being one of the forms in which Marxism, as a meta-theory, has been developed in the twentieth century. Laughlin himself poses the question about the validity of using critical theory at the micro-organisational level of functioning accounting systems. Even assuming that it can be employed in this way, a further problem arises: the feasibility of applying the perspective to study (let alone change) concrete accounting systems. Once again it is a matter of weighing the potential benefits of rich and insightful case materials against the various costs which gaining them will entail. Taken together, these issues demonstrate the underlying difficulty of integrating critical theory into management accounting research work: determining the parameters of the contribution that it can realistically make.

The Foucauldian perspective

Michel Foucault was not a sociologist, nor is his work neatly categorisable as a sociological perspective in the sense of structural functionalism, conflict theory or interactionism. In this way he may be designated a critical theorist along with Horkheimer, Adorno, Marcuse, or Habermas (cf. Chua, 1986). Like them he was concerned with the task of producing social analyses which were permeated by philosophical insight. Foucault's work differs from that of the Frankfurt school in two major respects however. It was always much more historically rich than theirs, and perhaps more importantly, it was never politically committed while still managing to be politically incisive. Foucault was very much a unique intellectual figure with a perspective of his own, sometimes idiosyncratic, always powerful. Merquior describes him as 'a historian of the present',

> the thinker who welded philosophy and history and in so doing developed a dazzling critique of modern civilisation.

(Merquior, 1985, p.16)

During his lifetime he produced a series of critiques of social phenomena including mental illness, sexuality, the human sciences, asylums and prisons. To produce his various analyses Foucault employed a methodology which was heavily reliant on two epistemological techniques: *archaeology* and *genealogy*. Use of the former was more evident in the period before Foucault published his methodological treatise *The Archaeology of Knowledge* (1972), being displaced in later years by genealogical analysis. Archaeological analysis is carried out on discourses, i.e. the complexes of concepts and terms which are employed in the context of discussing, describing, theorising, etc. a social phenomenon such as mental illness (or accounting). The object of the analysis is not to reveal some hidden meaning or deep truth but to document in a critical way that which passes for knowledge. Genealogical analysis is carried out in order to demonstrate that history is not linear, that the actual course of events that constitutes history is marked by discontinuities, contingencies and most significantly continual power struggles. Foucault seeks to question the facticity of history through genealogical analysis. In many ways the more untidy the history which emerges, the more perceptive the understanding it produces. At a more substantive level Foucault's later work exhibits a growing interest in the *power/knowledge* relationship. His general theme is that it is possible to understand the development of modern societies in terms of a shift in the mode of exercise of power. Whereas in the past sovereign power was the characteristic mode for the exercise of power, in modern society there has been a move towards knowledge-based disciplinary power. This permits a much wider, deeper exercise of power giving rise to a growing management of social life. These themes are explicit in his *Discipline and Punish* text (1977) although once outlined they are equally evident in much of the earlier work. In his subsequent analysis of sexuality, Foucault presents it as one of the most important and far-reaching ways in which power has been exercised over life in modern Western societies.

Even had he lived, Foucault probably would not have turned his attention to accountancy. Yet the points of contact are quite plain to see especially for those interested in developing a more radical perspective: archaeologies of accounting discourses; genealogies of accounting techniques; the critical analysis of accounting as the exercise of disciplinary power. As early as 1980 Burchell *et al.* had indicated an interest in the work of Foucault. Five years later three members of the same research group offer a genealogical approach to the study of the value-added concept in the UK in an attempt to 'avoid the assumption that accounting has some essential purpose or role' (Burchell, Clubb & Hopwood, 1985). The following year Hoskin & Macve published an essay in which they use

Foucault's work to demonstrate the links between the disciplinary power of the (accounting) examination and the history of double entry book-keeping (see also Hoskin & Macve, 1988a, 1988b). Anne Loft uses a Foucauldian perspective to fashion a provocative genealogical history of the rise of cost accounting in the UK in the period 1914–1925 (Loft, 1986). Hopwood himself has written on the archaeology of accounting systems although he admits that what is on offer is as much genealogy, evidence of the complementary nature of the two techniques. The paper is built around three case studies in accounting change, one historical the other two being much more contemporary (Hopwood, 1987). The use of Foucault's work on disciplinary power to inform the analysis of historical materials has also been illustrated by Walsh & Stewart (1988).

To date perhaps the best example of the use of a Foucauldian perspective in the context of management accounting research is Miller & O'Leary's 'governable person' essay (1987). Their underlying objective is to demonstrate the ways in which social and organisational factors determine the nature of accountancy (cf. Burchell et al., 1980). To achieve this they use a historical case study, the development of standard costing and budgeting between 1900 and 1930. They begin by making a case for using Foucault's philosophico-historical perspective rather than either a conventional/functionalist or a Marxist approach, and continue by offering a brief but highly instructive account of Foucault. Moving on to standard costing and budgeting, they suggest that the development of these activities can best be understood in terms of a more general desire on the part of a highly influential group of ideologues to promote a complex of practices of 'social and organisational management'. This would involve making the individual more efficient in the workplace, something which would result in benefits for the individual, the organisation and the broader social order. Although the individual's work life would become subject to greater regulation, this was necessary in order to promote general well-being. Miller & O'Leary support their thesis by showing how standard costing and budgeting techniques are consistent with a discourse of national efficiency current in the period 1900–1930, while at the organisational level they complement the development of both scientific management theory and early industrial psychology. All are to be seen to form part of a complex of social and organisational management through the creation of a 'governable person'. In keeping with Foucault's 'history of the present' philosophy they offer some thoughts on the introduction of the 'behavioural' into accounting, concluding that accounting continues to be concerned with 'the active engineering of the organisationally useful person'.

A study of this quality obviously commends the Foucauldian perspective to anyone looking for an alternative to a behavioural approach to the study of management accounting. It is insightful in the most obvious ways, being both suggestive and provocative. It focuses on the social and the organisational levels which Hopwood identified in his founding *AOS* editorial, yet it still manages to focus on the individual. Unlike either the labour process or critical theory perspectives, the Foucauldian perspective is not politically constituted in some *a priori* way. Foucault's own interest in the power/knowledge relationship results in a perspective that more consciously focuses on power than much interactionist research, arguably the mainstream sociological counterpart to Foucauldianism. Finally, and in some ways most importantly, it appears to be a perspective which can readily be embraced and employed. Some trivialisation and emasculation seem inevitable but on balance work like that of Miller & O'Leary or Hoskin & Macve shows what can be achieved.

There is, however, a major question to be asked of the perspective: is it anything other than a radical historical perspective which can only furnish insightful and provocative alternative histories of accounting? This should not be taken to imply that historical enquiry of whatever sort is valueless. The issue is how to learn from history? What is the lesson to be drawn from the history of the development of standard costing and budgeting in the first three decades of the twentieth century? For those who might adopt a labour process or a critical theory perspective, the lesson would be that accounting can easily become part of a complex of techniques which are unlikely to serve the interests of the working class. A politically radical (as opposed to an intellectually radical) management accounting tradition needs to be conscious that its techniques and its theories not only have social and organisational determinants, they also have social, organisational and behavioural consequences. To understand the world, either in a historical way (Foucault) or as it is socially constructed (interactionism), is one thing. To do so in order to change it is another. This is arguably the fundamental dilemma of sociology: the choice between a genuinely radical sociology or what is in effect a conservative, or in this case, a managerial sociology (Shaw, 1975). This provides a neat link into the final section of the chapter where attention will focus on the revolution which is presently being witnessed in the sphere of technical management accounting.

JOHNSON & KAPLAN: RELEVANCE LOST: THE RISE AND FALL OF MANAGEMENT ACCOUNTING

Johnson & Kaplan's 1987 text presents the most far-reaching and provocative critique of management accounting to be published in recent years. As such it offers an obvious focus for considering the significance sociology may have for the more strictly 'technical' or 'quantitative' aspects of management accounting. It is the result of two decades of research and writing during which time its authors have become increasingly concerned about the relevance of much present-day cost and management accounting theory and practice. The basis for their concern is the view that what presently constitutes cost and management accounting simply does not and cannot provide the information necessary for effective planning, control and decision-making in either modern manufacturing industry or in the newer, rapidly expanding service industries of the post-industrial age. Although pronouncedly US-centric their thesis is intended to apply wherever conventional cost and management accounting is practised, including Britain. To the extent that other industrial nations employ the same approach, they too will come to face similar problems. Japanese manufacturing industry, however, provides some significant pointers as to how it might be possible to refashion cost and management accounting argue Johnson & Kaplan. On what basis do they arrive at this conclusion? What are the particular lessons of the Japanese experience? To answer these questions it is necessary to consider their study in some detail.

At the outset they offer the provocative claim that management accounting is not a development which can be traced back to the 1950s. Although there have been some major developments in management accounting thinking since then, e.g. capital budgeting, most of what serves as conventional wisdom was in place by 1925. Management accounting as a means to enhanced managerial control must be traced back a further century. This gives rise to a second highly provocative claim that there is a line of continuity from the development of the simple costing techniques required by the managements of armories and textile mills in the early nineteenth century to the widespread installation of effective management control systems in the highly diversified manufacturing organisations by the early 1920s. Along the way more complex systems of product costing were developed with their characteristic reliance on simple overhead absorption techniques. To emphasise the idea that costing is legitimately viewed as the first phase in the development of management accounting, they term it *cost management* rather than cost accounting. They reserve the latter title for what they see happened to costing after 1925 when it was appropriated by financial accounting for the purpose of stock valuation. Johnson & Kaplan take the view that by the mid-1950s cost accounting was really little more than an appendage to the financial reporting function, as discussed at the beginning of the chapter, being principally concerned with *cost allocation* which they distinguish from cost management.

It is their view of the supposedly progressive post-war management accounting tradition that gives rise to their third and probably their most contentious claim. In their view these 'new' internal accounting systems with their potential for improved planning, control and decision-making are not serving management in anything like the positive way that the earlier cost management had invariably done. Not only had much costing activity become geared to the needs of financial reporting, the same was the case with many other practical management accounting developments, e.g. capital budgeting and return on investment techniques. The real problem was the short-termism which characterises financial accounting with its focus on short term results rather than longer term performance. Even where supposedly sophisticated management accounting systems were in existence, they commonly failed to deliver the information management needed timeously, despite the rapid advances in information technology in the 1980s.

Johnson & Kaplan believe that academic management accounting researchers have not served practitioners well either. Most have been too interested in the financial accounting framework, e.g. advocating direct costing as opposed to full absorption costing, and from the early 1960s increasingly divorced from manufacturing reality. Their main reservation is that while such developments as single-person information economics modelling, agency theory and transaction cost theory may be highly sophisticated in content, they are based on 'simplified, stylised production settings' which are not characteristic of advanced manufacturing industry. One reason for this was that many of those involved in such research actually had little experience of the settings they were seeking to model. The bulk of the literature is of only limited interest to practitioners, whose situation by the early 1980s had deteriorated so much that neither they nor their cost accountant colleagues were in the position to provide information that was of use to senior managers:

> Contemporary cost accounting and management control systems . . . are no longer providing accurate signals about the efficiency and profitability of internally managed transactions.

> (p.205)

In a period of sixty years whatever relevance cost and management accounting once had for the effective financial management of manufacturing industry had been progressively lost. As a consequence America's position as the world's pre-eminent industrial nation is under severe threat. Corrective action is needed as a matter of great urgency.

Johnson & Kaplan conclude with two chapters intended to provide the foundations for such action. In the first of these a new cost accounting is sketched out. They begin by stressing that it is necessary to develop three cost accounting systems simultaneously rather than simply aim to make use of a single, all-inclusive system. The first of these is required for financial reporting purposes and is only briefly discussed by them. The second is for *process control* purposes, being an analytical approach to the task of devising cost centre budgetary procedures which maximise effective managerial responsibility. Cost centres are viewed as activity centres which incur costs in the course of performing their intended activities. It is the understanding of what costs can be identified with activities and more importantly how these vary with activity levels which is the novel idea here. The concept of a *cost driver* is first introduced in this connection, being the particular activity which 'drives' the costs of an activity centre. For example, in a shipping department the number of orders shipped may be the relevant cost driver so in order to understand the behaviour of costs in a shipping department it is necessary to establish how these vary with activity levels in the relevant time period (p.229). Only those costs which are traceable to particular activity centres should be assigned there. There is no benefit to be had for process control purposes from allocating any non-traceable costs to activity centres in the conventional way (p.232). Johnson & Kaplan are confident that the currently available technology will make this a relatively simple exercise but an extremely effective one in terms of budgetary control.

It is the third system, however, which has rapidly become the most widely known and discussed. A separate product costing system completes the set of cost accounting systems proposed by Johnson & Kaplan. *Activity-based costing* or ABC as this has become known in the literature which has subsequently appeared is a second essentially analytical approach to the problem of accurate product costing in the age of hi-tech, short run, customised, added value, quality goods (and an increasing range of services). Products are argued to consume activities rather than simply attracting costs. Activities can be costed and a *cost driver rate* established for each of them. In turn a product can be costed on the basis of the amount of activity it consumes. So if two hundred units of product each require six different machine set-up activities and the cost driver rate of each set-up is known (or is projected in an activity budget) then it is possible to establish this particular component of the product cost. The novel idea in ABC is that it is based on the premise that because of the pattern of development of an increasing number of goods and services more and more of their costs are becoming variable, contrary to the view underpinning much management accounting thinking. It is now possible to establish very accurately the cost of any particular variant of a product if its activity profile is known. In association with Robin Cooper, Kaplan has demonstrated how many companies simply don't understand the costs of many of their products (Cooper & Kaplan, 1987). The message is again very simple: understand the activities associated with any product and you are on the way to a more accurate measure of their cost.

A complementary new management accounting is suggested in the concluding chapter of the text. Unfortunately it is only very generally discussed both here and in subsequent papers, a serious limitation which few commentators seem to have recognised to date. The Japanese connection which underlies so much of their thesis is also clearly evident here although only to readers who have persevered with the preceding chapters. The new management accounting should concern itself with performance measures preferably not of the short term financial kind which characterise much contemporary practice. Instead it is desirable to follow the Japanese example and measure performance in terms of reduced levels of scrap, rework, defects, machine breakdowns, etc. Cutting down on set-up times, stock holdings, throughput times, delivery times are all necessary factors in increasing competitive advantage in the new manufacturing environment which the Japanese have been so successful in exploiting in the post-war period. They have achieved this in part by a pursuit of excellence which can be measured in terms of increased performance across the enterprise. Understanding where and why costs are incurred, linking back to both process control and ABC, predates their control and results in increases in competitive advantage. Performance measures have also been developed to assess levels of employee satisfaction on the basis that the workforce plays the key role in the added value process. Customer satisfaction, measured in terms of loyalty, growth in the level of business, cooperation in product design and development, etc. are equally legitimate performance indicators to establish. The message again is very simple: management accountants should concern themselves with the development and operation of a company's system of performance measurement. There can be no standard packages of measures, each system being contingent upon prevailing conditions and broader corporate objectives. The challenge is to develop these to their fullest value and to make a further contribution to the entity's effective operation.

In the light of this account of Johnson & Kaplan's thesis, what significance does sociology have for technical or quantitative aspects of management accounting? Perhaps the first point to make is that if there ever was a major division between these and the social, organisational and behavioural aspects this study demonstrates that it can no longer serve any useful purpose. Henceforth, 'good' management accounting thinking and practice will mirror its multi-faceted nature. Secondly, the clear message of the text is that it is crucial to spend rather more time thinking about what cost and management accounting is about rather than simply doing it all by numbers. The need to adopt an analytical approach was commented on several times in the previous paragraphs. One of the qualities of any sociological perspective is that it promotes analysis and for this reason it would seem desirable that those who are responsible for teaching contemporary management accounting increase the sociological content of their courses wherever possible. Of course an economics perspective also promotes analysis but few seem to disagree with Johnson & Kaplan's view of its contribution to management accounting. Equally their new cost and management accounting is reliant on critical thinking, again a quality which sociology promotes in abundance, together with thinking systemically and where necessary strategically. It is also inherently change-oriented, something which would commend it to the authors. Finally, most sociology is committed to the fullest involvement of people into all aspects of society, not least their work. It is true that a great deal of organisational psychology, organisation theory and contemporary management thinking embraces the same ideals but perhaps not as zealously as many in sociology. The belated recognition by the Japanese that the human factor is the source of added value is not too far removed from the thoughts of Marx which have inspired many sociological analyses of the social organisation of work. Clearly there is a great deal to be gained from further integration of the sociological imagination into the mainsteam of cost and management accounting.

Adopting a sociological perspective can also offer some interesting thoughts on the Johnson & Kaplan thesis, no better illustrated than in the recent critique written by Ezzamel, Hoskin & Macve (1990). Adopting a Foucauldian perspective but integrating many broader insights fom sociology and beyond, their paper questions many aspects of *Relevance Lost*. They suggest that it was always Western management's intention to manage by way of (financial) accounting numbers and it is not that somehow cost and management lost its way in the 1920s. It was never going anywhere else. To correct things it doesn't make much sense to attend to only management accounting. On the Japanese solution Ezzamel *et al.* are very sceptical. Japanese management have devised their own ways of managing, exhibiting many features which do not promote the human factor quite as fully as some suggest. Nor is it certain that financial accounting considerations will continue to take second place as Japan's economic strength increases. For their part a growing number of young Japanese workers are actively questioning many of the traditional values which have contributed so much to the country's success. Why should Japan prove the exception ask Ezzamel *et al*.? Their concluding thoughts are worth recounting at length as they illustrate admirably the power of a sociologically infused management accounting viewpoint:

> Perhaps therefore, instead of attempting to merely improve Western MAS systems by the importation of techniques that are currently successful in Japan, we should be thinking systematically about the underlying accounting problem that has been there from the outset. How best can we make the accounting numbers work within the overall system of control so that they become really effective complementary and interlocking ways of both describing and driving real world performance while being aware of and responsive to the ways that a population of calculable persons changes and evolves? A convincing solution to that problem of 'managing by the numbers' will be irresistible to managerialism everywhere.

Chapter 7

Finance

The third foundation of contemporary accountancy is provided by the branch known as finance, or alternatively as corporate finance, business finance, financial management or managerial finance. The most recently emergent branch of accountancy, finance dates back little more than three decades which makes it quite different to both financial and management accounting. It is also the branch of accountancy most in flux, as yet uncodified and seemingly open-ended. As a fashionable branch of the discipline it is currently being expanded by an enthusiastic body of supporters. It has been said that finance, or perhaps financial management, is where financial accounting and management accounting come together, but a more apposite description might be that finance is the branch of accountancy which deals with what the other pair omit (along with some of the topics which they conventionally include, e.g. capital budgeting or financial statement analysis). Equally it is possible to study, research and write on finance without any significant accounting knowledge; indeed some would say that it is a positive benefit if the latter is lacking! Authorities in the field are quite explicit about the origins of their subject – economics not accountancy. For Copeland & Weston (1988) finance (or 'modern finance theory') has developed from applied microeconomics while Brealey & Myers (1988) take the view that corporate finance is based on financial economics. With such a foundation is it any wonder that to date this branch of accountancy has remained virtually untouched by ideas drawn from the literature of sociology. And that it can benefit from the exercise of the sociological imagination should by now be a readily acceptable contention. The following pages are offered as proof that this is in fact so.

THE NATURE OF FINANCE

It has already been intimated that it is no easy matter to offer a definition of finance or any of its synonyms. Writers of texts on finance don't often begin by offering a trite definition of their field, preferring to simply get into the thick of things as quickly as possible. So rather than attempt a futile definitional exercise, and not being in any position to write another text on finance to illustrate what it is about, the tactic to be adopted here is to identify a series of parameters which mark out the field of finance. The first of these is that finance is concerned with issues and matters of a business or commercial nature. Much more so than either financial and management accounting, finance immediately conveys the impression that it is concerned with 'live' business or commercial situations. The widely understood objective of maximising shareholders' wealth is the normal starting point for most finance writers, being the premise upon which much of the rest of the subject is constructed. The identification of profitable investment opportunities is the most common means of achieving this objective and so a key issue in finance is the study of the investment process. Nobody would willingly invest funds in projects which are likely to prove a drain on the wealth of a business, and therefore management, as the agents of shareholders, need to be able to rely on techniques which will guard against this to a large degree. Thus the development of net present value models and their underlying discounting techniques are a major feature of contemporary finance. They are immediately understandable to anyone who thinks in a commercial way: a potential investment opportunity over a period of time at a particular cost for funding – will it pay? And what changes in the meantime might affect this return?

Live business or commercial situations such as this require actual decision-making and it is the decision-making emphasis which forms the second parameter of finance. Once a net present value has been established for an investment then a decision about going ahead or not must be made. If there is only one project and the promise of a favourable return then the decision can readily be made. Where there are competing projects, uncertainties about the future availability of finance and a complex of non-financial factors to be considered, decision-making is not so straightforward. However, in even the most simple investment appraisal situation a critical decision is necessary before any computations are carried out. This is the decision about the discount factor to be used in the appraisal exercise. Establishing the cost of capital is a popular examination topic although in live situations the amount of information available to the financial management team will be both more extensive and more problematic. On the one hand the sources of finance available at any time will reflect the financial status of the organisation, while the reality of alternative gearing arrangements will certainly be more constraining than in examination questions. It is necessary that any financial manager is fully aware of both these aspects of finance, however unconnected they may sometimes appear in the pages of textbooks. To complete the decision-making aspect of finance there is the whole question of deciding on dividend policies in the short, medium and long terms. This decision can in turn have significant effects on the cost of the capital available to the company which may result in changes in investment plans, either favourable or otherwise.

Financial management also involves a number of rather more modest but no less important activities which might best be described using a term borrowed from management accounting, those of a management control nature. This control emphasis complements the decision-making emphasis and forms a third parameter marking out the field of finance. While considerations such as gearing, the cost of capital, dividend policy, risk, etc., all involve significant bodies of finance theory, the management of working capital is an eminently practical activity. The financial management of stock, debtors, creditors, liquid assets, etc. is a much less grand affair than deciding on financing and investment issues. But it is of crucial significance to the day-to-day liquidity of any business and potentially an opportunity for lucrative short term investment in many instances. Any business or commercial enterprise which fails to manage or control this aspect of its activities is failing in the objective of maximising shareholders' wealth. Why search for profitable investment projects only to let funds trickle away through inefficient treasury management. The management of foreign exchange activity is a parallel focus of financial management, again involving a need to control on the part of management. As businesses have extended the boundaries of their activity they have become involved in foreign exchange transactions on a regular basis. At the same time the global market place has evidenced increasingly fluctuating exchange rates which can have highly significant consequences for individual companies. While it might well be true that for the system as a whole the swings and roundabouts effect will operate, for individual companies there is nothing to be gained from such a policy. All foreign exchanges must be managed if the company is to achieve its underlying objective of wealth maximisation. A third example of this sort of day-to-day financial management might be the effective use of the various forms of short term credit that are increasingly available in the market. It is for this reason that the study of a range of short term sources of financing including overdrafts, factoring, leasing, mortgaging, etc., complements the attention paid to the sources of finance available for investment purposes.

The fourth parameter which can be identified should already have become clear: the organisational context of finance and financial management. Real or live business or commercial situations, managerial decision-making about financing investment projects and the day-to-day control or financial management of working capital, foreign exchange and short term borrowing all take place within organisational settings. Implicitly all finance texts are concerned with finance in the context of large-scale organisations. Why else do many of them, particularly British texts, find it necessary to include specific chapters on small business finance? This organisational emphasis also explains why many US texts term finance *corporate* finance, the study of the financial decision-making and control in large organisations. The same emphasis also goes some way to explaining why in recent years the early chapters of many texts discuss the relevance of the theories and practice of corporate finance for financial management in state-owned and other not-for-profit settings. As large-scale organisations they share the need for effective management decision-making and control despite their differing objectives. The rise of the *value for money* philosophy with its reliance on the three E's: economy, efficiency and effectiveness is a response to the recognised need for financial management in these settings.

Characterising finance in these ways, drawing attention to its business and commercial emphases, its managerial dimensions such as control and decision-making behaviour and its organisational contexts, suggests that its foundations extend beyond economics to the other social sciences. Finance inevitably has a strong and growing reliance on the recently emergent business and management sciences including organisation theory, organisation behaviour and behavioural science. This is not a radical viewpoint of course and surely few finance writers, teachers or researchers would disagree if confronted with it. The difficulty is that to a very great extent the voluminous corpus of finance literature does not reflect this view and remains pronouncedly economics oriented and technique based with sizeable chunks of descriptive material as a welcome supplement. There is very little attention paid to managerial, organisational and behavioural issues, even in passing. Part of the explanation lies in the fact that this other body of knowledge is also growing very quickly and so cannot easily be embraced even by those who recognise its value. It is also comparatively abstract and may need to be worked at a little too much. And without many examples of such integrated work to emulate, it is always difficult to know how or where to begin. Thus the temptation to stay with the established pathways is difficult to resist and the cross-fertilisation process is further postponed.

In planning and researching this chapter two topics of importance to finance which were heavily reliant on the wider social sciences immediately presented themselves. The first of these is *decision-making theory* which has developed almost in parallel to finance in the past three decades and is a well-established part of the literature of management science. On the basis that so much of practical financial management is concerned with decision-making it seems reasonable that the latter literature be brought to the attention of students of finance. The second topic already features in the body of finance literature and beyond, being known as *agency theory*. As agents of the owners of any business, management may not have the interests of the owners at heart when they carry out their allotted tasks and so must be subject to a measure of control. Agency theory is concerned with this problem but to date has tended to be rather narrowly focused in its explanations. Within the broader social sciences the debate about the significance of the replacement of owners by managers as the controllers of corporation has long been debated in a much fuller way and this literature may also usefully be brought to the attention of students of finance. The choice of a third topic was rather longer in the making but on reflection equally obvious. In the past decade the study of *corporate culture* has become increasingly important, particularly to those interested in the dynamics of contemporary large-scale organisations. Since finance is also intimately associated with such organisations it is important that those involved in its study have some insight into the debates about organisations and their cultures.

The order in which these three topics are considered is agency theory, followed by decision-making or behavioural theory, with corporate culture last. In this way the chapter moves from issues which should be reasonably well known to those involved in finance to those which are probably rather more implicit before concluding with some very contemporary debates. Where a distinctly sociological perspective fits into all of this will become clear as the chapter progresses.

AGENCY THEORY

Agency theory is a major theory within modern finance, being viewed by one commentator as 'the most general theory of finance we have' (Beranek, quoted in Lister, 1984). A measure of its importance can be judged by reflecting on the nature of the 'problem' which has given rise to it: do managers have the correct incentive to maximise shareholders' wealth? (Copeland & Weston, 1988, p.20). Agency theory is concerned with the problem of agency costs which arise in the modern business corporation. These costs are the direct consequence of the now well-established arrangements in business corporations whereby management are charged with the task of running the organisation on behalf of its owners. These managers are the *agents* of the owners who are known in turn as their *principals* and who can reasonably expect to receive the benefits of successful business and commercial enterprises. In terms of the three types of decisions commonly taken in modern business organisations, the principals are the recipients of the dividends which their agents determine to be appropriate given the present and projected state of the investment and financing decisions' scenario. At a previous point in time, exactly when is not itself a relevant issue for agency theory, there was no such division between principals and agents since the owners of any business managed it and thereby controlled the various decision-making processes involved. Developments in business practice have replaced the traditional structure of ownership and control with the new arrangements of separation and thus the problem of agency costs (Jensen & Meckling, 1976, p.328).

The essence of the problem is not the *separation of ownership and control per se*. Rather it is the fact that both parties to these arrangements are viewed as being self-interested or *utility maximisers* as Jensen & Meckling term them in their seminal essay on agency costs. While shareholders seek the optimum dividend/ capital value combination for their equity holding, management are portrayed as being liable to act in ways which do not always serve the best interests of principals. They may not seek to maximise profitability at every opportunity, they may choose to work only as hard as they believe necessary, or they may elect to acquire for themselves a variety of perquisites at the expense of principals. All of these ultimately cost the latter party and it therefore pays principals to expend resources in an attempt to encourage agents to act in their interests. Among the means available to principals are incentive plans for agents and various *monitoring activities* designed to limit the aberrant practices of agents. Examples of these monitoring activities include the requirement to submit financial reports for auditing, the introduction and operation of formal control systems and introduction of budgetary restrictions. All of these also constitute a cost to principals of course, but they are borne because they hopefully will amount to less than the costs involved in leaving agents free to pursue their own interests. According to Jensen & Meckling, agents normally wish to reciprocate and these monitoring activities are complemented by a range of *bonding activities* which are undertaken by agents. Examples given by the Jensen & Meckling are contractual guarantees to have the financial accounts audited, explicit bonding against malfeasance on the part of the manager, and contractual limitations on the manager's decision-making power (p.325). Again these constitute a financial cost to principals but in addition they also 'cost' agents in terms of the introduction of restrictions on their freedom of action as the controllers of the enterprise. Even where it is possible to achieve a situation of optimal monitoring and bonding activities Jensen & Meckling argue that there will rarely be a perfect accord between agents and principals and as a result some divergence will occur between the interests of the two parties. This gives rise to the third element of agency costs, *residual loss*.

The widespread use of contracts for service has been the practical response of owners to the emergence of the agency problem attendant on the separation of ownership from control. These contracts specify the basis upon which an agent is engaged to perform certain designated tasks on behalf of a principal. In his contribution to agency theory Fama (1980) begins by accepting the view that the firm should be viewed as a set of contracts among factors of production and that self-interest is a major motivational factor for all the members of any firm. However, Fama feels that it is necessary to provide a much fuller understanding of some of the issues involved in the agency problem, i.e. to develop (agency) theory in the sense discussed in Chapter 5. He first considers the owners or equity holders who have become the principals of agency theory. Despite the insights provided by agency theory, Fama argues that there is still too great a tendency to portray owners in the image of entrepreneurs who have certain specified property rights in the corporation. A more accurate view is that nowadays there are no owners *per se* of large corporations, only owners of capital. They have a contract with the corporation in the same way that managers (and workers) do. In the case of owners of capital the contract is 'to accept the uncertain and possibly negative difference between total revenues and costs at the end of each production period' (p.290). Should any individual decide that this contract is unfavourable, the existence of the capital market allows the contract to be teminated. Equity (or bonds) can be sold and the resulting funds transferred to other stock.

The concept of markets is at the heart of Fama's contribution to agency theory. Moving on to consider managers, i.e. agents, he argues that they are also subject to the operation of managerial labour markets. Since the owners of capital are not in a position to monitor and discipline management there will always be the possibility of managerial aberration and thus agency costs. However, there will always be individual managers both within and outside the corporation willing, for their own career purposes, to incur less of these costs. In this way the resolution of the agency problem lies not in well-written contracts between principals and agents but in the operation of effective managerial labour markets. This type of argument is characteristic of much economic thinking of the time and has a very obvious appeal to certain elements. Being essentially tautologous it is also extremely difficult to refute. Fama's thesis, however, should not be dismissed on these grounds as it adds the all-important rider that although there may not be the opportunity for owners of capital to monitor and discipline the controllers, the existence of boards of directors provides a vital mechanism for ensuring the effective operation of the managerial labour market. Bearing in mind that it is a convention that these boards include non-executive directors (for whose services there is also a market of course) there is every likelihood that the agency problem arising from the separation of ownership from control will not threaten the survival of the firm. The problem will not disappear but the market will serve to reduce the level of agency costs to a very great extent and with little recourse to elaborate contract writing.

In 1983 Fama & Jensen produced a pair of papers which integrated their thinking and so further theorised the agency problem. In the first of these they characterise the problem as being 'the survival of organisations in which important decision agents do not bear a substantial share of the wealth effects of their decisions' (1983a, p.301). It is the owners of capital who take on the risk-bearing function, and management (agents) as the controllers who are responsible for the decision function. Fama & Jensen argue that where there is a separation of ownership and control it is also common to find that there is a further separation between those agents involved in *decision management* and those involved in *decision control*. It is in this way that the agency problem is resolved and the survival of the organisation ensured. By decision management they mean the twin functions of *initiation*, the generation of proposals for resource utilisation and structuring of contracts and *implementation*, the execution of ratified decisions. Decision control involves *ratification*, the choice of decision initiatives to be implemented and *monitoring*, the measurement of the performance of decision agents and the implementation of rewards. This schema is a major development of the theory, providing a means to analyse the actual structure of agency relationships in the organisation and a basis upon which to understand organisational survival. Fama & Jensen describe the organisation as being a *decision hierarchy* in which higher level agents ratify and monitor the decision initiatives and performance of their subordinates up to the level of the board of directors who effectively control the entire structure and by implication the organisation itself. Agency relationships exist between all the various levels of management necessitating a complex nexus of agency contracts while simultaneously providing the basis for the internal managerial labour market previously invoked by Fama.

Outlining the development of agency theory in this way readily illustrates that while it emerged as a response to a set of major financial economic problems it very quickly becomes transformed into a theory concerned with a much wider range of issues. In particular it raises a series of broader questions about the organisation and management of large organisations which cannot be answered within the framework of economics. This perhaps explains why in most finance texts the discussion of agency theory remains with Jensen & Meckling and the more information economics oriented approach of Alchian & Demsetz (1972). The tradition of research which has derived from these foundations has tended to be highly mathematical and reliant on abstract formal models. As Johnson & Kaplan (1987) say of the agency perspective in management accounting research, its potential to inform and understand practice is still many years in the future (p.175). So what about the broader organisation and management issues?

The separation of ownership and control has long been of interest to sociology and while it may never have been one of the key issues in the way that social mobility or alienation and job satisfaction or the decline of the family have been, it has given rise to a sizeable literature. The question which has given rise to this interest is whether the form of capitalism experienced for much of the twentieth century is significantly different to that characteristic of the nineteenth century? The Marxist undertones of the question are ever-present in the literature and while Berle & Means are widely cited as the writers who first drew attention to the separation of ownership and control and its significance, many would argue that Marx himself appreciated the coming of the phenomenon. In volume III of *Capital* he makes the following observations on the 'divorce' of ownership from control attendant on the emergence of the joint-stock form of business enterprise:

> the actually functioning capitalist [is transformed] into a mere manager, administrator of other people's capital and the owner of capital into a mere owner, a mere money capitalist . . . . The total profit (for the salary of the manager is, or should be, simply the wage of a specific type of skilled labour) . . . is henceforth . . . mere compensation for owning capital that now is divorced from the function in the actual process of reproduction, just as this function in the person of the manager is divorced from ownership of capital.
>
> (Marx, quoted in Cottrell, 1984, p.79)

At this stage in his life Marx was less optimistic about such changes in the capitalist order than he had been as a younger man. Although the divorce of ownership from control was a major development, he could no longer be sure that it was destined to give rise to any significant socio-political change.

Writing half a century later, Berle & Means (1932) were convinced of the positive benefits of the twin processes of increased managerial control and widespread share ownership. Their optimism was based on the belief that these arrangements would give rise to a freedom for managers to act in more socially responsible and responsive ways. The primary objective of wealth maximisation would now be tempered with the need to consider the situation of employees, the integrity of products, the consequences for the environment as it is now termed, etc. Educated managerial cadres were now emerging equipped to reap the benefits of economic and technological progress in a much more socially beneficial way. The passing of entrepreneurial capitalism was occurring peacefully, without the revolution predicted by Marxist writers. It is interesting to note that in the context of agency theory although reference is invariably made to the work of Berle & Means, their enthusiastic support for the rise of *managerialism* is rarely acknowledged. From their perspective, there would not be such a thing as the agency problem since they took the view that the coming of managerial control was a wholly positive advance which should be supported as widely as possible. Nichols (1969) termed Berle & Means' position as an example of *non-sectional managerialism* since in opposition to *sectional managerialism* it took the view that the motivations of the new managerial cadres were essentially altruistic rather than self-interested. It is for this reason that the origins of agency theory are in the work of writers such as James Burnham rather than Berle & Means.

In *The Managerial Revolution* (1941) Burnham offered a counter-thesis to the optimistic and radical work of Berle & Means. He agreed that there had been a process of managerial ascendancy in large organisations and that managers were now firmly in control. The future promised more of the same which was a cause for some concern since most managers were viewed by Burnham as being motivated by self-interest and self-aggrandisement. In this way they were akin to the utility maximisers described by Jensen & Meckling, managers invested with great power, able to manage their organisations as they chose and thus commonly in need of some persuasion through compensatory inducement and contractual restraint. On the question of the broader significance of the managerial revolution Burnham took a fundamentally different view to Berle & Means. The emergence of widespread managerial control in all forms of organisation and the rise of the professional manager did not signal the emergence of a new managerial tech-nocracy as implied by Berle & Means. For Burnham, the twentieth century had seen only the rise of a new form of capitalism, *managerial capitalism*, and not a new social order. As a consequence the lot of employees on the one hand and society in general on the other had not changed significantly regardless of these new organisational forms. At this point it is interesting to reflect on a common theme implicit in the position adopted by Fama & Jensen. In their view the real locus of power in the organisation lies with the board of directors who control the decision hierarchy staffed by the various levels of manager, the returns to shareholders or residual risk bearers, the employment experiences of the whole workforce and the role which the organisation plays in the broader society. Is this not suggestive of a quite different and more far-reaching 'agency problem' perhaps: what are the motivations of the members of boards of directors and what consequences are these likely to have for all of those who come into contact with them?

A third position on the ownership versus control debate is evident in the literature of the later 1950s and 1960s. This is sometimes described as the conservative or Marxist response to the claim that, for good or for ill, manager-ialism has become increasingly important in the twentieth century. A series of counter-arguments, some empirically supported, were assembled to convey a 'no change' scenario: dispersed share ownership results in small groups being able to control management; offering even modest numbers of shares to the most senior managers is likely to assure their compliance; the existence of patterns of inter-locking directorships serves as a constraint on erring managements; many of the most senior managerial posts remain and will continue to remain closed to more radical managerial elements; in the last analysis it is always possible to restrain managers by disposing of a company to 'friends' (Child, 1969; Zeitlin, 1974). Later work was to draw attention to the growing role of the financial institutions in advanced capitalism, arguing that they too were unlikely to readily tolerate much managerial autonomy. All of which suggests that the problem of agency, as it is conventionally posed, is not really a serious problem at all with managerial employees fully recognising what is expected of them in fulfilling their contracts of employment. Once again, however, the key role seems to fall to those most senior managers who sit on the boards of companies and effectively control everything around them. It is this comparatively small group who seem to be responsible for making contemporary organisations 'work' and in so doing succeed in shaping the broader social order. Are these arrangements not the basis of the real agency problem attendant on the separation of ownership and control in modern society?

The supposed separation of ownership from control was one of the issues which led a later generation of Marxist writers to begin to rethink the nature of the class structure of contemporary capitalism. The twentieth century had also seen a contraction in the size of the working class, a growing and increasingly diverse middle class, an ill-defined bourgeoisie together with the spread of affluence, opportunity and social mobility. The old orthodoxies of class analysis could no longer seemingly offer much insight to those interested in charting the topography of present-day class struggle. During the 1970s a new class analysis was formulated in an attempt to understand the changing nature of the economic, social and political class structures of contemporary capitalism (Cottrell & Roslender, 1986). Many of the insights which emerged in this re-analysis are also relevant to an understanding of the problem of agency since it was quickly recognised by these writers that managers and their work were crucial to the reproduction processes underpinning advanced capitalism.

Much of the foundation for the new class analysis was provided by Nicos Poulantzas in two texts entitled *Political Power and Social Classes* (1973) and *Classes in Contemporary Capitalism* (1975). Poulantzas himself, however, offered a rather orthodox analysis in which the ownership and control debate was viewed as little more than a mystificatory thesis designed to obscure the fact that this aspect of contemporary capitalism had changed very little. Top managers with their real economic ownership of capital and thus their effective control are a key fraction of the modern bourgeoisie. And while some members of the managerial cadres might be employed in work which gives them an identity similar to the working class, their involvement in the reproduction processes of the existing social order ensures that they are members of the new petty bourgeoisie and thus the enemy of labour. Gugliemo Carchedi's view was much more insightful, being based in a broad-ranging economic analysis of the contemporary class structure (1977). He also takes the view that the most senior of managers are members of the capitalist class or bourgeoisie due to their economic owner- ship and thus effective control of the means of production. The majority of managers perform what he terms work of control and surveillance or the global function of capital, together with either work of coordination and unification which he sees to be one aspect of the modern function of the collective worker, or perhaps technically skilled, e.g. professional, work. In this way they are identified as members of the *new middle class*. The more of either of the latter type of work that is performed, the lower the level of management engaged in and the closer those involved are to the working class in economic class identity terms. At the same time Wright (1976, 1978, 1980) was in the process of identifying a similar order of managerial hierarchy which stretched from top executives (the modern day equivalent of the traditional capitalist) to top man- agers through middle managers to professionals and at the base of the managerial ladder, foremen and supervisors.

In *Marx's 'Capital' and Capitalism Today* (1977,1978) Cutler, Hindess, Hirst & Hussain argued that in modern joint-stock capitalism it is the capitalist enter- prise itself which is the agent possessing, i.e. controlling, the means of production with managers of all ranks being employees. Managers merely direct production or investment processes on behalf of a capitalist enterprise or a *capital* and thereby make effective that capital's possession of the means of production. They support their view by pointing out that in law such an enterprise is a distinct legal subject with definite powers, adding that even the most senior managerial employees can be dismissed. Exactly who dismisses them is never very clear, although it would seem reasonable to conclude that once again it may very well fall to non-executive directors to act in the interests of all parties on these occasions. In fact much of what Cutler *et al.* have to say is complementary to the position adopted by Fama in 1980. However, to focus on the situation of top managers detracts from the analysis of the structure of contemporary managerial work or as agency theory terms it the structure of agency relationships. Cottrell & Roslender (1986) conceptualise these in terms of a *social division of labour* between those managers at the apex of such structures who are charged with the task of performing a wide range of important control, surveillance, coordination and unification functions (cf. Carchedi) down to lower-grade supervisory staff, e.g. senior secretaries or senior clerks whose work involves managing other staff in a direct way (see also Kelly & Roslender, 1988). One of the more significant consequences of such analyses is to demonstrate that increasingly many pro- fessional workers are not involved in managerial work although they may well receive attractive salaries in exchange for their skills, as discussed in the case of accountants in Chapter 3 above.

The relevance of the new class analysis for agency theory can be summarised very succinctly. It can help agency theory answer a series of important questions which it has already drawn attention to: who manages; on what basis; by what means; with what consequences for those directly associated with a particular enterprise; and at what cost to the broader society?

BEHAVIOURAL THEORY

Implicit in most finance literature is the assumption of decision-making rationality. When studying various techniques such as investment appraisal or foreign exchange hedging the question of rationality is rarely addressed. These techniques are intended to be viewed in a wholly normative way so that in any particular situation it is necessary to follow a set procedure, assess the results and then decide how best to proceed. The objective of shareholder wealth maximisation is the basis for such decisions and therefore the substance of the implicit rationality. In most texts comparatively little attention is paid to the practical aspects of decision-making. There is rarely any consideration of the factors which may affect it apart from the identification of certain technical constraints which inevitably reduce room to manoeuvre. It might be objected that it is unreasonable to single out finance as the only branch of accountancy which fails to address many of the realities of decision-making since the other branches also tend to sketch over the issues involved. However, because finance is so crucially concerned with making decisions, failing to consider the issues which may be involved is a serious self-imposed limitation on finance theory. It is for this reason that students of finance would benefit from a knowledge of some of the insights provided by decision-making theory or as it is termed here, *behavioural theory*.

This is already a well-established theory dating back to the late 1940s. Judging by the frequency with which it is referred to in the literature of business and management science it is a widely known theory but equally it is not a popular theory in the same way as Herzberg's or Peters & Waterman's are. The reason for this is not difficult to understand since in many ways behavioural theory is an inherently critical theory, being concerned with understanding and explaining managerial decision-making processes rather than setting out prescriptions. It has an obvious appeal to academics in the fields of business and management, especially those who profess the need to adopt a more critical perspective. Despite being derived from economics and psychology, many of the insights of behavioural theory are commensurate with those emanating from the sociological study of organisation and management. For this reason it is common to find that behavioural theory is more fully discussed in sociology texts than it is in the pages of business and management science texts. Behavioural theory is also known to some management accounting researchers including the group who carried out the NCB study discussed at length in the last chapter. But it still has not had much of an impact on finance thinking despite the claim made some time ago by David Cooper:

The investment process within the firm should be regarded as a social as well as a financial process . . . affected by the concepts of rationality appropriate to social man, administrative man and political man.

(Cooper, 1975, p.200)

In many ways this brief proposition expresses admirably the underlying premise of this section. To fully appreciate decision-making it is necessary to view it in a much broader way than is conventionally the case in finance theory, in a way typified by behavioural theory.

The agenda for behavioural theory was drawn up in the work of Herbert Simon in the late 1940s as part of his attempt to construct a theory of rational choice to understand and explain the influences which come to bear upon decision-making in an organisational context. Simon was concerned that the implications of the *economic man* view which characterised the existing literature were not fully appreciated. He also questioned their value for understanding the practices of what he termed *administrative man*. Economic man was endowed with a global rationality which provided him (*sic*) with the capacity to view behaviour alternatives prior to decision-making in a panoramic fashion, consider the whole complex of consequences that would follow on each choice and single out one from the set of alternatives (Simon, 1957, p.80). Simon took the view that actual behaviour falls short of this in a series of ways including the possibility of having only a fragmentary knowledge of alternatives, a limited appreciation of consequences and a capacity to anticipate only imperfectly. As a result the decision-maker is only able to operate within a limited rationality rather than the global rationality ascribed to him. Simon termed this limited rationality *bounded rationality*, being the basis upon which administrative man operates. In his words:

Administrative theory is peculiarly the theory of intended and bounded rationality – of the behaviour of human beings who satisfice because they do not have the wits to maximise.

(Simon, 1957, p.xxiv)

In contrast to the maximising objective implied in the global rationality of economic man, a *satisficing* philosophy gives rise to searching out alternatives which are good enough. While economic man deals with the real world in all its complexities, administrative man prefers to operate in terms of a simplified view of the world with its limited alternatives, easier choices and satisfactory outcomes.

A similar perspective was evident in Lindblom's characterisation of management as 'the science of muddling through' (Lindblom, 1959; see also Braybrooke & Lindblom, 1963). The rational deductive ideal evident in classical theory with its premise of a comprehensive informational base gives rise to a synoptic model of decision-making argued Lindblom. The model, however, is open to a series of questions: as well as the reality of man's limited intellectual capacities, there are cost considerations to bear in mind, together with the possibility of restrictions on the availability of knowledge, the intrusion of values into the realm of fact and the need for a strategic sequence to guide analysis and evaluation. As a result decisions are normally made on a much more restricted basis reflecting the widespread adoption of a strategy of *disjointed incrementalism*. They are normally made incrementally, tending to be restricted in nature both in terms of the number of alternatives which are considered and the number of consequences which are considered for any alternative. Much decision-making is either reconstructive or remedial and thus tends to be fragmented in nature. Disjointed incrementalism scales problems down to size: it limits the information which is available, restricts choice and shortens horizons. As a result, unlike the managers and administrators who feature in classical theory, real ones muddle through, often flying by the seat of their pants as Lindblom was to term it.

In a later formulation (1960) Simon was to develop his theory by drawing attention to the tendency to programmed decision-making. He describes the decision-making process in terms of four phases, the first of which is searching the environment for conditions calling for a decision – the *intelligence activity*. This is followed by inventing, developing and analysing possible courses of action – the *design activity*. Next comes the selection of a particular course of action from those available – the *choice activity*. Finally there is an on-going assessment of past choices – the *review activity*. Instead of the various phases being enacted in an open-ended way which would give rise to extensive uncertainty and thus instability, Simon argues that decision-makers normally seek to programme as many decisions as they possibly can. To do this they are heavily reliant on their past and present successes the foundations of which they endeavour to deploy wherever possible. In essence all Simon was doing was to provide a different explanation of the meaning of bounded rationality and the satisficing philosophy. However, he also argued that with the coming of computer technology in the later 1950s, the prospects for a further programming of decision-making were increased and that as a result those in managerial positions would find themselves with more time available to devote to their other managerial roles.

The next major landmark in decision-making theory was the publication in 1963 of Cyert & March's *A Behavioural Theory of the Firm*. The intention of the authors, at the time both colleagues of Simon, was to introduce into the theory of the firm, then a predominantly economic debate, a much-needed measure of organisational and behavioural insight. They did this in the belief that theorising about the firm was best conceived of in terms of theorising about decision-making in complex business organisations which in turn was best understood from a behavioural perspective. At various times they describe their work as 'our theory of business decision-making' (p.116), 'an understanding of the decision-making process in a modern, large-scale business organisation' (p.125) and 'a theory of decision-making in complex organisations' (p.128). In contrast to Simon who focused on decision-making at the individual level, Cyert & March's interests were at the collective, i.e. the organisational level. Their theory was developed in the form of three sub-theories of organisational goals, organisational expectations and organisational choice. In respect of goals they make the now widely accepted observations that organisations don't have goals only members who come together to form coalitions and thereby formulate sets of goals by way of mutually beneficial compromises. At all times some members are excluded from the *dominant coalition* as it was later termed but since alliances are always changing, new coalitions are constantly being formed and thus the organisation's goals are subject to perpetual reformulation. Turning to expectations, Cyert & March are concerned with the practices expected of any firm in providing the bases upon which to make decisions. If goals are the rationale for having to make decisions, expectations are the procedures entailed in arriving at a position of being able to make a decision – Simon's design activity phase. In theory the organisation is expected to pursue a rigorous process of gathering information, extensive calculative activity in order to arrive at the best decision and an equally intensive competition for resources. In practice, organisations, i.e. their dominant coalitions, are much more restricted in these activities, confining their attention to a limited number of possibilities and approaching these in established ways. As a result organisational choice is made from among the resulting limited alternatives. Choice is determined very much by the pre-existence of certain states rather than others, states which the organisation prefers. Decision rules which lead to a preferred state are more likely to be used when making choices, although at all times there is a reality of externally induced changes which may necessitate novel decisions. As far as possible, the organisation will seek to be as adaptive as it can in the face of a changing environment, giving rise to the characteristic *adaptive rationality* of the business firm.

Cyert & March continue by restating their theory in terms of four *relational concepts* intended to convey the nature of the decision-making process in complex organisations. The first of these concepts is the *quasi-resolution of conflict*. Organisations are unable to fully resolve all of their internal conflicts, yet despite the lack of consensus most do succeed and many thrive. They manage this in a number of ways. One way is by employing a series of *local* rationalities so that the various sub-units of the organisation deal with only one set of decision problems rationally and without concern for the consequences which this may have for the broader organisation. Because organisations seldom pursue overall optimisation, as long as individual decisions are sufficiently consistent with each other interested parties generally accept them, hence the idea of 'acceptable level' decision rules as means to resolve internal conflicts. A third tactic is to attend to different goals and make the necessary decisions in a sequential manner. All of these inevitably give rise to a quasi-resolution of conflict but in most cases this is adequate Cyert & March argue. The second concept is *uncertainty avoidance*. Because organisations are constantly faced with an uncertain environment they develop decision processes to avoid its consequences. So rather than adopt a long term perspective or develop long-run strategies, whenever possible they tend to operate on an incremental, here and now basis, making essentially short term decisions to stay ahead of the game. At the same time every effort is made to negotiate the external environment to further avoid its inherent uncertainty.

Cyert & March's third concept is *problemistic search*. Search in this sense is problem-driven and answer-seeking rather than seeking out problems and devising solutions in the course of regular or planned search. Problemistic search is narrowly focused and is inevitably subject to individuals trying hard to apply their favoured past solutions to problems. It is not uncommon to find solutions looking for problems, a theme which March was to develop in later work. The final concept is *organisational learning*. Like individuals and indeed the individuals who constitute them, organisations learn. By learning Cyert & March have in mind the process of adaptation whereby organisations in effect exhibit changes in their goals over time, shift their attention, e.g. to different aspects of their environments perhaps in line with the views of particular groups within the dominant coalition, and also adapt their search rules as necessary. The concept is consistent with the idea of adaptive rationality mentioned earlier in the context of their theory of organisational choice, but equally it is related to the issues of goals and expectations, the other dimensions of their theory.

In the 1970s March developed behavioural theory initially by way of the *garbage can model* and then by analysing the role which *ambiguity* plays in all decision situations. However, before this he published a short but illuminating essay in which he introduced the *technology of foolishness* into the literature of management thought (March, 1971). He views this as a necessary counterbalance to what he terms the *technology of reason* which he argues has pervaded civilisation in general and management science in particular, to its detriment. The following quotation admirably captures his position:

> Interesting people and interesting organisations construct complicated theories of themselves. In order to do this, they need to supplement the technology of reason with a technology of foolishness. Individuals and organisations need ways of doing things for which they have no good reason. Not always. Not usually. But sometimes. They need to act before they think.
>
> (March, 1971 quoted in March, 1988, p.259)

The technology of foolishness is presented as having two aspects: *sensible foolishness* which involves the relaxation of strictures against imitation, coercion and rationalisation; the promotion of *playfulness* which involves the suspension of rational imperatives towards consistency and its replacement by a willingness to explore alternatives and engage in experimentation. Establishing a balance between the prescriptions of rationality and the value of staying loose as the jargon of the time termed it clearly appealed to March, the essay taking on a normative tone in places. The outcome is conceived of as being highly beneficial and not at all likely to degenerate into anarchy. In terms of the development of behavioural theory the essay is best seen as a subtle critique of those management theorists who continue to advocate the pursuit of formal rationality. Much management practice is necessarily a departure from this ideal, being in great measure no bad thing.

In his 1972 paper with Cohen and Olsen, March characterised organisations as *organised anarchies* in which the basis for decision-making or organisational choice is the garbage can model. Organisations as organised anarchies have three general properties. They operate on the basis of a variety of inconsistent and ill-defined preferences with the result that instead of being a coherent structure, organisations are better conceived of as being a loose collection of ideas. They discover preferences in the course of action rather than acting on the basis of preferences, hence the property of *problematic preferences*. Secondly, organisations manage to survive on the basis of trial and error procedures, learning from accidents of past experience and necessitous pragmatism. Invariably its processes are not understood by its members, hence the property of *unclear technology*. The third property is *fluid participation*, relating to the members of organisations. As well as constantly changing, participants vary their involvement in the organisation over time and as a result the boundaries of organisations are uncertain and fluid. Against this backcloth Cohen *et al.* question the value of any theory of organisational decision-making which implies clear goals, well-defined techniques and extensive participant involvement. In its place they advance what they believe to be a more perceptive account, one consistent with the three properties of organisations as organised anarchies, the garbage can model of organisational choice.

They characterise the organisation as a collection of choices looking for problems, issues and feelings looking for decision situations in which they might be aired, solutions looking for issues to which they might be the answer and, of course, decision-makers looking for work. Thus it is possible to view an opportunity to make a decision, i.e. a choice opportunity, as a garbage can into which various kinds of problems and solutions are dumped by participants as they are developed. Any particular decision is the outcome of the interaction between these four streams within an organisation: problems, solutions, participants and choice opportunities. A major consequence of this state of affairs is a partial uncoupling of problems and choices so that only some decisions are made on the basis of *resolution*. Many decisions are made by *oversight* where problems are perceived as ancilliary to other choices which when made lead to the former's resolution or by *flight* where decisions are delayed with the consequence that they are resolved in the context of other problems. What is generally viewed as a rational process is now presented as one in which every decision should be viewed as being essentially fortuitous. As March & Olsen were later to say:

> an organisational choice is a somewhat fortuitous confluence [of the four streams within the organisation]. It is a highly contextual event, depending substantially on the pattern of flows in the several streams.
>
> (March & Olsen, 1976, p.27)

In this way one decision is as likely as another, so on those occasions where the 'right' decision is made, it may be more by accident than design. This conclusion is never spelled out by March and his colleagues but it is quite consistent with their own:

> It is clear that the garbage can process does not resolve problems well. But it does enable choices to be made and problems resolved, even when the organisation is plagued by goal ambiguity and conflict, with poorly understood problems that wander in and out of the system, with a variable environment, and with decision-makers who may have other things on their minds.
>
> (Cohen *et al.*, 1972 in March, 1988, p.32)

The study of the role which ambiguity plays in the process of decision-making has been the principal focus of March's later work. This is hardly suprising since ambiguity is arguably the most fundamental feature of the environment for any organisation and its participants and must inevitably influence decision-making in a myriad of ways. In a recent retrospective essay March (1988) identified four types of ambiguity which serve to summarise his thinking on the issue. First there is ambiguity about *preferences*: most organisations are characterised by their inconsistent and ill-defined objectives. They do not have a specific meaningful preference function which calls into existence consistent choices. Actors drive preferences as much as preferences drive actors. Next is ambiguity about *relevance*: organisations are far less tightly coupled than classical theory would have us believe. There are commonly deep ambiguities in the causal linkages among the various activities of an organisation, between problems and their solutions, between how managers talk and act. Means and ends are not mechanically and systematically linked. Thirdly there is ambiguity about *history*: the past is important and its clarity is vital for future activity. In practice it is clearly and notoriously ambiguous. It can be reinterpreted, restructured, rewritten, etc. with the result that what happened and what is said to have happened need not be related. Because of this what an organisation can learn from history may be partial or selective (or both) and thus ambiguous. Finally there is ambiguity about *interpretation*: information is presented as a way to clarify decision-making and thus decision-outcomes. It is also always subject to interpretation and in turn a lack of clarity. If anything, the collection and deployment of information is a ritualistic activity, a symbolic activity. Although individuals care about outcomes they also care about the symbolic meaning of the process and its outcome. Thus decision-making is a highly contextualised, sacred activity, surrounded by myth and ritual and as much concerned with the interpretative order as with the specifics of particular choices. March summarises his thesis in the following words:

> The argument is that ambiguity about preferences allows goals to develop through experience . . . about relevance allows relevance to be explored . . . about history facilitates motivation to cope with it . . . about interpretation allows communication to evoke more than a communicator knows.
>
> (March, 1988, p.15)

In other words, wherever there is decision-making there is behaviour, and wherever there is behaviour there is a pressing need to adopt a critical perspective.

CORPORATE CULTURE

If a growing literature becoming increasingly influential in business and management education is to be believed, there is a very grave danger faced by anyone who is not apprised of the crucial role which *corporate culture* plays in contemporary organisations. Presently one of the buzz words, along with related terms including *excellence*, *quality* and *added value*, corporate culture is having a significant impact on the way in which committed corporate managements are conceptualising and discussing their organisational realities. And since corporate managements normally include many trained in accountancy, it is appropriate to devote some attention to the debates surrounding organisations and their cultures in a text claiming to consider the nature of modern accountancy. The choice of the chapter on finance as the place to address the issues involved needs a little justification perhaps. One reason has already been discussed in the introduction to the chapter, i.e. the organisational context of a large part of finance practice or 'corporate finance'. Secondly, the various implications of basing an organisation's long term strategy on building a successful or 'strong' corporate culture could have rather negative connotations for a section of corporate management who have become associated with returns on investment, positive net present values, optimal gearing ratios and similar financial performance measures. Perhaps more than most accountants, such individuals need some knowledge of current thinking on corporate culture.

The treatment of the topic in the following paragraphs is to begin by reviewing the ideas of Chester Barnard the American management writer who is credited with being the progenitor of the idea of corporate culture. This is followed by a necessarily brief account of two highly influential texts which popularised the value of corporate culture, those of Peters & Waterman (1982) and Deal & Kennedy (1982). The theme which links all three together, that of managerially driven excellence, is highlighted before turning to some sociologically-informed commentary which acts as a necessary counterbalance to the favourable impression of corporate culture conveyed by advocates and adherents in the managerial tradition.

The rediscovery of the work of Chester Barnard has paralleled the development of the corporate culture concept in modern management theory. Peters & Waterman (1982) cite Barnard as their principal inspiration, along with others including Mayo, McGregor, Selznick, and more recently, Lawrence & Lorsch, Chandler, Weick and March. Barnard was an executive who in the 1930s was associated with a number of Harvard's sociology faculty, including Mayo. Over time they persuaded Barnard to communicate the benefits of his wealth of organisation and managerial experience to a broader audience which he did in his text *The Functions of the Exexcutive* published in 1938. In keeping with contemporary Harvard thinking, Barnard characterises the organisation in essentially systems terms, something which is carried over to the corporate culture concept in the 1980s. For Barnard the organisation is best seen as a cooperative entity involving a number of individuals who share the pursuit of a common purpose. By implication he also takes the view that unless the organisation is constructed in this way it is unlikely to be successful, a premise shared by those who advocate the creation of corporate cultures. Looking at the same issue from another point of view, Barnard can see no other reason for participating in organisation, a position which underscores the moral tone of his work. This is the context in which Barnard's executive functions to sustain the equilibrium of the organisation. Three essential functions must be performed: the formulation and definition of purpose; securing the efforts necessary from participants to reproduce the organisation; and providing the appropriate systems of communication to sustain the organisation. The key point in Barnard's theory is that management perform these functions by playing a full part in the organisation. Unlike most earlier thinking, the executive is not some kind of visitor who is present only to control and coerce. On the contrary the executive is there to make things happen by securing commitment and actively managing all aspects of the organisation, a key feature of a successful corporate culture.

The purpose of Peters & Waterman's highly influential study was to identify the practices which have made certain corporations, e.g. IBM, Delta Airlines or McDonald's 'excellent'. Their view is that such corporations characteristically feature eight attributes of excellence which have been put in place and are consistently promoted by management, hence the theme of managerially driven excellence. It is these attributes which constitute the foundations of the culture of an organisation, i.e. its corporate culture. Since it is successful companies that are the focus of enquiry, the corporate culture concept is endowed with a highly positive connotation being something to aim at in any 'search for excellence' which a management team may decide to embark on. The actual practices which Peters & Waterman commend are far from being esoteric. Three are essentially commonsense: a bias for action; seek to be close to the customer; do what you do best, i.e. 'stick to the knitting'. Three are prescriptions about structuring an organisation: autonomy and entrepreneurship are to be encouraged; try to keep the bureaucracy at a minimum; balance the need for control with the benefits to be had from autonomy. The remaining pair are perhaps a little more radical: 'productivity through people' is the principle that employees are people as well as being the major resource of the organisation. Management must recognise that it needs to be people-oriented to be successful. 'Hands-on, value-driven', the remaining 'prescription', perfectly encapsulates the concept of corporate culture: the organisation must be guided by a clear sense of shared values, mission and identity, relying on inspirational leadership rather than bureaucratic control. In order to build a corporate culture it is imperative that everyone involved knows and shares the same set of ideas and ideals at all times.

Deal & Kennedy (1982) complement these ideas in a number of ways. First they stress the idea that there are corporate cultures and *strong* corporate cultures, so if management are seeking to be successful they must ensure that they create and reproduce a strong culture. They then move on to consider in some detail the elements of corporate culture. In their view the business environment is the single greatest influence on the shape of any corporate culture. The business environment determines what it requires to be successful so it is crucial that management is able to read and respond to the environment at all times. In this way management must be flexible and adaptable if they seek to ensure the continuity of a strong culture. While values are the basic concepts and beliefs at the heart of a corporate culture, two additional elements have key roles to play: *heroes* and *rituals* and *ceremonies*. Heroes are those individuals who personify corporate culture, the individuals who form its role models such as Jim Treybig of the Tandem Corporation or Bill Hewlett and Dave Packard. Deal & Kennedy take the view that there are some heroes who are born to assume this role while others grow into heroes as they find themselves in certain situations. Rituals and ceremonies both serve to spell out the corporate culture for consumption by those who participate in it. Rituals are more mundane events such as weekly 'beer-busts' while ceremonies are extravaganzas such as company-wide celebrations staged on important holidays. In their different ways they both provide opportunities for all parties to reaffirm their integration. The final element identified by Deal & Kennedy is the *cultural network*. This is the primary means of communication within the organisation, the carrier of corporate culture which is so crucial to its effective reproduction. Being able to work the cultural network is essential both for knowing what is going on in the organisation and for getting things done.

The employment of a culture concept in the organisation and management literature was already well-established by the time that these two texts were published, argued Linda Smircich in 1983. Corporate culture was only one of five 'themes' in organisation and management research which she identifies as integrating a culture concept from anthropology and an organisation concept from organisation theory. In the case of the corporate culture theme, culture acts as an adaptive–regulatory mechanism uniting individuals into social structures while organisations are viewed as adaptive organisms existing by process of exchange with the environment. It is heavily reliant on the structural-functionalism of Radcliffe-Brown and contingency theory respectively (Smircich, 1983, p.342). Whereas writers on corporate culture see culture as something which organisations have (or should have), those such as Ouchi (1981) or Pascale & Athos (1983) who typify the 'comparative management' theme in the literature see organisations as being subject to culture. In this case the most obvious example is a national culture being an external variable which affects organisations in important ways, hence interest in Japanese management success. Smircich continues by pointing out that these two themes are similar in that they present culture as a *variable*, either an independent variable in the latter case or an internal variable as in corporate culture. Conversely the other three themes in the literature share the belief that organisations can usefully be understood as cultures, i.e. culture as a *root metaphor*. Instead of seeing culture as something an organisation has, such writers favour the view that a culture is something an organisation is. The different root metaphors provide different ways of understanding organisations (and management) or in Smircich's terms (p.348):

> the research agenda stemming from this perspective is to explore the phenomenon of organisation as subjective experience and to investigate the patterns that make organised action possible.

Thus to view organisations and their cultures in the sense of corporate culture is only one way of seeing and for Smircich an impoverished one at that. Better to adopt a root metaphor approach which shifts attention from:

> concerns about what organisations accomplish and how they may accomplish it more efficiently, to how is organisation accomplished and what does it mean to be organised?
>
> (p.353)

In his chapter on organisations as cultures Morgan (1986) provides a number of insights which must be taken into account when seeking a balanced view of the promise of corporate culture. He begins by making explicit a point implicit in Deal & Kennedy that every organisation has its own unique culture which reflects its history, its membership, its capacity to adapt and so on. Those involved in the sociological study of work and organisations have long recognised the existence of organisational cultures and have established a rich literature on them. Some organisations have exhibited strong cultures in the sense of Deal & Kennedy while others have been successful in creating them. And in many cases it is in no small part due to the efforts of inspirational leaders such as Bill Hewlett and Dave Packard. However, not all strong cultures are quite so appealing as H-P's. He singles out the case of ITT under Harold Geneen as an example of an unsavoury corporate culture describing it as a 'dog-eat-dog world' where the success of the corporate culture 'was achieved at great private and public cost' (p.126). The unspoken question in the minds of those who popularise the idea is, therefore, is it desirable to create a successful corporate culture at any cost? Moving on, Morgan draws attention to the existence of powerful counter-cultures which inevitably make the creation of strong cultures more difficult. The most obvious example of such a culture is that of organised labour with its history, ideology, traditions and integrity. In an ideal world, one with no history, no conflict, no mistrust, the offer of a progressive, people-oriented, participative alternative would be hard to refuse. But this is not the offer as it is perceived, and not without some cause given the emphasis which is commonly placed on the role of management in the quest for excellence. Equally problematic are highly fragmented organisational cultures in which there is a tradition of sub-cultures, e.g. those of professional groups. These are frequently powerful and resistant to change and cannot suddenly be dispersed overnight after attending a few seminars on the virtues of building a corporate culture. In his view:

There is a certain ideological blindness in much of the writing about corporate culture, especially by those who advocate that managers attempt to become folk heroes shaping and reshaping the culture of their organisations . . . . To the extent that the insights of the culture metaphor are used to create an Orwellian world of corporate newspeak, where culture controls rather than expresses human character, the metaphor may thus prove quite manipulative and totalitarian in its influence.

(Morgan, 1986, p.138–9)

Like Smircich, Morgan advocates the use of the 'organisation as culture' metaphor to help make sense of the complex reality which is an organisation. This should provide a better understanding of organisations upon which more effective strategies can be constructed. But it will never be an easy task as Morgan himself concludes:

An understanding of organisations as cultures opens our eyes to many crucial insights that elude other metaphors, but it is unlikely that these insights will provide the easy recipe for solving managerial problems that many writers hope for.

(p.139)

Chapter 8

Auditing

For generations, auditing and accounting have been almost synonymous for many young accountants employed in public practice. Their professional training has often amounted to little more than an extended period of learning through practice the procedures which constitute the audit function. Many remain in auditing after they qualify and some go on to have highly successful careers in what has traditionally been a very lucrative branch of accountancy. Most of those who leave auditing to pursue their individual career paths never seem to fully escape the rigours of their early training and not simply because they often find themselves on the other side of the audit relationship. The reason for this is evident in some of the terms used here. Auditing is first and foremost a practical matter; it is predominantly about following procedures designed to achieve a specified end. These procedures form a rigorous framework and thus a discipline to be embraced at all times. The same is also true of accountancy taken as a whole from book-keeping through budgeting to insolvency work or treasury management. Auditing could easily be described as accountancy in microcosm which in turn could provide a sound rationale for more auditing training. This is not the purpose of the present chapter, however, although a good deal of attention will be paid to the socialisation of auditors and accountants. The main aim is to offer a broader account of auditing, something which seems to be absent in most auditing texts. The particular sociological perspective adopted is interactionism, one ideally suited to providing a basis for auditors to think about the social, organisational and behavioural dimensions of their work rather than simply the means and ends involved.

THE NATURE OF AUDITING

The history of the auditing function was considered briefly in Chapter 2. Although auditing can be traced back to before the rise of the Roman Empire, in Britain it was only in 1900 that every company was required to have its balance sheet and underlying accounting books and records audited. The object of the exercise was to provide an audit report for the shareholders of the company which attested to the *truth and correctness* of the balance sheet. If the directors did not permit the proper performance of an audit or if an audit report was unfavourable, the shareholders had the legal right to call the directors to account for their stewardship of the company and if necessary to have them replaced by new directors willing to accept the responsibilities of running the company in the interests of the shareholders. These arrangements are still in force today although they have been augmented in a number of important ways. From 1948 only suitably qualified accountants could act as auditors and from that time they were called upon to audit both balance sheet and profit and loss account, and where appropriate consolidated accounts. In the 1948 Act the auditor was required to report on the *truth and fairness* of a company's profitability for the financial year in question and its financial position at the end of that year. Disclosure requirements have become more extensive in the post-war period and in 1981 the form and content of the financial statements to be audited was prescribed. The same Act saw the auditor being required to review the directors' report as well as any company transactions in its own shares. The scale and complexity of business operations has certainly kept pace with the enhanced statutory role of the auditor but the objective of being able to provide an annual audit report to the shareholders remains unchanged.

As a result the performance of an audit of even the most modest business enterprise is much more demanding than it was at the beginning of the century when the statutory provision was introduced. It takes much more time to complete, the number of financial items is normally much larger and their value far greater. In many cases the term auditor is best understood in a collective sense since it would be unrealistic to expect an individual to be able to perform the work which now constitutes an audit within acceptable time parameters. Consequently the audit of most companies other than the smallest ones is achieved by employing a number of divisions of labour. In most cases there is a division of labour in a temporal sense between the interim, year-end and final review audits. The former normally takes place three-quarters of the way through the financial year and in the main involves the auditor in work designed to assess the efficiency of the system of internal control which the client operates. In the case of an on-going audit the auditor should already have a knowledge of the systems in operation and have formed an opinion as to their effectiveness. The interim audit provides an opportunity to detemine whether the system is still working efficiently. As the term suggests, the year-end audit takes place at the end of the company's financial year and is normally more concerned with the verification of the company's balance sheet items rather than their systems. If there was some concern with the latter at the interim stage the year-end audit also provides an opportunity for further enquiry. The third audit should not really be a time-consuming exercise, being concerned with completing the audit for the year. It might involve adjustments to financial statements or resolving matters of concern to the auditor. The outcome will hopefully be the signing of an unqualified audit report which will be attached to the financial statements which the company will publish and make available to shareholders. In the largest companies it may be necessary to adopt what is known as a continuous audit approach where there are a series of interim audits throughout the year or where there is auditor presence in the organisation on a continuing basis in order to complete the scale of audit work involved.

A second division of labour is often necessary to carry out the audit function in the case of companies which carry on their activities in a geographically dispersed way, e.g. a chain of department stores or a multidivisional manufacturing company. In order to complete the audit work on time it will be necessary to use local auditors to carry out the work at the various operational centres although there may be some opportunity for audit teams to perform a small number of parallel audits in the year, geography permitting. There are both advantages and disadvantages in these arrangements. On the positive side the auditor who performs a series of audits in one company may come to better understand the company and in turn provide a better service. Equally the loss of variation as between different types of client could lead to boredom and a deterioration in standards. From the client point of view, the benefits of an informed audit team have to be weighed against the cost of keeping it together. If individuals are called upon to work away from home this must inevitably be reflected in the fees charged. On balance, in the case of the more junior auditing staff the work is often so routine that any means to increase variety would seem to commend itself to all concerned, hence the normal practice of rotating staff between assignments on a regular basis in most medium- and large-sized accountancy firms.

As a consequence of using audit teams, the need to perform a series of audits each year and the various developments which favour deployment of staff in a distinctly atomistic way, the modern audit function must be managed effectively if it is to be successful. On a day-to-day basis someone must supervise the team which is on site at any point in time. At the same time it will be necessary to ensure that all of the different phases of the work are completed satisfactorily and that where operations are carried out across a wide geographical area the work of the various auditors can be readily integrated, on time and profitably. There are several other tasks to attend to at all times: acquiring new business; staff recruitment, training and development; quality control; etc. Within the auditing function a clear technical division of labour exists between partners, audit managers, audit seniors and juniors and trainees. Audit teams are normally under the control of audit seniors who are qualified accountants with experience in the function. They will be responsible for the performance of the routine work which is undertaken by their less experienced and part-qualified junior staff together with a couple of new recruits or trainees. Since these latter would tend to move between jobs on a regular basis the audit senior and some junior staff are also responsible for introducing a degree of continuity into the audit function. The audit manager would normally be responsible for a number of teams and thus a number of audits. It is audit managers who plan and coordinate the more complex audits as well as taking on responsibilities for training and staff development, and liaison with senior management in the client company. By contrast, the function of the partner might best be described as strategic (rather than administrative or operational) and would encompass marketing; research; public relations and general 'profile work' (Harper, 1988). And of course they also sign audit reports on behalf of the firm.

It must also be remembered that this technical division of labour is also a social division of labour in the sense discussed in Chapter 3. Seniors not only plan and coordinate the work of less experienced staff, they also control and supervise it. Matters of a disciplinary nature are their responsibility whether it be about unsatisfactory work or conduct in its performance. Trainees often find themselves reporting to their more experienced junior colleagues but the latter have no authority and in the event of misdemeanours both can find themselves disciplined by their seniors. In the same way the seniors are responsible to audit managers who are concerned to ensure that the budget for an audit is not exceeded and that the audit is completed satisfactorily, both technically and in terms of the behaviour of those involved. Partners and senior partners exercise control over their various middle-management staff in exactly the same way and in the largest firms are able to use the promise of promotion into their ranks as a powerful control strategy. The implications of these arrangements have also already been fully discussed and there is little value in repeating the same arguments here despite their importance. More insight into the nature of auditing can be gained by moving from considering its organisational structure to consider its operational structure.

Even if the birth of auditing is traced back only to the passing of the Joint Stock Companies Act of 1844 it is still difficult to believe that the operational structure of auditing can be set out in a few hundred pages. Yet it is, in the form of a series of Auditing Standards and Guidelines which have been published during the 1980s. The 'Explanatory Foreword' to these standards and guidelines, first published in 1980 by the Auditing Practices Committee (APC) and revised in January 1989, defines an auditing standard in the following terms:

8 Auditing Standards prescribe the basic principles and practices which members of the Accountancy Bodies are expected to follow in the conduct of an audit. Auditing Standards apply whenever an audit is carried out by them.

The foreword continues by making the point that it would be impracticable and indeed undesirable to provide detailed prescriptions for all situations and circumstances. Consequently the auditor must exercise 'his' judgement in order to determine the necessary auditing procedures to be adopted. To assist in this Auditing Guidelines are necessary and in 1980 five operational guidelines were issued to complement the 'Auditor's Operational Standard' together with a lengthy reporting guideline to complement the 'Audit Report' standard. Subsequently over twenty further guidelines have been introduced and currently there are around a dozen exposure drafts and six audit briefs. In the words of the APC:

14 Auditing Guidelines are intended to be persuasive. They are not prescriptive and there are many occasions when the auditor considers it appropriate to depart from the guidance given. However, they should normally be followed, and the auditor should be prepared to explain departures if called upon to do so.

This paragraph makes it very clear that in the normal course of events the auditor is intended to view both standards and guidelines in the same way, as constituting the elements of a normative operational framework. In the jargon of the auditing profession these standards and guidelines outline what is regarded as 'best practice', the APC indicating that they are likely to deemed 'good practice' by a court of law, further strengthening their prescriptive status.

It is possible to argue that there is much more to auditing than an operational framework of standards and guidelines. There are organisational issues some of which were touched on above. There are philosophical issues which have long been debated: the nature of auditor independence and auditor responsibility; the meaning of truth and fairness or materiality; the status of audit evidence, etc. Less abstract issues also feature in the pages of textbooks, study manuals and professional journals: the value of the small company audit; the need for more informative audit reports; the role of audit committees, etc. On the legal side there is the fundamental issue of the liability of the auditor, concern about which has been heightened in recent years as a result of several widely publicised actions raised against the Big 6 firms. All of these are important areas for debate and discussion and all impinge on every auditor. However, on a day-to-day basis the vast majority of auditing staff are involved in putting into practice the prescriptions of the 'Auditor's Operational Standard'. That is they are involved in the various aspects of planning, controlling and recording their work which extends to ascertaining and evaluating both the system of recording and processing transactions adopted by an enterprise and its structure of internal controls. In order to perform the audit effectively it is necessary to collect sufficient evidence of a relevant and reliable nature about the enterprise and to carry out a review of the enterprise's financial statements. Having followed these procedures the auditor will then be in a position to arrive at an opinion on these financial statements which is communicated in a (prescribed form of) audit report. Only in the smallest-scale audits will an individual carry out all of these procedures. Most auditors will only be involved in part of the work employing the techniques adopted by their firms to translate the prescriptions of the standards and guidelines into practical operating procedures.

In their training, younger auditors learn both the theory and practice of auditing. The theory is the standards and guidelines. The practice actually involves two aspects: firstly, the techniques which form the procedures of their firm, secondly, the experience of doing audits. In their professional examinations they may find themselves called upon to answer questions about philosophical or legal issues but in the main they are tested on their appreciation of the theory and practice of auditing. Some questions require answers which amount to little more than a precis of the main points of a guideline. Case study type questions are a little more analytical but usually they can be answered in a not dissimilar way. In any such answers it would not be desirable for students to begin to talk about their own experiences in similar circumstances or how they think that the techniques that they are called upon to use are flawed and why they have arrived at this conclusion. Although they are examined on the practical aspects of auditing, this is done in a highly technical way. There is no place here for critical thinking, for reflecting on doing audits. You either know the prescriptions or you are a waffler (who might just get through on the discussion questions). In the last analysis passing the examination is only a means to an end.

This situation and its rationale are symptomatic of a fundamental problem which auditing as a branch of accountancy exhibits. It has always conceived of itself in a highly technical way. An audit is performed to produce an audit report which is required by the directors of a company for a sound legal (and moral) reason. The various standards, guidelines, procedures, organisational arrangements and so on are necessary to perform effective audits. The examination and training programmes are the means to produce good auditors. In this way auditing is represented as a mainly technical activity. It is rarely viewed as an activity which has social, organisational and behavioural dimensions and for this reason it is dangerously myopic. There is a literature on the problems of motivation among auditors (Dillard & Ferris, 1989) but it is such an obvious research topic that it would be difficult to miss. To date it has tended to be considered in a behavioural way as that term was used in the early paragraphs of Chapter 6. Adopting a labour process perspective might provide more insights perhaps. However, this is only one aspect of the non-technical side of auditing and an advanced topic in many ways.

There is a series of more basic aspects which seem not to have attracted much attention. One is the study of the social, organisational and behavioural processes involved in becoming an auditor, some of which have been briefly mentioned in the previous paragraphs. Then there is the complementary study of the processes involved in being an auditor. Doing audits is a social, organisational and behavioural activity and this too should be studied. Because auditors audit other people's activities it is an interactive activity which involves a perpetual negotiation process. All of these aspects should be apparent to anyone who has had any involvement with auditors and auditing. Few could disagree with the contention that in order to fully understand the practice of auditing it would seem desirable to have an appreciation of some of these issues, aspects and problems as well as the technical ones which take up the greater part of the conventional wisdom of auditing. Yet they are studiously avoided almost without exception and to the detriment of all concerned. In the next two sections an attempt is made to cast some light on this, the hitherto unstudied side of the practice of auditing.

THE ELEMENTS OF ROLE ANALYSIS

The perspective to be adopted to consider auditing is that of interactionism. More specifically the analysis will be informed by the symbolic interactionist tradition rather than the action frame of reference tradition since the former offers more insight into the processual and negotiational aspects of action than the latter which is more concerned with meanings. *Role analysis*, or role theory as it is sometimes termed, makes extensive use of a series of concepts which have a general currency within modern sociology. Not all of these concepts originated in the symbolic interactionist tradition but they are normally deployed most effectively by writers such as Erving Goffman or Howard Becker who are firmly part of this tradition.

The first task is to introduce the various concepts of role analysis. Although the role concept is the fundamental one it is easier to understand it after considering the concept of a social position. A *social position* is some slot in the social structure of a society, the most obvious example being an occupation such as a lecturer which is a slot in the occupation structure which in turn is a part of the social structure. Equally husband, son, parent, jogger, etc., are social positions. The most commonly used definition of a role is 'a set of expectations impinging on an individual occupying a social position' (Berry, 1974). The *role* concept refers to the expectations which society has of individuals who occupy any social positions. For example, a lecturer is expected to offer lectures to students which bear some relationship to the name of the course they are taking; they are expected to learn from their time in the lecture room and their learning will normally be evaluated in some way, to their benefit. Although society's expectations are a major constraint on an individual's role performance, this should not be taken to mean that roles are totally constraining. There is always a degree of leeway which provides an opportunity for individuals to interpret their roles. In this way individual role performances are negotiated between the individual and society. Those who simply play out their roles wholly as expected Merton terms ritualists (see Chapter 5), deviant individuals just as much as those who seek to interpret their roles in more obviously socially unacceptable ways.

Individuals learn of the expectations associated with a particular role and the limits placed upon interpretation by way of a socialisation process. The term socialisation is used to describe any process by which individuals become social beings. *Primary socialisation* is the many faceted process which everyone experiences as they grow up. It involves a number of agencies whose collective contribution is the formation of a socially acceptable and responsible member of society. The family of origin is the first and most important primary socialising agency; in time the school and a series of peer groups combine with the family to fashion a social being able to make her or his own way in the world. In Western culture, primary socialisation is completed in the mid-teens at which time the young adult goes out to work. Once in employment it is necessary to learn the demands of the chosen occupation. This is the first experience which the individual has of *secondary socialisation*. Among the things to be learned are how the tasks which are allocated are supposed to be done and how they are actually done, the formal and the informal aspects of the task. Then it is necessary to learn how to work as part of a team, how to get on with colleagues and of course how to get on with the boss. Where a job requires an individual to interact with the public it is equally important to learn how to do this effectively, both formally and informally. These different parties with their various expectations constitute what was termed 'society' in the previous paragraph. They are the parties with whom an occupational role performance is negotiated. Mistakes will inevitably be made as the individual learns the demands of the role; in the early days these mistakes are normally tolerated but as time passes the tolerance of colleagues, clients and superiors alike can become strained and unless the individual is able to demonstrate an acceptable level of learning over time they can find themselves out of a job.

Work group socialisation, as this experience is sometimes termed, is typical of secondary socialisation in general. Take for example the individual who decides to stay on at school rather than leave to find a job. They will have to learn to live without the pleasures that their friends in work can now enjoy and at the same time with the demands of advanced study and the possibility of failure. Going up to university brings with it its own learning experience: there is now no one to watch over you; living away from home can be so much fun with all those parties, five hours of lectures a week and the union bar. But if the individual doesn't learn how to be a student, failure and a more painful learning experience follow. Moving on a little, deciding to marry involves much learning, with taking on a mortgage or becoming a parent requiring yet more. In fact all adult life is a continual process of secondary socialisation, so much so that some sociologists talk about the ultimate example of learning how to die with dignity. By comparison with primary socialisation, secondary socialisation is a more active process with the individual being able to exercise more choice about what learning to engage in. Once the decision is made, unless the learning is effective, failure and some social disorientation are a strong possibility.

Returning to the case of socialisation into an occupational role, the picture sketched out earlier now needs to be considered in a more detailed way. When a young person enters a job they must learn its demands if they are to enjoy a worklife with a minimum of stress. Five years on they may move to a new job as a mature, experienced adult. Obviously there will be a need to learn the demands of the new role but now they may have more confidence in their own view of the role. Equally they may find themselves subjected to new demands and expectations which they have never experienced before. Alternatively, someone who has held the same job for a period of time may begin to think more deeply about the various expectations which are associated with their occupational role. In all of these cases the possibility of *role conflict* is present. Which particular group(s) in society are you going to be more responsive to? This type of role conflict is normally termed *intra-role conflict* because it occurs within the role itself. The various groups which have expectations of the individual role player (and who constitute 'society') are termed the *role set* (Merton, 1957). The role set of a lecturer includes students; colleagues; the management of the teaching institution; prospective employers; the government; the lecturers' union; the broader community not to mention a spouse, children, friends and so on. Each one of these groups could well hold different expectations: students may seek an interesting but not too testing course while colleagues expect that the individual will not act in ways which will put pressure on them. Management may expect compliance while the union may be engaged in a campaign for better conditions. Employers and the government normally seek well-trained employees while the community is concerned to have the traditions of education continued. At all times it is for the individual to decide which set(s) of expectations to go with. This is sometimes dependent on which of these other parties is taken as the individual's *reference group*(s). It is always a matter of making choices and living with the consequences. At different times the various groups may be viewed differently and as a result the individual's role performance may change. Learning how to deal with the demands of the various groups and producing a socially acceptable role performance is never an easy matter.

Every individual is more than just an employee, the performer of an occupational role. Adults are normally spouses, parents, children, friends, members of clubs and societies, etc. These various social positions make up an individual's *status set* and in turn give rise to the possibility of further role conflicts. Known as *inter-role conflict* they occur as a result of having to fill a series of roles in the course of everyday life. For example, the conscientious lecturer will inevitably find that the demands of family life will limit the time which can be spent preparing lectures, carrying out research and writing academic papers. The keen gardener may find that the demands of the garden reduce the time available to have a drink down at the local or prepare for the annual 10km fun run or help out at the church bazaar. Choices have to be made, time and relationships have to be managed as a result of the need to fulfil a series of roles, further complicating an already complex scenario of intra-role demands. Some writers talk of the existence of a further form of role conflict which exists between the individual and the role itself, the conflict which happens when individuals find themselves having to fill roles which they no longer believe in. If this is a temporary situation it is sometimes referred to as *role strain*. Where it goes much deeper and is likely to be permanent, it often gives rise to ritualistic role performances which see the individual doing exactly what is expected, going through the motions and thus giving a bland role performance which is of little value to anyone in the long run. In this connection Goffman has identified the phenomenon of *role distance* where the individual actively communicates that they are not really gaining any enjoyment from performing a particular role. A good example of this would be the lecturer who keeps on apologising for the material being delivered and who clearly enjoys talking about football or music rather more than the intended lecture topic. The individual who chooses to go through the same material with no verve or vigour and whose performance is completely devoid of any sign of enthusiasm has probably given up long ago.

AUDITING: A ROLE ANALYSIS

What insights does this set of concepts offer on the process of becoming an auditor? The following account has made extensive use of a recent paper by Richard Harper and should perhaps be read in conjunction with it (Harper, 1988). Filling a new occupational role for the first time, the young auditor will be subjected to a comprehensive process of occupational socialisation. Most recruits will already have some impression of their chosen role which they may have employed at their interview for the job, but the new member of the firm will normally have no practical experience of the role. At this stage the role set will be a comparatively narrow one for most individuals. Two groups will be ever present: audit seniors and colleagues who will have varying degrees of experience of the work. The former will be in a position of controlling the formal socialisation process, the latter the more informal aspects. Each of course recognises the existence and the activities of the other since all audit seniors were once trainees and all but the most recent of fellow recruits recognise the existence of both a formal and an informal socialisation process. Audit managers, staff trainers and partners form a third group in the role set who have expectations which differ in detail but in the main their demands, like their presence, is rather distant at this stage. Usually their expectations are transmitted through audit seniors but occasionally they may turn up on the job and communicate these directly if needs be. Likewise the client's demands exist but these are initially the senior's problem. One of the things that is learned very quickly is the need to look busy whenever there is anyone outside of the audit team present who just might have some authority. The accountancy profession's role in the role set is initially equally distant but as examination time approaches it becomes more important. This in turn is the source of a major conflict in the trainee's role set, whether to do a first rate job during the day and comparatively little studying in the evening or to save yourself during the day and make some progress after work with the books. The need to study can often give rise to a second conflict, in this case between the role of trainee and the various others which constitute an individual's status set (Power, 1988).

Exactly what constitutes the culture of auditing that is being learned in this socialisation process? The need to work very hard and to always give the impression of working hard are certainly at the heart of this culture. Auditors and accountants in general have a reputation for their industriousness which must be communicated to all new recruits and internalised by them if they are to succeed. Their work is also recognised to be methodical, carefully planned and executed and very thorough, and it is expected that an intending auditor will accept these demands quickly and enthusiastically. On the other hand, there are always opportunities to play games in the course of everyday auditing, as long as you don't get caught and manage to get the job done. Those who have been through the process know that the work is boring but it has to be done. The challenge is to have a bit of fun but deliver the goods at all times. The more formal aspects do not end at being able to do a good job. There are a number of qualities that a good auditor must demonstrate. As part of their socialisation process young auditors are expected to develop the following qualities in addition to their technical and examination skills (BPP, 1984; cf. Hastings & Hinings, 1970). An auditor is expected to be a person of integrity, the sort of person whose word or opinion you will trust. This is a necessary quality for a professional whose work culminates in the signing of an audit report with all that this entails. The qualities of independence and objectivity are complementary in that an auditor must always be his or her own person and must always approach an audit with an open mind. Who would place any credence in the word of an auditor who exhibits a variety of biases or who can be easily swayed by other people? An auditor is expected to exhibit an inquiring mind, to be ever vigilant and to develop the skill of knowing intuitively when something may be amiss. There is no point simply knowing all the standards and guidelines and mastering all the firm's techniques if you can't sense when things are wrong.

The quality of tact is viewed as being of particular importance judging by the following quotation:

if the auditor was to adopt a dictatorial approach and march around insisting on his statutory rights, it is likely that this would serve only to make his own duties more onerous. Tact involves dealing with people in a sympathetic and considerate way and it is also a quality which will enable the auditor to handle awkward situations . . . a friendly and polite approach costs the auditor nothing and may go a long way to improving the effectiveness of his audit.

(BPP, 1984, p.2)

While the qualities of integrity, independence, objectivity and inquisitiveness are skills of a more technical nature, the ability to be tactful involves the development of a crucial social skill. It is this which makes it a different sort of quality to the others, and ultimately perhaps the most difficult to develop. It is much easier to inculcate integrity and independence and to promote objectivity and inquiry in the majority of people. But trying to develop social and interactional skills in many people is a much more difficult task. Although it is comparatively easy to give someone lessons in how to handle other people it is quite different when they find themselves confronted by real situations. Temperament, manner, confidence, personality, some of the bases of tact, cannot easily be changed and it is for this reason that tact and social skills in general are so difficult to master. In practice it may be that only modest developments of social skills are expected of the trainee given the other pressures which they experience. As long as they act in a socially acceptable way they will be judged to be adapting to the role satisfactorily.

How does becoming an auditor look from the perspective of the trainee? The work itself is normally very routine, repetitive and seemingly rather meaningless, not the sort of activity which is consistent with lofty ideals such as being objective or inquisitive. Any opportunities to have some fun are seized upon by most trainees in an attempt to distance themselves from their role. This is particularly true in the early stages of training. The challenge is not to get caught, not to attract the attention of seniors, certainly not audit managers or partners and definitely not managers in the client organisation. Once the decision is made to persevere with the role and to qualify as an accountant then the more negative aspects of the work must be afforded less significance. In this second stage of training the guiding notion might be summed up as making the most of a bad job. Qualification now becomes the goal with a need to study on the one hand and to gain whatever practical experience is on offer on the other. The work is often no less boring of course and it is still enjoyable to take part in some of the pranks of new recruits. Now the job is recognised to be the basis for developing new skills and needs to be embraced in a more enthusiastic way. It is at this point that audit seniors and their managers can begin to develop in their trainees the various skills identified above, particularly those of a more technical nature. There is a disturbing sense of instrumentalism evident in the later stages of training, something which is quite consistent with the conclusion that in the auditor's socialisation process only a modest development of social skills can be expected. It is far easier to impress superiors by becoming methodical and conscientious than by being able to develop an effective set of social skills. Integrity, independence and inquisitiveness can be more readily communicated than a successful disposition with the client's staff. And since the majority of trainees are aware of the need for impression management at this stage they will tend to display the qualities which promote the best impression. At a practical level senior staff simply do not have the time to observe the social skills of their trainees at length but they do have to review their working papers and discuss their thoughts and conclusions with them. Because many trainees have decided that auditing is not the career for them, they would not place too much importance on the possession of social skills and besides they don't get many examination questions on the topic either! Even for the most committed trainee, becoming an auditor is essentially a technical process of mastering techniques, passing exams and displaying several well-recognised professional qualities.

Having qualified, many trainees remain in the job because they wish to make a career in this branch of accountancy. Some do the work because they have as yet found no other employer willing to offer them an alternative career. The former usually find themselves promoted to the post of audit senior soon after they qualify, this being the first step on a career ladder that stretches up to the level of senior partner with the number of intervening steps depending on the size and structure of the firm. The audit senior carries out audits together with the juniors and trainees who constitute the audit team. Audit managers are normally

one step removed from the actual act, being responsible for several audits at any one time and thus several audit seniors. For this reason when moving on to discuss 'doing audits' attention might most usefully focus on audit seniors. The audit senior has a much more extensive role set than the trainee. First there are the members of the audit team being managed who expect their senior to perform the work in a reasonable manner, to plan it properly, provide the necessary guidance and training for junior staff, to be available for consultation, etc. The client is the second member of this role set and normally expects an audit which is professionally administered on the one hand and at a reasonable price on the other. It is the audit senior who hears complaints from clients about the behaviour of staff or the escalating cost of the exercise. In the end it is the manner in which the audit senior interacts with the client that determines whether the audit will be placed with the firm in the future. A third set of expectations are transmitted by the senior's own superiors, audit managers and partners. There are expectations about the quality of the audit which is being performed and about profitability. There is no virtue in performing a perfect audit if it makes a loss. The job of the audit senior is to ensure that an acceptable audit is provided, one which is to the satisfaction of the client and which makes a profit for the firm. It is on these criteria that the senior will be judged and, to some extent at least, selected for promotion.

Fellow seniors are another group in the role set who have their own particular expectations. They expect their colleagues to conduct their audits in a manner which will not reflect badly on them. Too much freedom of action devolved to subordinates may be fine for one individual but colleagues may not be quite so able to manage on this basis. Conversely when colleagues spend valuable time counselling trainees dismayed by the treatment they have received on other audits, nobody benefits. Also colleagues expect the individual to have some integrity in dealing with superiors and not simply seek favour and promotion at any price. The broader profession is also a group which will have expectations of the auditor. Standards and guidelines are expected to be employed as a matter of course and the individual auditor is also expected to act in an ethical manner, each of the professional institutes having gone to some lengths to communicate a code of ethics to all members. Courts of law and the general public have their various expectations of the auditor, these having become more significant in recent years as a result of a number of well-publicised legal actions against auditing firms. Finally there are the expectations which the auditor's family has, particularly those which relate to the nature of the commitment which the individual makes to the job. If this commitment is believed to be excessive because too much time on the job is required or if the rewards for the work being performed are insufficient, damaging conflicts may occur. These can result in marital problems or a deterioration in the standard of work, or both, which can become translated into reasons for client dissatisfaction.

It is up to the individual to determine how to manage the demands which these various groups impose. There can be no ideal solution because every individual is different and as a result seeks something different. It is part of the secondary socialisation process to learn how to live with the choices which have been made in the past and indeed how to come to terms with the consequences of any change in priorities which are presently being considered. The one outcome which perhaps should be avoided at all costs is that the auditor gives a ritualistic role performance and simply goes through the motions, employing the prescribed techniques, carrying out the work according to the book, subjecting subordinates to excessive boredom and the client's staff to unnecessary disruption. This said, in practice it is sometimes difficult to avoid such a role performance particularly in the case of the highly experienced audit senior who has not been promoted and who sees many colleagues and an increasing number of younger people gain promotion. In an attempt to gain the attention of superiors the audit senior may take to playing out the role in a highly stylised way, trying to correct for mistakes made in the past and to project a model image which of course is not terribly positive in most circumstances. Such role performances are a problem for senior management since they often signify a loss of interest and impetus which dates back some time and indeed probably explains the individual's lack of career success. A good employer should not have allowed this to happen and at this stage can still rescue things by offering some career counselling. Most, however, leave the individual to find new challenges in other environments.

Irrespective of which particular groups in the role set are the individual senior's reference groups it is imperative that they interact with clients in the appropriate manner. As the individual in charge of the audit on a day-to-day basis it is the audit senior's responsibility to ensure that the necessary rapport exists between the audit team and their counterparts on the client's staff. During the pre-qualification training process only a modest extent of social skills will have been picked up so a further socialisation process will be necessary immediately on assuming this new role. If the individual senior is committed to a career in auditing then it is more likely that they will be willing to pay more attention to the social skills aspects of the new role than if they simply drift into it. However enthusiastic someone may be, this is still a difficult learning process to engage in. For one thing most clients have preconceived notions about the intrusions of the auditors. They are perceived to make excessive demands upon staff in the accounting function and charge excessive fees for this privilege. They ask the same questions year after year, often seemingly irrelevant questions, with the result that staff don't always take them seriously. Many of them seem to be interested in comparatively small amounts of money and probably wouldn't recognise a case of fraud if they found one. To suggest that the way to overcome these problems is by being polite and considerate, friendly and sympathetic is rather wishful thinking. Anyone who adopts this as a basis for communicating with a client is likely to find that the efforts of both their staff and themselves are unlikely to succeed since they are much too defensive and apologetic in nature. After a series of difficult audits it may be the case that the audit senior has learned the lesson that whilst friendliness and politeness don't cost anything they also don't get you too far either. The result is that the successful audit senior quickly develops the appropriate way to perform an audit, and in time a repertoire of different approaches to the work. These will reflect the individual's own accommodation to their role, the corporate culture of the firm which will be communicated by audit managers and partners, and of course the cumulative experience of the other party to any audit, the client.

Up to this point it has been the auditor who has been the principal focus for attention. Every audit, however, is an interactive process involving two principal parties: the auditor and the client. In law the former has a whole range of rights and powers but as the earlier quote indicated, marching around insisting on your rights is only likely to make the task more onerous. In practice it needs to be recognised that what any audit actually becomes depends very much on what the client and the client's employees allow it to be. For this reason it is important that auditors, from trainees through to the most senior partners, recognise that every audit is a negotiated order the outcome of which fully reflects the involvement of both parties. The auditor comes to each audit as a new situation no matter how much experience has been gained in previous audits of this or any other clients. Together with their practical experience auditors also have a stock of standard procedures which they will be expert in applying. But this experience and expertise is necessarily historical in nature and while it obviously serves a basis upon which to predict effective audit performances in the future it does not guarantee them. The next audit always presents the possibility of being the most problematic yet encountered or the one where something crucial is missed or where a breakdown in relations with the client results in chaos. It really all depends on the other party. It is in their power to make an audit difficult, to present information in such a way as to cause the auditor to overlook important matters or to goad the auditor into acting in an unprofessional way. All of the rights and powers which are characteristic of the auditor's position cannot ensure that the audit will proceed as laid down in a textbook or audit manual.

It is in this way that the outcome of any audit is a *negotiated order* involving two parties. If an auditor were to be involved in an audit of a situation wholly within their control, then if any problems are encountered they are entirely the fault of the auditor. Any errors would be unforced. In such cases you are negotiating the order with yourself. When another party is involved it is only possible to be as effective, successful, thorough, competent, etc., as the other party will allow. In the context of modern day professional football this situation has given rise to the universally embraced objective of 'getting a result' which is a euphemism for avoiding a defeat by at least managing to achieve a draw. Defeat is unacceptable, something to be avoided at all costs. If there were no other team involved as in the case of playing against the dustbins in the car park then of course a victory would be assured. Since there will be an opposing team, in all probability equally motivated to get a result, settling for a draw will usually be a mutually acceptable outcome, hence its appeal to managers, players and fans alike.

The strength of the client's position can easily be overlooked. It should be remembered that in the same way that the auditor is involved daily in carrying out audits, their clients design, develop, operate, manipulate, customise and corrupt the very systems the auditor is called upon to review. It is only logical that in the last analysis the client has a superior appreciation of these. They are also in an ideal position to claim that they do not understand the various requests which the auditor might legitimately make. Alternatively, they are equally well placed to provide the information they believe they are being asked for, perhaps on the pretence that this is all that is available. Deliberately offering evidence of minor mistakes would seem an easy way to misdirect the auditor's attentions and provide a cover for more serious defalcations. The age old trick of passing enquiries from person to person is well rehearsed in all spheres of business and commercial life and it would be naive to believe that the auditor will be able to avoid this sort of treatment during the time spent in the client's offices. In short, like auditors, clients have their own cultures with their constituent norms and values, necessitous learning and socialisation processes, workgroup ethics and convincing role performances. Periodically this comes into contact with the auditing profession in the pursuit of a favourable audit and attendant audit report. To make the trite observation that it is not in the interests of the client to secure the latter against a backcloth of lies and misrepresentations is in fact to miss the point. In the last analysis perhaps the most satisfactory outcome is for both parties to 'get a result' as they say in football even if this is largely negotiated behind closed doors. But that is perhaps another story that could more usefully be told elsewhere!

INTERNAL AUDITING

In the previous sections attention has been focused exclusively on the form of auditing known as statutory or external auditing. This is understandable given that the great majority of professionally qualified accountants employed as auditors have traditionally been involved in this sort of work and that of necessity most of their formal auditing studies will be of the theory and practice of external audit. Nevertheless it would be unwise to omit to consider *operational* or *internal auditing* in this or indeed any account of auditing as a major branch of modern accountancy. A number of reasons can be given for this: firstly, external auditors have always found themselves working in close association with their clients' internal auditors and therefore need to understand something about their work. However, during the past twenty years the role for, and in turn the significance of the internal audit function has become increasingly crucial in all types of organisations and promises to continue doing so in the future. This being so, an increasing number of professionally qualified accountants might reasonably expect to find themselves working in the internal audit functions of such organisations during their careers. Finally, from a specifically sociological perspective internal auditing is a function involving a number of aspects which admirably repay even the very limited amount of enquiry possible here.

The obvious starting point is with a definition of internal auditing. The US-based professional body set up in 1941 to promote internal auditing and its practitioners, the Institute of Internal Auditors (IIA), defines it in the following terms:

An independent appraisal activity within an organisation for the review of operations as a service to management. It is a managerial control which functions by measuring and evaluating the effectiveness of other controls.

From this statement it is immediately apparent that internal auditing is in effect a marriage between the traditions of external auditing and certain aspects of contemporary management accounting, hence the admission of its predominantly managerial nature. CIPFA has recently defined internal audit in the public sector in essentially the same terms overlaid with the philosophy which has characterised UK political economy for the past decade or so:

an independent appraisal function within an organisation for the review of activities as a service to all levels of management. It is a managerial control which measures, evaluates and reports upon the effectiveness of internal control and the efficient use of resources within an organisation.

In the UK it has been the public sector rather than the private sector which has served as the proving ground for the function although in recent years more and more private sector organisations, like their US counterparts, have begun to expand their own internal audit work in the pursuit of greater economy, efficiency and effectiveness, i.e. value for money. So much so that the big accounting firms are themselves rapidly attempting to integrate the *management audit* service into their portfolios (Humphrey & Turley, 1990).

The popular view of internal audit, i.e. the one advanced by the bodies which provide the personnel who fill the ranks of external audit, can be seen in the tone adopted in the auditing guideline 'Reliance on Internal Audit' issued in November 1984. To say the least this guideline is condescending, evidencing a conscious attempt to convey the impression that those involved may be fine chaps doing sterling work but they are not like us. The relationship between the two parties is prescribed in the following way:

7 Unlike the internal auditor who is an employee of the enterprise or a related enterprise, the external auditor is required to be independent of the enterprise, usually having a statutory responsibility to report on the financial statements giving an account of management's stewardship.
8 Although the extent of the work of the external auditor may be reduced by placing reliance on the work of internal audit, the responsibility to report is that of the external auditor alone, and therefore indivisible and is not reduced by this reliance.
9 As a result, all final judgements, relating to matters which are material to the financial statements or other aspects on which he is reporting, must be made by the external auditor.

If reliance is to be placed on the work of internal audit, the external auditor is called upon to assess the effectiveness of their counterparts in terms of their degree of independence from management, the scope and objectives of their work, their professionalism and technical competence, and the quality of the work which they normally carry out. Only if entirely confident in the function are external auditors encouraged to place any degree of reliance on internal audit. Little wonder that even the most enthusiastic of advocates of internal audit such as Richard Roy acknowledge that it is often viewed as the 'step-child of the external audit' and that its practitioners are thereby 'second class citizens' (Roy, 1989).

Why does the accountancy profession feel the need to be so defensive? Obviously there is a lot of money involved in the statutory audit function and if it were to be seen that the in-house team could carry out more of the work equally competently and, perhaps more importantly, more economically then pressure would inevitably mount to reconsider the accountancy profession's monopoly of this work. It is in the interests of the profession to talk down the value of internal audit, at least as a substitute for certain aspects of the conventional audit process. However, it is not simply a matter of the proponents of enhanced professional status for internal audit to expose the self-interest of their more illustrious colleagues in external audit. To be able to organise effectively it is necessary to establish the legitimate nature of the internal audit function within the organisation. Only then is the occupation able to seriously begin to pursue a more favourable professional status. Both of these issues provide interesting foci for sociological enquiry.

There is no point in denying that internal audit is not an independent function in the organisation. Together with a growing number of management services including accounting and finance it constitutes part of the collective management function in the organisation. And like all those who work in these functions, internal auditors perform the tasks set out for them by executive management. By contrast the external auditor does not provide a service for these latter individuals, being the party responsible to a third party, the members. However, while the auditor may be independent of a client organisation's executive management, those employed by even the most modest sized firm will find themselves performing audits in the manner set out by their own management. In this sense independence is perhaps not the substantial issue implied in the view which the accountancy profession presents of internal audit and its practitioners.

Of much more interest in this connection is the view which an organisation's management has of the role of those who perform the internal audit function. It has long been recognised that within the organisation the internal auditor is the subject of a fundamental intra-role conflict as a result of the different expectations which members of the role set have (Mints, 1975; Morgan & Pattinson, 1975; Chambers, 1986; Vinten, 1988). In a study undertaken in association with CIPFA Morgan & Pattinson identified this conflict in the following terms. Both internal auditors and those who were being audited were in agreement that the objective of internal audit was the provision of a protective function geared to inspection. However, while the auditees took the view that invariably auditors adopted the role of a policeman to achieve this objective, auditors saw themselves adopting the role of a friendly adviser, some kind of in-house expert seeking to educate the rest of the staff in the interests of all concerned. The researchers were already aware that many auditors recognised that they were seeking to wear two hats but felt that this did not compromise them in any serious way. From the auditees point of view Morgan & Pattinson concluded that 'it may be difficult to seek meaningful advice from someone who is perceived as being primarily an inspector' (p.28). It also depends on what auditors mean when they say that they give advice, an issue which their report then goes on to consider.

Morgan & Pattinson are unconcerned with the question of how management view the role of internal audit. In his brief account of the behavioural aspects of internal auditing Chambers (1981) takes a fairly pessimistic view of the role which management has of the work: to prevent and detect error and loss, whether fraudulent or accidental; to comment on the competence and effectiveness of individual employees; to limit review to only financial and accounting areas all of which would run counter to the wide-ranging advisory role conceived of by many of its practitioners. More recently Chambers has reiterated this view, arguing that:

> Line management should resist using internal audit for political reasons as their shock troops. A request from a line manager to conduct an audit may be in order that the resulting audit report will give the line manager a pretext to take unpopular action – the need for which was already obvious . . . To conduct audits in such situations is to cast internal audit . . . in the role of an instrument of punishment – which is counterproductive to effective internal auditing.

> (Chambers, 1986, p.22)

Behind Roy's rhetoric on the importance of a strong internal audit function is the acceptance that in most instances it remains what management want it to be (Roy, 1989). Advocates of internal audit like Chambers and Roy who envisage internal audit as a radical management function committed to education and participation recognise that at this point in time the internal consultant role for internal audit is difficult to have accepted as legitimate by the majority of senior management. The possibilities for a softer, more constructive, people-oriented approach to internal auditing are consistent with the ideas of contemporary writers such as Peters & Waterman. They may, however, be some time in gaining widespread support.

The signs are present to indicate that internal audit is an occupation which is intent on attaining a favourable professional status. For years its practitioners' efforts have been denigrated by large sections of the accountancy profession. They have experienced the antipathy of most of those who have been subject to its enquiries but little positive support from their masters. The chosen way forward is that of arguing for the technical aspects of the occupation rather than its more qualitative ones. In this way Roy stresses the multidisciplinary nature of internal audit, its broad theoretical base and a recognition that it is now a profession which needs to train a growing number of its members in the universities. This strategy is almost identical with that identified by Wilensky in the early 1960s as the characteristic mode of attempting to attain a professional status: the emergence of a full time occupation followed by the establishment of some form of training school, and by implication a body of knowledge, associated with a professional association. The latter in turn lobbies for a measure of legal protection which will help it to project itself as it develops a code of ethics which it enforces in an attempt to demonstrate the goodwill, importance and value of the occupation. In Chapter 1 it was noted that Wilensky himself was very sceptical about the possibility of there being many new professions which would achieve the same levels of acceptability as the established professions such as medicine, law and of course (chartered) accountancy. The advocates of internal auditing obviously don't agree and seem to believe in the self-evident virtues of their profession. They direct their appeal to their employers, stressing the technicality of their work as it was termed by Jamous & Pelloile (1970).

These same writers drew attention to the role that indeterminate factors played in the success of the established professions. By definition indeterminate factors are not readily identifiable but skills such as a doctor's bedside manner, a lawyer's talent for advocacy, a minister's ability to allay anxiety and, in the case of accountants, an ability to determine the level of profitability of an enterprise are all significant factors in explaining the success of these professions. What indeterminate skills has an internal auditor? Or more importantly, what skills do the mass of the community believe the internal auditor to have? To the extent that the occupation sets out its prospectus as an occupation which has a mastery of purely technical skills, it is unlikely to gain any positive community sanction. For their part employers may well be impressed by the enhanced skill levels of their internal audit staff. But as long as they wish to deploy these in ways which management determine, and which are widely resented by the rest of the workforce, there is little chance that the internal audit function will increase its professional status. What is required is a serious rethink on the definition of internal audit as a service to management – such an open affiliation is always going to make it extremely difficult to convince the broader community of the universally beneficial function which the profession performs. But is this what internal audit specialists are really interested in or for that matter what motivates their counterparts in the external audit function and in the broader accountancy profession? Is it not simply that everyone has been seduced by the spirit of the age and now believes that you are what you can command in the marketplace?

Chapter 9

Summary and conclusions

In the course of the last eight chapters a wide range of sociologically informed insights on accountancy has been presented and a whole series of questions, issues, themes, problems, controversies, etc., raised. Most of the content of the preceding pages is obviously very different to the knowledge of accounting which is found in mainstream texts. However, there are also many points of contact between them and in this way the text is presented as a complement to them. Taken together they should provide a better knowledge of modern accountancy. This concluding chapter is in three sections, the first of which summarises the contents of the previous chapters and highlights some of the points made there. The second section considers the case for, and some of the difficulties associated with thinking about accountancy rather than simply 'doing' it. And finally some thought is given to the ways in which looking at accountancy sociologically can be of equal benefit to the discipline of sociology.

SUMMARY AND THE MAIN POINTS OF THE TEXT RESTATED

Chapter 1 on the profession was the obvious starting point for the sociology of accountancy part of the text. In the first section the lengthy review of the sociology literature on the professions and professionalisation concluded with the view that nowadays relatively few professional accountants are found in the traditional situation of collegiate control. The majority are employed in large organisations rather than being members of small practices. As a result they do not experience the freedom and autonomy commonly associated with professional persons. As corporate professionals in industry and commerce, the public sector and increasingly in public practice firms, they are very much professional employees. Moving on to consider the organisation of the modern accountancy profession in the UK and elsewhere in the developed world, the question of why six bodies are needed in the UK to service around two hundred thousand members (and an equal number of students) presents itself. Given the size and stature of the ICAEW it would seem reasonable to conclude that it should be in a position to structure the agenda for the UK profession in the twenty-first century. Instead it is under severe pressure on a number of fronts and seems to stumble from one crisis to another in a distinctly reactive manner. In the section on the recruitment and socialisation of accountants an implicit theme was the problems which exist in establishing the appropriate balance between the educational and training elements of the professional formation process. The rising proportion of women in the ranks of trainees was also noted but it will be a long, long while before they become as successful in the profession as their male counterparts, one of the points considered in the final section of the chapter.

The purpose of Chapter 2 was to try and set out what it is that professional accountants do in their work. The starting point was a critical appraisal of the modern public practice role, traditionally the perceived job of accountants. In the main a series of problematic features was highlighted. There is evidence that too many accountants do too much auditing. As the 'stock in trade' of public practice there will always be a great deal of auditing work to do. But as it is presently structured it seems to be a misuse of talent, especially among trainees. In the case of the large firms which have increasingly come to dominate public practice, they are effectively a source of cheap labour who can readily be replaced by others who seek to become chartered accountants (and live very comfortably ever after). Even if a trainee does survive the auditing apprenticeship the need to specialise in the early stages of a professional career seems to be equally problematic. The fact that so many leave public practice on qualification has contributed to the decision to introduce a measure of training provision outside of practice. This seems something of a contradiction in terms and may yet give rise to a further measure of disintegration. Others are leaving public practice to pursue their careers in smaller firms, a growing number of which offer only a limited range of consultancy skills in direct competition with their former employers. All things considered, unless you are a senior manager or a partner in a large or medium-sized public practice firm work is unlikely to be very fulfilling.

Nor is it likely to be much better in industry or commerce, or in the public sector, unless you are in senior post. Both were argued to be increasingly subject to a formalisation process which has had the consequence of reducing much accounting practice to little more than the application of accounting formulae. Standardisation, routinisation, the importation of procedures and systems, the emergence of extensive specialisation of function, etc., are all evidence that the principles of management control have now been extended to the accounting and finance function in the interests of greater economy, efficiency and effectiveness. Whether the individual accountant is engaged in an external audit role or in a specific organisational function, there is a great deal of evidence that most of the time work is simply a matter of following procedures and operating within systems. At the very least there has been a massive increase in the level of bureaucratisation of the work of most accountants. In the UK public sector there is the added dimension of increasing political intervention which has the consequence of imposing more pressure on the ranks of accountants employed there. While there is much scope to improve the performance of financial management in this sector, the tendency to withdraw any funds which are saved rather than to employ them in a more beneficial way only serves to further disaffect many employed there. Chapter 2 concluded with some provocative comments on longer term significance of the emergence of a formal accounting technician role in recent years. Given the moves toward formalisation, bureaucratisation, management control or whatever among the ranks of professional accountants, this might prove to be the profession's own Trojan Horse.

Chapter 3 built directly on Chapter 2 and is essentially an attempt to conceptualise accountants' work experiences in terms of labour process theory and class analysis. The general conclusion was that many accountants experience their own form of labour process and in this way they are simply another group of workers who have come to experience the negative consequences of the social organisation of work. The twin divisions of labour, the technical and the social, were argued to be increasingly evident among accountants in large organisations. The technical division of labour gives rise to the division and sub-division of tasks which result in accountants finding themselves engaged in narrow, routine and fragmented work activities. The social division of labour can be seen in the development of managerial hierarchies within the accounting and finance function, the result of which is accountants being managed by other accountants who in turn find themselves managed by more senior accountants. This was argued to have great significance for the question of whether accountants can properly be designated management in large organisations. While they may be involved in a management function, only those who actually exercise any direct function of management content in the work role are properly identifiable as management. The opportunities to move into genuinely managerial roles were argued to be less commonplace nowadays, all of which points to the progressive economic proletarianisation of large sections of the accountancy profession in recent times. While accountants may still be well rewarded and seemingly guaranteed a career for life, the reality of their work experiences is often as negative as that of most lower-level employees.

The final chapter given over to considering the sociology of accountancy focused on the nature of the relationship between accountancy and ideology. While ideology has been one of the key concepts in its lexicon, little or no attention has been paid to the ideological nature of accountancy by sociology. However, the critical accounting tradition which developed in the 1980s has provided a body of literature on the topic. This was reviewed in the second section of the chapter revealing a wealth of valuable insights on the question of the neutral or objective status of accounting as a practice and the broader institution of accountancy itself. One of the more interesting consequences of this conclusion is how consistent this is with the previous arguments about the class identity of many lower-level accounting roles. Although all those who practise accounting are in effect implicated in the reproduction of the dominant ideology it should not be concluded that they are themselves committed to it. Like every group of employees they also experience ideology in its various material forms. In the second half of the chapter the focus of attention switched to a discussion of the status of some of the proposed alternatives to conventional accounting and reporting. Generally these have tended to be viewed as supplementary to conventional accounting and as long as they remain categorised in this way they will not seriously challenge the latter's contribution to the reproduction of the existing social order. In the final section of this chapter particular attention was paid to human resource accounting. After two decades of unfulfilled promise, the prospects for some reconstituted form of human resource accounting appear more promising as a complement to recent radical developments in management thinking. However, in the last analysis the extent of the challenge that these present to the prevailing relationship between capital and labour will be the determining factor in their long term success.

The second part of the text constituted an attempt to break away from merely developing a sociology of accountancy. It was conceived of as assembling some insights drawn from sociology which were believed to be of value in understanding a variety of topics and issues within some of the different branches of modern accountancy. In this way it is perhaps best viewed as a sociology *for* accountancy rather than a sociology *of* accountancy. The first branch of accountancy to be considered was financial accounting. Here the principal focus of attention was theory and theory construction which often seem to be pursued in an uninformed way. Initially an attempt was made to consider the meaning of some of the terminology employed in the debate over theory including a series of commonly invoked oppositions, e.g., between normative and descriptive theories, between explanation and prediction, between *a priori* and empirical theory, etc. Where appropriate these oppositions were collapsed revealing how theories and theory construction involve both elements. This led to the conclusion that financial accounting and indeed accounting in general should be very wary of seeking to emulate the approach to theory and theory construction which characterise the natural sciences. As a social science discipline, accounting should endeavour to learn more from sister disciplines such as sociology. The middle-range approach to theory construction in the social sciences exemplified by Robert Merton was discussed with particular attention being paid to its emphasis on explanation rather than on comparatively trivial predictions. The chapter concluded with a discussion of the work of Watts & Zimmerman, two of the major figures in the accounting theory debate. In line with other commentators it was concluded that their work might reasonably be described as an insightful contribution to the sociology of accounting choice.

The chapter on sociology for management accounting was in great part a critique of recent attempts by some working in this branch of the discipline to make use of a number of the various sociological perspectives on offer. The purpose of this critique was to highlight the partial nature of the insights which are provided by work informed by any particular perspective. Examples of some of the most insightful analyses using the different perspectives were also outlined and discussed. Without doubt some of these have made a major contribution to the development of management accounting and management control research in recent years. It is imperative that this sort of work is continued in the future, ideally by academic accountants and sociologists working together. In the final section of the chapter Johnson & Kaplan's recent critique of contemporary management accounting was briefly outlined and discussed. Perhaps the most important lesson to be learned from their theses is that management accounting must be developed as something more than simply a set of techniques. It must become more analytical, more critical, more questioning, etc., if it is to fulfil its potential as a valued management function. For this reason management accounting should be even more open to the central issues, theories and concepts of sociology than it has been to date.

The finance branch of modern accountancy has traditionally been very heavily reliant on economics as its source discipline. The benefits of this association are evident for all to see. Chapter 7 was written on the basis that since much of the activity known as corporate finance or financial management actually takes place within large organisations and involves behaviour, it might be of value for finance to begin to pick up on a wider range of literature. Agency theory is a major theory within finance but to date it has normally been conceptualised in a narrow, economistic way. It is concerned with the consequences of the separation and divorce of ownership from control in modern capitalist enterprises. This development has also been of interest to several generations of sociology and as a result has given rise to a complementary literature. The general conclusion of this literature is that the new managerial hierarchies found in large organisations have been constructed in such a way as to minimise agency problems, with effective control residing only in the hands of executive management who invariably share the same objectives as the owners of capital. Corporate finance is intimately bound up with decision-making and for this reason the third section of the chapter considers the literature of decision-making or behavioural theory. This particular literature provided a rather stark contrast to the implicit rational decision-making approach of conventional finance theory. The final section focused attention on recent management thinking on the value of developing strong organisational cultures as a means of ensuring corporate success. This is very much in opposition to the perspective inherent in much finance theory. The section concluded with a few cautionary words on the emergence of the new panacea known as corporate culture.

Auditing is inherently a social, organisational and behavioural activity but to date it has rarely been considered as such. Of the four branches of accountancy chosen for consideration here this is the one where the value of sociology for accountancy is most readily apparent. The specific aspect of sociology relevant for considering auditing is role analysis with its foundations in the interactionist perspective. The principal elements of role analysis were outlined and discussed in section two of the chapter before being applied in the third section. The audit was characterised as a negotiated order involving two principal parties, the audit staff and the client's staff. Both parties have been subject to an extensive socialisation process and as a consequence come to the audit fully prepared for the appropriate performance of their respective roles. What ensues is negotiated between the two parties, the actual outcome of the negotiation process being determined by the conviction with which those concerned play out their roles. Rather than only focusing on the statutory powers of the auditor or the methodical fashion in which auditors are intended to pursue their work, an audit can also usefully be characterised in the same terms as a game of football where the intention is to at least manage to avoid being defeated by the opposing team. Internal auditing was discussed in the final section of the chapter. Its relationship with statutory auditing was considered together with the difficulties attendant upon being cast in the role of policeman by senior management. For these and other reasons the internal audit function faces a major uphill struggle in its attempt to enhance its professional status.

THINKING ABOUT ACCOUNTANCY: THE PROMISE AND THE PITFALLS

So what have you learned from reading the last eight chapters with their 80000 words, many of them rather obscure, and hundreds of references, some of them years old? Part I might have left you a little disillusioned with its emphasis on the more unrewarding side of being an accountant: negative work experiences across the board; the threat posed by the emergence of accounting technicians; limited opportunities for real career progression; the role of accountancy in reproducing the existing social order and so on. On the other hand Part II might have left you a little more intrigued as a result of its closer relationship with a subject matter you are more familiar with as students of accounting. But in the final analysis how will having another view on financial accounting theory or on the complexities of the management control problematic, on the social, organisational and behavioural aspects of corporate finance or auditing help you be a better account-ant? What exactly is the benefit to be gained from thinking about accountancy in a sociologically informed way or indeed from thinking about it at all?

There can be little doubt that accounting as the practice of accountancy is very much a hands-on activity. This was certainly brought home to me sitting in an examination room trying to make sense of the suspense account entry in the trial balance from which I was intended to produce a balance sheet and profit and loss account. Had I been a trainee accountant I would probably have been very aware of the practical value of such accounts. Alternatively, had I come across suspense accounts in the course of my previous studies I might have remembered what to do with them, i.e. how to account for them. This is what a great deal of accounting is, a routine practical activity the purpose of which is to provide an account of, or a particular kind of story about, a specified aspect of economic reality. A 'good' accountant is someone who can provide a good story, one which is useful to the party who commissioned it. Conversely a 'bad' accountant is a contradiction in terms since nobody would willingly keep faith with someone who is unable to provide at least a satisfactory account when required to. Therefore it is perhaps better to think in terms of accountants and good accountants, rather like wine and good wine, leaving the bad accountants to look to their own failings.

This of course begs the question: what distinguishes a good accountant? It is not simply a matter of successfully completing professional qualifications since these are only an indication that an individual can pass a set of accounting examinations. In the UK, to gain admission to the accountancy profession it is necessary to demonstrate that you have also gained the appropriate practical experience either during a training contract or in the course of the early years of your career as an accountant. These two criteria taken together still provide no guarantee that an individual is able to keep and/or provide good accounts. A good accountant is a *creative* accountant. The choice of the term creative should not be taken to signify any affinity with the rather 'sharp' practice known as creative accounting. A creative accountant is adaptable, dynamic, inventive, open to new ideas, able to take a broader view, aware of different perspectives and prepared to defend a chosen alternative. Although accounting is at base an inherently practical and often a highly routine activity, mastery of its conventional practical content is a necessary but not a sufficient foundation for ensuring the performance of good accounting. In other words, simply being able to keep and provide accounts is no guarantee of their ultimate value.

The development of these skills or talents in aspiring accountants has long taxed accounting educators. It has been particularly problematic to those employed in university and polytechnic accounting departments in the past twenty years or so. In the case of the university departments offering degrees in accounting the problem has often been to achieve the appropriate balance between an educational experience which would seem to mirror the traditions of the university and the fact that those taking the courses wished to become accountants and were able enough to gain university entrance. In the case of the polytechnics the problem has been to offer accounting degrees which are clearly distinguishable in content from the various professional courses taught in the same department, often by the same overworked lecturers. The most common solution has been to introduce a greater 'theory' content into the curriculum. This is designed to encourage students to think about accountancy at the same time as they are mastering the basic techniques, the intention being to develop the analytical, critical and communication skills which the creative accountant should possess. The need to gain accreditation as a relevant degree (for professional examination exemption purposes) has obviously served to constrain excesses in curriculum development. Nevertheless what is acceptable as part of an accounting degree course is sometimes surprising. One of the enduring difficulties with introducing a major element of theory into the curriculum is that while we the educators can recognise and appreciate the crucial role which it plays in the development of a stock of creative accountants, our students commonly see it as material to be assembled, learned and regurgitated as effortlessly as possible, leaving more time for mastering 'real' accounting. At the root of the problem is the fact that there is too great a similarity between the two parts of the curriculum for most students to recognise the complementary demands which are being made on them.

In recent years an alternative approach to developing the skills of the creative accountant has gained support both in higher education and among those who devise the professional examination programmes. This is the integration of a case approach to accounting into the curriculum. The obvious benefit which it has over a theory approach is that it is a set of activities which are clearly distinct from but complementary to a concern with accounting techniques. The case approach provides a means of developing problem-solving and decision-making skills, something which any managerial employee should not be without in the present era. For this reason we find more case work in degree courses and in the professional examinations, particularly at the more advanced stages. Even the most technical papers seem to include some questions which require close reading and reflection before you switch the calculator on! Although an advance on the theory approach to thinking about accountancy, case work has its own difficulties. It was originally developed in the context of post-experience training programmes where students were commonly long on business and management experience but short on formal education. Although it soon filtered down to MBA programmes and ultimately undergraduate business degrees, it still works best with those who bring their own experiences to the classroom. This precludes most accounting undergraduates of course. And while the majority of professional accountancy students are in employment, the case approach doesn't serve them too well either. This is due mainly to the fact that we are talking about instructing and examining several thousand students at any one time rather than small groups of managers with whom we have close contact. In short this way of promoting thought about accountancy is surrounded by too many operational difficulties to exploit to its full potential.

This conclusion has the consequence of returning the focus back to the possibility of devising a theory-type approach which is sufficiently different to the study of accounting techniques that it impacts on the student in the desired way of encouraging thinking about accountancy and in turn the development of the skills which characterise the creative accountant. It must therefore be different from the greater part of the accounting curriculum but not too different. And it must be able to provide the opportunity to develop the necessary skills. Another way of describing it is as a truly complementary study, one which interacts with, builds upon and simultaneously poses questions against its counterpart. Few disciplines are able to do this of course but one which can is sociology. The previous eight chapters have, I hope, gone a long way to establishing some substance for what the more cynically minded might dismiss as an unashamed piece of disciplinary empire building. As a separate discipline, sociology has something to say about the accountancy profession and its members, the work they do and the problems they experience when doing it, the critical role which accountancy plays in structuring the social order and the potential for alternative contributions. Other disciplines, e.g. history or political science, also provide their own sort of insights but none is perhaps so broad in focus as sociology.

At this point it might be imagined that I am advocating that all accounting students will learn to think about accountancy, and in time stand a greater chance of becoming creative accountants, by simply assembling, learning and regurgitating the 'facts' of the sociology of accountancy. This would make the exercise almost identical to that which presently exists in the case of the theory approach discussed earlier. In the case of sociology it is the form which it assumes rather than its content which is of the greatest importance. It has developed the many perspectives which I described in the introduction in an attempt to gain a better purchase on its subject matter. It is the way in which what passes for sociological knowledge is arrived at rather than the knowledge itself that is its greatest strength. Another way of expressing this view is to say that it is the questions which sociology asks rather than the answers which it provides which are the basis of its value. In the case of accountancy I hope that I have managed to demonstrate this to be the case whether one is interested in either the sociology of accountancy or, more ambitiously, sociology for accountancy.

As a good sociologist, rather than a good accountant, I must conclude this section with some mention of the pitfalls of introducing a significant slab of sociology into the accounting curriculum. I have decided to highlight three which should be considered in the first instance. Firstly, it is not going to be an entirely comfortable experience, having to come to grips with not only the demands of accountancy and its associated disciplines, e.g. economics, law, information technology, etc., but also with a seemingly quite unrelated discipline. Where the real problem might lie is in coming to grips with a quite different approach which emphasises reading, thinking, arguing, changing your mind, never being certain that you've got it right. This has to be compared with doing examples, checking them against solutions, building up speed, mastering techniques and moving on to the next stage. A second problem is that if we are seriously intent on developing a stock of creative accountants then in all probability it will be necessary to lengthen the education and training period. An extra year for an accounting degree would also provide an opportunity to increase the technical content of programmes. It would also significantly increase the cost of producing accounting graduates, arguably the prime consideration in the present climate in the UK. And finally there is the question of how creative do those who employ accountants really want them to be? Few if any prospective employers would deny that they are seeking adaptable, dynamic, inventive, open-minded, lateral thinking, etc., staff. But the evidence assembled in Chapters 2 and 3 suggested that these qualities, if widely distributed, might prove problematic given the existence of the social and technical divisions of labour, the general application of accounting formulae, the intrusion of politics and so on. One of the dangers of encouraging students to think about accountancy is that they might be tempted to think about other things as well.

ACCOUNTING FOR SOCIOLOGY

When I was discussing sociology and the sociological perspective in the introduction I mentioned that in Britain the discipline was no longer viewed in a
positive way by the Establishment. There are a number of reasons for this, not
least the fact that for many people sociology still has the radical political reputation which it gained for itself twenty years ago. While this may be a somewhat
oversimplistic view it is certainly true that sociology has a number of characteristics which result in its having a less than favourable image. Without doubt it
appears as a rather negative discipline, one which can leave non-sociologists
pessimistic. Trained sociologists recognise that in general the discipline adopts
an even-handed approach but to outsiders the lasting impression is often one of
things being wrong with society. A related characteristic is that sociology often
seems well supplied with ideas and 'theories' but is much less forthcoming on the
practical side of things. The stock defence of many sociologists that it is not their
role to actually change things is irrelevant to most people. In the same vein is the
criticism that sociologists are often a little smug, implying that they know best
and that the rest of society should listen to them. Viewed objectively, this is not
an unreasonable proposition and after all we don't complain about intellectual
arrogance in the case of natural scientists or medical scientists. In this context
another of sociology's difficulties is apparent. It has a reputation for providing
excuses, for being an apologist for all sorts of disreputable parties and practices.
Again the point of its being a liberal discipline is lost in a world of prejudice and
the desire for 'quick-fixes'. I am not the first to conclude that if sociology were
to issue damning indictments against football hooligans, gays, or plant-level
union activists and recommend positive ways of dealing with them it would be
much more favourably received both by the Establishment and the majority of the
population.

Thankfully this sort of sociology does not seem to be forthcoming, despite the
Thatcher years and the emergence of the radical right. But the mainstream of
British sociology has certainly moved to try and influence the public perception
of the discipline and what it has to offer society. In recent years there has been
much evidence of a comprehensive campaign to reconstruct sociology and to
present it in a favourable way at every opportunity. In terms of actually doing
sociology, there has been a pronounced move towards an empirical approach, one
built upon the methodological self-awareness which was gained alongside
theoretical self-awareness in the 1960s and 1970s. The shortage of funding to
carry out major research projects has had the consequence of giving rise to much
more modest enquiries. Many of these are characterised by a level of sophistication that should do much to dispel some of the more unfounded criticisms of
the past decade or so. It is not that sociology doesn't consider controversial
questions or issues any more. It does but in a way that makes the whole endeavour
seem less threatening and more constructive. New interests have emerged and
continue to do so. Old ones are subjected to division and sub-division, a sure

means of emasculating them perhaps. And in the end it is possible to pick up issue after issue of sociology's leading journals and find little that you recognise as being part of the discipline's central thrust and less still that must be read. In short British sociology in the hands of British sociology seems to have lost its way to a very great extent.

In the summer of 1984 I certainly recognised that I had lost my way. The previous year I had asked to be transferred from my teaching on a 'science in society' degree course which had occupied me for much of the previous six years, to teaching on several business degrees. I had now completed my doctoral work which was partly sociology of science oriented and had no wish to continue in that specialism. I was interested in continuing my research into proletarianisation among professional employees, however, and thought it might be useful to turn my attention to business professionals such as accountants. It seemed logical to try to get some idea about business and management hence the move to these degrees. During the next academic year sociology was finally expunged from the curriculum of the business studies degree, to be replaced by behavioural science and organisation behaviour courses. The projected common first year for all of the business degrees meant that in a short time there would be no place for sociology on this sort of course. Clearly there was no future with sociology in this scenario. Equally there was no immediate opportunity to return to previous teaching. On the research and writing front a general lack of interest in what I had to say only compounded the problem. The only sensible decision was to begin a retraining process which might eventually provide a means of escape. There was never any question that the much hyped MBA experience would appeal; I was already a generalist with proven analytical, critical and communication skills. A career in accountancy was far more attractive and certainly presented much more of a challenge. In November 1984 I became a student member of the ACCA and enrolled for my first accounting class two months later.

For the past two years I have spent much of my time teaching a variety of managerial accounting courses and enjoy this every bit as much as I ever did teaching sociology. I still plan to research proletarianisation among accountants, empirically and hopefully with some methodological self-awareness. Arguably the most important reason for wanting to pursue this research, apart from my own long-standing interest in it, is that in the intervening period I have found that many of my academic accountant colleagues are also interested in it. It promises to provide a provocative counter-perspective on the accountancy profession to the one which has emerged from critical accounting in recent years. But this is only half of the appeal of accountancy as a subject to pursue research in and in many ways the least attractive half. Looking at accountancy from the outside in the manner of the sociology *of* accountancy is less rewarding than looking at it from within. In this way writing the second part of this text has proved much more fulfilling and thus easier than writing the first part. Becoming involved in the study of accountancy as an insider, providing sociology *for* accountancy, seems to me to be a much more useful activity than standing on the sidelines offering a comparatively narrow range of insights about it. To do this it is not necessary to go to the lengths that I chose to. A number of sociologists have succeeded in making a contribution to the development of accounting research without submerging themselves in a formal study programme. There are many academic accountants anxious to foster links with sociologists who are interested in their discipline. They will willingly provide the necessary technical insight for any joint research project. Such is the present level of acceptance for sociology in accounting research circles.

In no sense am I advocating that sociologists should *en masse* decamp into accounting research. That would be a pointless exercise even if it were a practical one. My point is that if the institution of accountancy is of interest to you as a sociologist then it would seem more beneficial to pursue that interest in some form of insider role. Accountancy is not the only place where this sort of work is possible. The whole spectrum of research into business and management activities and functions is equally open to the importation of the sociological perspective. During the last fifteen years a growing number of sociologists have made their homes in university and polytechnic departments of this sort and have engaged in a great deal of insightful joint work. Much of it has been critical and some as radical as any sociology in recent years, thereby challenging the stereotype of managerial sociology. The point of contact is that both sociology and inherently practical activities such as accounting, marketing, personnel management, business policy, etc., are concerned with social phenomena. After a period of involvement with economics and psychology, academics working in these fields have come to recognise this and in turn, the potential of employing a sociological perspective. Because of the social science connection it is possible for sociologists to work in these fields in a way that is different to science, engineering, data processing, etc. All of these are themselves social phenomena and have been studied as such by sociologists. But they are not concerned with social phenomena in the same way as accounting or personnel management are. For this reason they do not offer the same opportunity to develop any sociology for science, engineering, data processing, etc.

The lesson to be learned from this is quite simple. The prospects for sociology in Britain in the coming years look rather uncertain despite all of the rhetoric issuing from the profession. As a consequence it seems sensible to take full advantage of any opportunities which exist to develop the discipline in a meaningful way. If it is only possible to develop a conventional *sociology of* perspective then this must be done as effectively as possible. However, where there is the chance to work more closely with fellow researchers in other disciplines to create a *sociology for* perspective then this should be a major objective of those sociologists interested in such work. These are complementary activities which can only serve to strengthen the discipline in the future in the same way as they have done in the past. Accountancy is one subject where this development process is possible and should be exploited for mutual benefit. The fact that many influential academic accountants are presently rather enthusiastic about what sociology can offer them should be seen as something of a bonus. The opportunity is one which should not be missed.

The title of this final section, *accounting for sociology*, was briefly considered as the title for the entire text. This was decided against on the grounds that it was a trifle too enigmatic for such an ambitious project. Nevertheless it captures much of the spirit of the past three years of research and writing. It is a most apt way to describe a potentially positive future for some within sociology while also neatly encapsulating the process by which I have eventually come to terms with the discipline of sociology. On the one hand accounting for sociology is a forward-looking ideal, an example of the way in which British sociology might regain some of its presently tarnished reputation. On the other it is a backward-looking view, a historical account of where I see I have come from. As an academic discipline, sociology unquestionably has an enormous amount to offer any society and its members. But in the last analysis, it will only do so if it can give a good account of itself!

Bibliography

Abercrombie, N. (1980), *Class, Structure and Knowledge*, Oxford, Basil Blackwell.

Abercrombie, N. & J. Urry (1983), *Capital, Labour and the Middle Classes*, London, Allen & Unwin.

Abercrombie, N., S. Hill & B.S. Turner (1980), *The Dominant Ideology Thesis*, London, Allen & Unwin.

Accounting Standards Steering Committee (1975), *The Corporate Report*, London, ASSC.

Alchian A. & H. Demsetz (1972), 'Production, information costs and economic organisation', *American Economic Review*, v.62, pp. 777–795.

Althusser, L. (1969), *For Marx*, Harmondsworth, Penguin.

Althusser, L. (1971), *Lenin and Philosophy and Other Essays*, London, New Left Books.

American Accounting Association (1966), *A Statement of Basic Accounting Theory*, Evanston, AAA.

Anthony, R.N. (1965), *Planning and Control Systems: a Framework for Analysis*, Harvard Graduate School of Business.

Argyris, C. (1952), *The Impact of Budgets on People*, New York, The Controllership Foundation.

Armstrong, P. (1985), 'Competition between the organisational professions and the evolution of management control strategies', *Accounting Organisations and Society*, v10/2, pp. 129–148.

Armstrong, P. (1986), 'Management control strategies and interprofessional competition: the case of accountancy and personnel management', in D. Knights & H.C. Willmott (eds), *Managing the Labour Process*, London, Gower, pp. 19–43.

Armstrong, P. (1987a), 'The rise of accounting controls in British capitalist enterprises', *Accounting, Organisations and Society*, v12/5, pp. 415–436.

Armstrong, P. (1987b), 'Engineers, management and trust', *Work, Employment & Society*, v1/4, pp. 421–440.

Arnold, J. (1989), 'Accounting education and research: the role of universities' in G. MacDonald & B.A. Rutherford (eds), *Accounts, Accounting and Accountability*, London, VNR/ICAEW.

Arnold, J. & T. Hope (1990), *Accounting for Management Decisions*, 2/e, London, Prentice-Hall.

Atkinson, P. & S. Delamont (1990), 'Professions and powerlessness: female marginality in the learned occupations', *Sociological Review*, v31/8, pp. 90–110.

Barber, B. (1963), 'Some problems in the sociology of the professions', *Daedalus*, v92/4, pp. 669–688.

Barnard, C.I. (1938), *The Functions of the Executive*, Cambridge, Mass., Harvard University Press.

Barnes, S.B. (1971), 'Making out in industrial research', *Science Studies*, v1, pp. 157–175.

Barnes, S.B. & D. Edge (eds) (1982), *Science in Context: Readings in the Sociology of Science*, Milton Keynes, Open University Press.

Becker, H.S. (1962), 'The nature of a profession' in The National Society for the Study of Education, *Education for the Professions*, Chicago, pp. 27–46.

Belkaoui, A. (1985), *Accounting Theory*, 2/e, San Diego, Harcourt Brace Jovanovich.

Berle, A.A. & G.C. Means (1932), *The Modern Corporation and Private Property*, New York, Macmillan.

Berry, D. (1974), *Central Ideas in Sociology*, London, Constable.

Berry, A.J., T. Capps, D. Cooper, P. Ferguson, T. Hopper & E.A. Lowe (1985), 'Management control in an area of the NCB: rationales of accounting practice in a public enterprise', *Accounting, Organisations and Society*, v10/1, pp. 3–28.

Bilton, T., K. Bonnet, P. Jones, M. Stanworth, K. Shead & A. Webster (1987), *Introductory Sociology*, 2/e, London, Macmillan.

Birkett, W.P. & W.F. Chua (1988), 'Situating management accounting practice', *Interdisciplinary Perspectives in Accounting* Conference paper, Manchester.

R. Blauner (1964), *Alienation and Freedom: the Factory Worker and his Industry*, Chicago: University of Chicago Press.

Blumer, H. (1969), *Symbolic Interactionism: Perspective and Method*, New Jersey, Prentice-Hall.

Boggs, C. (1976), *Gramsci's Marxism*, London, Pluto Press.

Boyle, C., P. Wheale & B. Sturgess (1984), *People, Science and Technology: a Guide to Advanced Industrial Society*, Brighton, Wheatsheaf Books.

BPP (1984), *Auditing*, London, BPP Publishing.

Brandenberg, M. (1987), 'The day of the accounting technician', *Accountancy*, December, pp. 105–106.

Braverman, H. (1974), *Labour & Monopoly Capital*, New York, Monthly Review Press.

Braybrooke, D. & C. Lindblom (1963), *A Strategy of Decision*, The Free Press of Glencoe.

Brealey, R.A. & S.C. Myers (1988), *Principles of Corporate Finance*, 3/e, New York, McGraw-Hill.

Bromley, P. (1986), *Corporate Capital Investment: a Behavioural Approach*, Cambridge, Cambridge University Press.

Bromwich, M. (1990), 'The case for strategic management accounting: the role of accounting information for strategy in competitive markets', *Accounting, Organisations and Society*, v15/1, pp. 27–46.

Brummet, R.L., E.G. Flamholtz & W.C. Pyle (1968), 'Human resource measurement: a challenge for accountants', *The Accounting Review*, v43/2, pp. 217–224.

Bucher, R. & A.L. Strauss (1961), 'Professions in process', *American Journal of Sociology*, v66/4, pp. 325–334.

Burchell, S., C. Clubb, A. Hopwood, J. Hughes & J. Nahapiet (1980), 'The roles of accounting in organisations and society', *Accounting, Organisations and Society*, v5/1, pp. 5–27.

Burchell, S., C. Clubb & A. Hopwood (1985), 'Accounting in its social context: towards a history of value added in the United Kingdom', *Accounting, Organisations and Society*, v10/4, pp. 381–413.

Burnham, J. (1941), *The Managerial Revolution*, New York, Day.

Burrell, G. & G. Morgan (1979), *Sociological Paradigms and Organisational Analysis*, London, HEB.

Carchedi, G. (1975), 'On the economic identification of the new middle class', *Economy & Society*, v4/1, pp. 1–86.

Carchedi, G. (1977), *On the Economic Identification of Social Classes*, London, Routledge & Kegan Paul.

Carlin, J.E. (1962), *Lawyers on their Own*, New Brunswick, Rutgers University Press.
Carlin, J.E. (1966), *Lawyers' Ethics: a Study of the New York City Bar*, New York, Russell Sage Foundation.
Carr, G.J. (1985), *Information Technology and the Accountant*, London, Gower.
Carr-Saunders, A.M. & P.A. Wilson (1933), *The Professions*, Oxford, The Clarendon Press.
Chambers, A.D. (1981), *Internal Auditing*, London, Pitman.
Chambers, A.D. (1986), 'The psychology of internal audit', *Managerial Auditing Journal*, v1/1, pp. 21–27.
Chartered Association of Certified Accountants (1990), *Accountants Guide*, London, Certified Accountants Educational Trust.
Cherns, A.B. (1978), 'Alienation and accounting', *Accounting, Organisations and Society*, v3/2, pp. 105–114.
Child, J. (1969), *The Business Enterprise in Modern Society*, London, Collier-Macmillan.
Child, J. (1984), *Organisation: a Guide to Problems and Practice*, 2/e, London, Harper & Row.
Child, J., M. Fores, I. Glover & P. Lawrence (1983), 'A price to pay? professionalism and work organisation in Britain and West Germany', *Sociology*, v17, pp. 63–78.
Christenson, C. (1983), 'The methodology of positive accounting', *The Accounting Review*, v58/1, pp. 1–22.
Chua, W.F. (1986), 'Radical developments in accounting thought', *The Accounting Review*, v61/4, pp. 601–632.
Chua, W.F. (1988), 'Interpretive sociology and management accounting research – a critical review', *Accounting, Auditing & Accountability Journal*, v1/2, pp. 59–79.
Cogan, M.L. (1953), 'Towards a definition of profession', *Harvard Educational Review*, 23, pp. 33–50.
Cohen, M.D., J.G. March & J.P. Olsen (1972), 'A garbage can model of organisational choice' in J.G. March (1988), *Decisions and Organisations*, Oxford, Basil Blackwell.
Colville, I. (1981), 'Reconstructing "behavioural accounting"', *Accounting, Organisations and Society*, v6/2, pp. 119–132.
Connerton, P. (ed.) (1976), *Critical Sociology*, Harmondsworth, Penguin.
Cooley, M. (1976), 'Contradictions of science and technology in the productive process' in H. Rose & S. Rose (eds.) *The Political Economy of Science*, London, Macmillan, pp. 72–95.
Cooley, M. (1981), 'The Taylorisation of intellectual work' in L. Levidow & R. Young (eds.) *Science, Technology and the Labour Process; Marxist Studies Vol. I*, Brighton, CSE Books, pp. 46–65.
Cooper, D. (1975), 'Rationality and investment appraisal', *Accounting & Business Research*, 19, pp. 198–202.
Cooper, D. (1980), 'Discussion of "Towards a political economy of accounting reports"', *Accounting, Organisations and Society*, v5/1, pp. 161–166.
Cooper, D. (1983), 'Tidiness, muddle and things: commonalities and divergences in the approaches to management accounting research', *Accounting, Organisations and Society*, v8/3, pp. 269–286.
Cooper, D. & M. Sherer (1984), 'The value of corporate accounting reports: arguments for a political economy of accounting', *Accounting, Organisations and Society*, v9/3, pp. 207–232.
Cooper, D. & T. Hopper (eds.) (1990), *Critical Accounts: Reorientating Accounting Research*, London, Macmillan.
Cooper, D. & K. Robson (1990), 'Understanding the development of the accountancy profession in the United Kingdom' in D. Cooper & T. Hopper (eds.), *Critical Accounts: Reorientating Accounting Research*, London, Macmillan, pp. 366–390.

Cooper, D., A.G. Puxty, E.A. Lowe & H.C. Willmott (1989), 'The accounting profession, corporatism and the state' in W.F. Chua *et al.* (eds.), *Critical Perspectives in Management Control*, London, Macmillan, pp. 245–270.

Cooper, R. & R.S. Kaplan (1987), 'How cost accounting systematically distorts product costs', in W. Bruns Jnr. & R.S. Kaplan (eds.), *Accounting and Management: Field Study Perspectives*, Harvard: Harvard Business School Press, pp. 204–224.

Copeland, T.E. & J. E. Weston (1988), *Financial Theory and Corporate Policy*, 3/e, Reading, Mass., Addison-Wesley.

Cotgrove, S. & S. Box (1970), *Science, Industry and Society*, London, Allen & Unwin.

Cotgrove, S., J. Dunham & C. Vamplew (1971), *The Nylon Spinners*, London, Allen & Unwin.

Cottrell, A. (1984), *Social Classes in Marxist Theory and in Post-War Britain*, London, Routledge & Kegan Paul.

Cottrell, A. & R. Roslender (1986), 'Economic class, social class and political forces', *International Journal of Sociology and Social Policy*, v6/3, pp. 13–27.

Covaleski, M.A. & M.W. Dirsmith (1983), 'Budgeting as a means of control and loose coupling', *Accounting, Organisations and Society*, v8/4, pp. 323–340.

Covaleski, M.A. & M.W. Dirsmith (1986), 'The budgetary process of power and politics', *Accounting, Organisations and Society*, v11/3, pp. 193–214.

Crompton, R. & J. Gubbay (1977), *Economy and Class Structure*, London, Macmillan.

Crompton, R. & G. Jones (1984), *White-Collar Professionals: Deskilling and Gender in Clerical Work*, London, Macmillan.

Cropper, K. (1990), 'The first ten years of AAT', *Management Accounting*, v68/8, p. 80.

Cutler, A., B. Hindess, P.Q. Hirst & A. Hussain (1977), *Marx's 'Capital' and Capitalism Today, Vol. I*, London, Routledge & Kegan Paul.

Cutler, A., B. Hindess, P.Q. Hirst & A. Hussain (1978), *Marx's 'Capital' and Capitalism Today, Vol. II*, London, Routledge & Kegan Paul.

Cyert, R.M. & J.G. March (1963), *A Behavioural Theory of the Firm*, New Jersey, Prentice-Hall.

Deal, T.E. & A.A. Kennedy (1982), *Corporate Cultures: the Rites and Rituals of Corporate Life*, New York, Addison-Wesley.

Dent, M. (1986), 'Autonomy and the medical profession: medical audit and management control', *Fourth UMIST/Aston Labour Process Conference* paper.

Dillard, J.F. & K.R. Ferris (1989), 'Individual behaviour in professional accounting firms: a review and synthesis', *Journal of Accounting Literature*, v8, pp. 208–234.

Dilley, S.C. & J.J. Weygandt (1973), 'Measuring social responsibility: an empirical test', *Journal of Accountancy*, September, pp. 62–70.

Drucker, P. (1981), 'Behind Japan's success', *Harvard Business Review*, v59/1, pp. 89–90.

Drury, C. (1988), *Management and Cost Accounting*, 2/e, London, Van Nostrand Reinhold.

Durkheim, E. (1933), *The Division of Labour in Society*, New York, Macmillan.

Durkheim, E. (1957), *Professional Ethics and Civic Morals*, London, Routledge & Kegan Paul.

Edwards, R.C. (1979), *Contested Terrain: the Transformation of the Workplace in the Twentieth Century*, London, HEB.

Elliott, P. (1972), *The Sociology of the Professions*, London, Macmillan.

Emmanuel, C. & D.T. Otley (1985), *Accounting for Management Control*, London, Van Nostrand Reinhold.

Estes, R.V. (1976), *Corporate Social Reporting*, New York, Wiley.

Ezzamel, M. & H. Hart (1987), *Advanced Management Accounting: an Organisational Emphasis*, London, Cassell.

Ezzamel, M., K. Hoskin & R. Macve (1990), 'Managing it all by numbers: a review of Johnson & Kaplan's "Relevance Lost" ', *Accounting & Business Research*, v78, pp. 153–166.

Fama, E. (1980), 'Agency problems and the theory of the firm', *Journal of Political Economy*, v88/2, pp. 288–307.

Fama, E. & M.C. Jensen (1983a), 'Separation of ownership and control', *Journal of Law & Economics*, v26, June, pp. 301–325.

Fama, E. & M.C. Jensen (1983b), 'Agency problems and residual claims', *Journal of Law & Economics*, v26, June, pp. 327–349.

Fanning, D. (1979), 'Employment reports – an appraisal', *Employee Relations*, v1/4, pp. 8–12.

Fayol, H. (1949), *General and Industrial Management*, London, Pitman.

Financial Accounting Standards Board (1976), *Scope and Implications of the Conceptual Framework Programme*.

Financial Accounting Standards Board (1978), *SFAC 1: Objectives of Financial Reporting by Business Enterprises*.

Financial Accounting Standards Board (1980), *SFAC 3: Elements of Financial Statements of Business Enterprises*.

Flamholtz, E.G. (1971), 'A model for human resource valuation: a stochastic process with service rewards', in *The Accounting Review*, v46/2, pp. 253–267.

Flamholtz, E.G. (1972), 'Assessing the validity of a theory of human resource value: a field study', in *Empirical Research in Accounting: Selected Studies*, pp. 241–266.

Flamholtz, E.G. (1973), 'Human resource accounting: measuring positional replacement cost', *Human Resource Management*, Spring, pp. 8–16.

Flamholtz, E.G. (1974), *Human Resource Accounting*, California, Dickenson.

Foucault, M. (1972), *The Archaeology of Knowledge*, London, Tavistock.

Foucault, M. (1977), *Discipline and Punish*, London, Allen Lane.

Freidson, E. (1970), *The Profession of Medicine: a Study of the Sociology of Applied Knowledge*, New York, Dodd, Mead & Co.

Freidson, E. (1986), *Professional Powers: a Study of the Institutionalisation of Formal Knowledge*, Chicago, University of Chicago Press.

Friedman, A. & B. Lev (1974), 'A surrogate measure for the firm's investment in human resources', in *Journal of Accounting Research*, Autumn, pp. 235–250.

Friedman, A.L. (1977), *Industry and Labour: Class Struggle at Work and Monopoly Capitalism*, London, Macmillan.

Friedman, M. (1962), *Capitalism and Freedom*, Chicago, University of Chicago Press.

Gambling, T.E. (1974), 'A system dynamic approach to HRA' in *The Accounting Review*, v49/3, pp. 538–546.

Gambling, T.E. (1984), 'Accounting to society', in B. Carsberg & A. Hope (eds.), *Current Issues in Accounting*, 2/e, Oxford, Philip Allan, pp. 136–147.

Giddens, A. (1986), *Sociology: a Brief but Critical Introduction*, 2/e, London, Macmillan.

Giddens, A. (1989), *Sociology*, Cambridge, Polity Press.

Glaser, B.G. & A.L. Strauss (1967), *The Discovery of Grounded Theory*, New York, Aldine.

Glautier, M.W.E. & J.L. Roy (1981), 'Social Responsibility Reporting', in T.A. Lee (ed.), *Developments in Financial Reporting*, Oxford, Philip Allan, pp. 223–250.

Glautier, M.W.E. & B. Underdown (1989), *Accounting Theory & Practice*, 3/e, London, Pitman.

Glover, I., M. Kelly & R. Roslender (1986), 'The coming proletarianisation of the British accountant?', *Fourth Aston/UMIST Labour Process* Conference paper.

Goffman, E. (1959), *The Presentation of Self in Everyday Life*, New York, Doubleday.

Goldthorpe, J.H. & D. Lockwood (1963), 'Affluence and the British class structure', *Sociological Review*, v11/2, pp. 133–163.

Goldthorpe, J.H., D. Lockwood, F. Bechhofer & J. Platt (1968a), *The Affluent Worker: Industrial Attitudes and Behaviour*, Cambridge, Cambridge University Press.

Goldthorpe, J.H., D. Lockwood, F. Bechhofer & J. Platt (1968b), *The Affluent Worker: Political Attitudes and Behaviour*, Cambridge, Cambridge University Press.

Goldthorpe, J.H., D. Lockwood, F. Beckhofer & J. Platt (1969), *The Affluent Worker in the Class Structure*, Cambridge, Cambridge University Press.

Goode, W.J. (1957), 'Community within community: the professions', *American Sociological Review*, v22, pp. 194–200.

Goode, W.J. (1960), 'Encroachment, charlatanism and the emerging profession: psychology, sociology and medicine', *American Sociological Review*, v25, pp. 902–914.

Gordon, L.A. & D. Miller (1976), 'A contingency framework for the design of accounting information systems', *Accounting, Organisations and Society*, v1/1, pp. 59–70.

Gouldner, A.W. (1971), *The Coming Crisis of Western Sociology*, London, HEB.

Gramsci, A. (1971), *Selections from the Prison Notebooks*, translated and edited by Q. Hoare & G. Nowell-Smith, London, Lawrence & Wishart.

Gray, R.H. (1990), *The Greening of Accountancy: the Profession after Pearce*, London, Chartered Association of Certified Accountants.

Gray, R.H., D. Owen & K. Maunders (1987), *Corporate Social Reporting: Accounting and Accountability*, Hemel Hempstead, Prentice-Hall.

Greenbaum, J. (1976), 'The division of labour in the computer field', *Monthly Review*, v28/3.

Greenbaum, J. (1979), *In the Name of Efficiency: Management Theory and Shopfloor Practice in Data Processing Work*, Philadelphia, Temple University Press.

Greenwood, E. (1957), 'Attributes of a profession', *Social Work*, v2/3, pp. 44–55.

Hales, M. (1980), *Living Think Work: Where Do Labour Processes Come From?*, London, CSE Books.

Harper, R.R. (1988), 'The Fate of Idealism in Accountancy', *Interdisciplinary Perspective on Accounting* Conference Paper, Manchester.

Harvey, M. & F. Keer (1983), *Financial Accounting Theory and Standards*, 2/e, London, Prentice-Hall.

Hastings, A. & C.R. Hinings (1970), 'Role relations and value adaptation: a study of the professional accountant in industry', *Sociology*, v4/3, pp. 353–366.

Hekimian, J.S. & C. Jones (1967), 'Put people on your balance sheet', *Harvard Business Review*, v45/1, pp. 105–113.

Hermanson, R.H. (1964), *Accounting for Human Assets*, Occasional Paper No. 14, Bureau of Business and Economic Research, Graduate School of Business Administration, Michigan State University, USA.

Hofstede, G.H. (1968), *The Game of Budget Control*, London, Tavistock.

Hopper, T. (1988), 'Social transformation and management accounting: finding relevance in history', *Interdisciplinary Perspectives on Accounting* Conference paper, Manchester

Hopper, T. (1990), 'The relevance of Weberianism to class analysis of accounting: a reply to Roslender', *Advances in Public Interest Accounting*, v3, pp. 213–225.

Hopper, T. & A. Powell (1985), 'Making sense of research into the organisational and social aspects of management accounting: a review of its underlying assumptions', *Journal of Management Studies*, v22/5, pp. 429–465.

Hopper, T., D. Cooper, T. Lowe, T. Capps & J. Mouritsen (1986), 'Management control and worker resistance in the National Coal Board: financial controls in the labour process', pp. 109–141 in D. Knights & H.C. Willmott (eds.), *Managing the Labour Process*, Gower, London.

Hopper, T., J. Storey & H. Willmott (1987), 'Accounting for accounting: toward the development of a dialectical view', *Accounting, Organisations and Society*, v12/5, pp. 437–456.

Hopwood, A.G. (1973), *An Accounting System and Managerial Behaviour*, Lexington, Mass., Lexington Books.

Hopwood, A.G. (1974), *Accounting and Human Behaviour*, New Jersey, Prentice-Hall.

Hopwood, A.G. (1976), 'Editorial', *Accounting, Organisations and Society*, v1/1, pp. 1–4.

Hopwood, A.G. (1978), 'Towards an organisational perspective for the study of accounting and information systems', *Accounting, Organisations and Society*, v3/1, pp. 3–14.

Hopwood, A.G. (1987), 'The archaeology of accounting systems', *Accounting, Organisations and Society*, v12/3 (1987), pp. 207–234.

Horkheimer, M. & T. Adorno (1973), *Aspects of Sociology*, London, HEB.

Horngren, C.T. & G. Foster (1987), *Cost Accounting: a Managerial Emphasis*, 6/e, London, Prentice-Hall.

Hoskin, K.W. & R.H. Macve (1986), 'Accounting and the examination: a genealogy of disciplinary power', *Accounting, Organisations and Society*, v11/2, pp. 105–136.

Hoskin, K.W. & R.H. Macve (1988a), 'The genesis of accountability', *Accounting, Organisations and Society*, v13/1, pp. 37–73.

Hoskin, K. & R.H. Macve (1988b), 'Cost accounting and the genesis of managerialism: the Springfield Armory episode', *Interdisciplinary Perspectives on Accounting* Conference paper, Manchester.

Hughes, E.C. (1958), *Men and their Work*, The Free Press of Glencoe.

Humphrey, C. & S. Turley (1990), 'Moving targets or poor shots – the continuing problem of the audit expectations gap', unpublished manuscript, University of Manchester.

Humphrey, C., L. Kirkham & P. Ciancanelli (1990), 'Balancing the scales', *Career Accountant*, July, pp. 24–25.

Hussey, R. (1979), *Who Reads Employee Reports?*, Oxford, Touche Ross.

Hussey, R. (1981), 'Developments in employee reporting', *Managerial Finance*, v7/2, pp. 12–16.

Jamous, H. & B. Pelloile (1970), 'Changes in the French university-hospital system', in J.A. Jackson (ed.), *Professions and Professionalisation*, Cambridge, Cambridge University Press, pp. 109–152.

Jensen, M.C. & W.H. Meckling (1976), 'Theory of the firm: managerial behaviour, agency costs and ownership structure', *Journal of Financial Economics*, v3/4, pp. 305–360.

Johnson, H.T. & R.S. Kaplan (1987), *Relevance Lost: the Rise and Fall of Management Accounting*, Boston, Harvard Business School Press.

Johnson, T.J. (1972), *Professions and Power*, London, Macmillan.

Jones, R. & M. Pendlebury (1988), *Public Sector Accounting*, 2/e, London, Pitman.

de Kadt, M. (1979), 'Insurance: a clerical work factory', in A. Zimbalist (ed.), *Case Studies on the Labour Process*, New York, Monthly Review Press, pp. 242–256.

Kelly M. & R. Roslender (1988), 'Proletarianisation, the Division of Labour Process', *International Journal of Sociology and Social Policy*, v8/6, pp. 48–64.

Kerr, C., J.T. Dunlop, F.H. Harbison & C.A. Myers (1962), *Industrialism and Industrial Man*, London, Heinemann.

Kraft, P. (1977), *Programmers and Managers: the Routinisation of Computer Programming in the United States*, New York, Springer.

Kuhn, T.S. (1962), *The Structure of Scientific Revolutions*, Chicago, University of Chicago Press.

Larson, M.S. (1977), *The Rise of Professionalism: a Sociological Analysis*, Berkeley, University of California Press.

Laughlin, R.C. (1987), 'Accounting systems in organisational contexts: a case for critical theory', *Accounting, Organisations and Society*, v12/5, pp. 479–502.

Laughlin, R.C. (1988), 'Accounting in the social context: an analysis of the accounting system of the Church of England', *Accounting, Auditing and Accountability Journal*, v1/2, pp. 19–42.

Laughlin, R.C. & A.G. Puxty (1983), 'Accounting regulation: an alternative perspective', *Journal of Business Finance & Accounting*, v10/3, pp. 451–479.

Laughlin, R.C. & A.G. Puxty (1984), 'Accounting regulation: a reply', *Journal of Business Finance & Accounting*, v11/4, pp. 593–596.

Laughlin, R.C., E.A. Lowe & A.G. Puxty (1982), 'Towards a value-neutral positive science of accounting: a comment', *Journal of Business Finance & Accounting*, v9/4, pp. 567–571.

Lawrence, P.R. & J.W. Lorsch (1967), *Organisation and Environment: Managing Differentiation and Integration*, Boston, Harvard University Press.

Lee, D. & H. Newby (1983), *The Problem of Sociology*, London, Hutchinson.

Lee, G.A. (1986), *Modern Financial Accounting*, 4/e, London, Van Nostrand Reinhold.

Lee, T.A. (ed.) (1981), *Developments in Financial Reporting*, Oxford, Philip Allan.

Lehman, C. & A.M. Tinker (1985), 'A semiotic analysis of "The Great Moving Right Show" featuring the accounting profession', *Interdisciplinary Perspectives on Accounting* Conference paper, Manchester.

Lehman, C. & A.M. Tinker (1986), 'The not-so-great society: the role of business literature in reshuffling Johnson's new deal', *Fourth Annual Aston/UMIST Labour Process Conference*.

Lehman, C. & A.M. Tinker (1987), 'The "real" cultural significance of accounts', *Accounting, Organisations and Society*, v12/6, pp. 503–522.

Lev, B. & A. Schwartz (1971), 'On the use of the economic concept of human capital in financial statements', *The Accounting Review*, v46/1, pp. 103–112.

Likert, R.M. (1961), *New Patterns of Management*, New York, McGraw-Hill.

Likert, R.M. (1967), *The Human Organisation*, New York, McGraw-Hill.

Likert, R.M. & D.E. Bowers (1971), 'Improving the accuracy of P/L reports by estimating the changes in dollar value of the human organisation', *Michigan Business Review*, v25, pp. 15–24.

Lindblom, C.E. (1959), 'The science of "muddling through"', *Public Administration Review*, v19/2, pp. 79–88.

Linowes, D.F. (1972), 'An approach to socio-economic accounting', *Conference Board Record*, November, pp. 58–61.

Lister, R.J. (1984), 'Capital budgeting – a survey paper' in R. Scapens, D. Otley & R.J. Lister, *Management Accounting, Organisational Theory and Capital Budgeting: Three Surveys*, London, Macmillan/ESRC.

Lockwood, D. (1958), *The Blackcoated Worker*, London, Allen & Unwin.

Loft, A. (1986), 'Towards a critical understanding of accounting: the case of cost accounting in the UK 1914–1925', *Accounting, Organisations and Society*, v11/2, pp. 137–169.

Lowe, E.A. & R.W. Shaw (1968), 'An analysis of managerial biasing: evidence from a company's budgeting process', *Journal of Management Studies*, v5, pp. 304–315.

Lukacs, G. (1968), *History and Class Consciousness: Studies in Marxist Dialectics*, translated by Rodney Livingstone, London, Merlin Press.

Lyall, D. (1981), 'Financial reporting for employees', *Management Decision*, v19/3, pp. 33–38.

Lyall, D. (1982), 'Disclosure practice in employee reports', *The Accountant's Magazine*, July, pp. 246–248.

Lynch, B. (1990), 'Learning from the Irish', *Career Accountant*, April, pp. 26–28.

Macintosh, N.B. (1990), 'Annual reports in an ideological role: a critical theory analysis' in D. Cooper & T. Hopper (eds.), *Critical Accounts: Reorientating Accounting Research*, London, Macmillan, pp. 153–172.

Macintosh, N.B. & R.S. Scapens (1989), 'Management control systems: a structuration theory analysis', *AAA/EMCA* Conference paper, London.

Mackenzie, D. & J. Wajcman (eds.) (1985), *The Social Shaping of Technology*, Milton Keynes: Open University Press.

Mannheim, K. (1954), *Ideology and Utopia*, London, Routledge & Kegan Paul.

March, J.G. (1971), 'The technology of foolishness' in J.G. March (1988), *Decisions and Organisations*, Oxford, Basil Blackwell.

March, J.G. (1988), *Decisions and Organisations*, Oxford, Basil Blackwell.

March, J.G. & J.P. Olsen (1976a), 'Organisational choice under ambiguity' in J.G. March & J.P. Olsen, *Ambiguity and Choice in Organisations*, Bergen, Universitetsforlarget.

March, J.G. & J.P. Olsen (1976b), *Ambiguity and Choice in Organisations*, Bergen, Universitetsforlarget.

March, J.G. & H.A. Simon (1958), *Organisations*, New York, Wiley.

Marcuse, H. (1954), *Reason and Revolution*, New York, Humanities Press.

Marcuse, H. (1964), *One Dimensional Man*, London, Routledge & Kegan Paul.

Marshall, T.H. (1939), 'The recent history of the professions in relation to social structure and social policy', *The Canadian Journal of Economic and Political Science*, v5, pp. 325–340.

Marsland, D. (1988), *The Seeds of Bankruptcy*, London and Lexington, Claridge Press.

Marx, K. (1956), *Economic and Philosophical Manuscripts*, Moscow, Institute of Marxism, Leninism.

Marx, K. (1974), *Capital Vol. II*, London, Lawrence & Wishart.

Marx, K. (1975), 'Theses on Feuerbach' in *Marx: Early Writings*, Harmondsworth, Penguin.

Marx, K. & F. Engels (1964), *The German Ideology*, London, Lawrence & Wishart.

Maunders, K.T. (1984), *Employment Reporting – an Investigation of User Needs, Measurement and Reporting Issues and Practice*, London, ICAEW.

Medawar, C. (1976), 'The social audit: a political view', *Accounting, Organisations and Society*, v1/4, pp. 389–394.

Merquior, J.G. (1985), *Foucault*, London, Fontana.

Merton, R.K. (1957), *Social Theory and Social Structure*, The Free Press of Glencoe.

Merton, R.K. (1967), *On Theoretical Sociology: Five Essays, Old and New*, New York, Macmillan.

Merton, R.K. (1973), *The Sociology of Science: Theoretical and Empirical Investigations*, Chicago, University of Chicago Press.

Miller, P. & T. O'Leary (1987), 'Accounting and the construction of the governable person', *Accounting, Organisations and Society*, v12/3, pp. 235–261.

Millerson, G. (1964), *The Qualifying Associations*, London, Routledge & Kegan Paul.

Mills, C.W. (1951), *White Collar: the American Middle Classes*, Oxford, Oxford University Press.

Mints, F.E. (1975), 'Behavioural patterns in internal audit relationships', *Research Report 17*, Institute of Internal Auditors, USA.

Morgan, G. (1986), *Images of Organisation*, Beverly Hills, California, Sage.

Morgan, G. & B. Pattinson (1975), *The Role and Objectives of Internal Audit: a Behavioural Approach*, London, Chartered Institute of Public Finance and Accountancy.

Morley, M.F. (1981), 'Value added reporting' in T.A. Lee (ed.), *Developments in Financial Reporting*, Oxford, Philip Allan, pp. 251–269.

Mouzelis, N.P. (1967), *Organisation and Bureaucracy: an Analysis of Modern Theories*, London, Routledge & Kegan Paul.

Neimark, M.D. & A.M. Tinker (1986), 'The social construction of management control systems', *Accounting, Organisations and Society*, v11/4, pp. 369–396.

Nichols, T. (1969), *Ownership, Control and Ideology*, London, Allen & Unwin.

Nichols, T. & P Armstrong (1976), *Workers Divided: a Study in Shopfloor Politics*, (1976), London, Fontana.

Nichols, T. & H. Beynon (1977), *Living with Capitalism: Class Relations and the Modern Factory*, London, Routledge & Kegan Paul.

Ogan, P. (1976), 'A human resource value model for professional service organisations', *The Accounting Review*, v51/2, pp. 306–320.

Otley, D.T. (1980), 'The contingency theory of management accounting: achievement and progress', *Accounting, Organisations and Society*, v5/4, pp. 413–428.

Otley, D.T. (1989), 'Some issues in management control', *AAA/EMCA International Conference* paper, London.

Ouchi, W.G. (1981), *Theory Z: How American Business Can Meet the Japanese Challenge*, Reading, Mass., Addison-Wesley.

Parker, L.D. (1986), 'Polemical theories in social accounting: a scenario for standard setting', *Advances in Public Interest Accounting*, v1, pp. 67–93.

Parkin, F. (1979), *Marxism and Class Theory: a Bourgeois Critique*, London, Tavistock.

Parry, N. & J. Parry (1976), *The Rise of the Medical Profession*, London, Croom Helm.

Parsons, T. (1954), 'The professions and social structure' in T. Parsons, *Essays in Sociological Theory*, The Free Press of Glencoe, pp. 34–49.

Parsons, T. (1968), 'Professions' in D. Sells (ed.), *The International Encyclopaedia of Social Science*, XII, New York, Macmillan/Free Press, pp. 536–547.

Pascale, R. & A. Athos (1983), *The Art of Japanese Management*, New York, Penguin.

Peasnell, K.V. (1982), 'The function of a conceptual framework for corporate social reporting', *Accounting & Business Research*, 48, pp. 243–256.

Peters, T.J. & R.H. Waterman (1982), *In Search of Excellence: Lessons from America's Best Run Companies*, New York, Harper & Row.

Poulantzas, N. (1973), *Political Power and Social Classes*, London, New Left Books.

Poulantzas, N. (1975), *Classes in Contemporary Capitalism*, London, New Left Books.

Power, M.K. (1985), 'Comments on Laughlin', *Interdisciplinary Perspectives on Accounting* Conference paper, Manchester.

Power, M.K. (1988), 'Educating accountants: towards a critical ethnography', *Interdisciplinary Perspectives on Accounting* Conference paper, Manchester.

Prandy, K. (1965), *Professional Employees: a Study of Scientists and Engineers*, London, Faber & Faber.

Preston, A. (1986), 'Interactions and arrangements in the process of informing', *Accounting, Organisations and Society*, v11/6, pp. 521–540.

Pugh, D.S. & D.J. Hickson (1976), *Organisational Structure in its Context: The Aston Programme I*, Farnborough, Saxon House.

Pugh, D.S. & C.R. Hinings (eds.) (1976), *Organisational Structure – Extensions and Replications: The Aston Programme II*, Farnborough, Saxon House.

Puxty, A.G. (1986), *Organisation and Management: an Accountant's Perspective*, London, Pitman.

Puxty, A.G., H. Willmott, D. Cooper & E.A. Lowe (1987), 'Modes of regulation in advanced capitalism: locating accountancy in four countries', *Accounting Organisations and Society*, v12/3, pp. 273–292.

Pyrhh, P. (1970), 'Zero-base budgeting', *Harvard Business Review*, v48/6, pp. 111–121.

Renshall, M. (1984), 'A short summary of the accounting profession', in B. Carsberg & A. Hope (eds.) *Current Issues in Accounting*, 2/e, Oxford, Philip Allan, pp. 23–38.

Rey, E. (1978), 'Corporate social responsibility and social reporting in France', in

H. Schoenfeld (ed.), *The Status of Social Reporting in Selected Countries*, Illinois, University of Illinois Press.

Richardson, A.J. (1987), 'Accounting as a legitimating institution', *Accounting, Organisations and Society*, v12/4, pp. 341–355.

Roberts, J. & R. Scapens (1985), 'Accounting systems and systems of accountability: understanding accounting practices in the organisational contexts', *Accounting, Organisations and Society*, v10/4, pp. 443–456.

Rockness, W.J. (1985), 'An assessment of the relationship between US corporate environmental performance and disclosure', *Journal of Business Finance and Accounting*, v12/3, pp. 339–354.

Rosenberg, D., C. Tomkins & P. Day (1982), 'A work role perspective of accountants in local government service departments', *Accounting, Organisations and Society*, v7/2, pp. 123–138.

Roslender, R. (1983a), 'Trade unionism among scientific workers in Great Britain: 1960–1975', Unpublished PhD thesis, University of Leeds.

Roslender, R. (1983b), 'The Engineers' and Managers' Association', *Industrial Relations Journal*, v13, pp. 41–51.

Roslender, R. (1988), 'The accountant: class, status and party', *Interdisciplinary Perspectives on Accounting* Conference paper, Manchester.

Roslender, R. (1990a), 'The accountant in the class structure', *Advances in Public Interest Accounting*, v3, pp. 195–212.

Roslender, R. (1990b), 'Sociology and management accounting research', *British Accounting Review*, v22/4, pp. 351–372.

Roszak, T. (1970), *The Making of a Counter Culture: Reflections on the Technocratic Society and its Youthful Opposition*, London, Faber & Faber.

Roth, J.A. (1974) 'Professionalism: the sociologist's decoy', in *Sociology of Work and Occupations*, v1, pp. 6–23.

Roy, R. (1989), 'Excellence in the administration of the internal audit department', *Managerial Auditing Journal*, v4/4, pp. 17–31.

Rueschemeyer, D. (1964), 'Doctors and lawyers: a comment on the theory of the professions', *Canadian Review of Sociology and Anthropology*, v1, pp. 17–30.

Sackmann, S.A., E.G. Flamholtz & M.L. Bullen (1989), 'Human resource accounting: a state of the art review', *Journal of Accounting Literature*, v8, pp. 235–264.

Saks, M. (1983), 'Removing the blinkers: a critique of recent contributions of the sociology of the professions', *Sociological Review*, v31/1, pp. 1–21.

Samuels, J., C. Rickwood & A. Piper (1989), *Advanced Financial Accounting*, 2/e, Maidenhead, McGraw-Hill.

Scapens, R. (1984), 'Management accounting – a survey paper' in R. Scapens, D. Otley & R.J. Lister, *Management Accounting, Organisational Theory and Capital Budgeting: Three Surveys*, London, Macmillan/ESRC.

Scarpello, V. & H.A. Theeke (1989), 'Human resource accounting: a measured critique', *Journal of Accounting Literature*, v8, pp. 265–280.

Schiff, M. & A.Y. Lewin (1970), 'The impact of people on budgets', *The Accounting Review*, v45/2, pp. 259–268.

Schonberger, R.J. (1982), *Japanese manufacturing Techniques: Nine Hidden Lessons in Simplicity*, New York, The Free Press.

Shaw, M. (1975), *Marxism and Social Science*, London, Pluto Press.

Sherer, M. & S. Turley (eds.) (1991), *Current Issues in Auditing*, 2/e, London, Paul Chapman.

Shillinglaw, E. (1980), 'Old horizons and new frontiers: the future of managerial accounting', in P. Hulzer (ed.), *Management Accounting in 1980: Proceedings of the*

University of Illinois Management Accounting Symposium, University of Illinois at Urbana-Champaign.

Silverman, D. (1970), *The Theory of Organisations*, London, HEB.

Simon, H.A. (1957), *Administrative Behaviour*, New York, Macmillan.

Simon, H.A. (1960), *The New Science of Management Decision*, New York, Harper & Row.

Smircich, L. (1983), 'Concepts of culture and organisational analysis', *Administrative Science Quarterly*, 28, pp. 339–358.

Solomon, D. (1974), 'Corporate social preferences – a new dimension in accounting reports?' in H. Edey & B.S. Yamey (eds.), *Debits, Credits, Finance and Profits*, London, Sweet & Maxwell, pp. 131–141.

Stewart, R. (1967), *Managers and their Jobs*, London, Macmillan.

Tawney, R.H. (1921), *The Acquisitive Society*, London, G. Bell.

Taylor, F.W. (1964), *Scientific Management*, London, Harper & Row.

Teulings, A.W.D. (1986), 'Managerial labour processes in organised capitalism: the power of corporate management and the powerlessness of the manager' in D. Knights & H.C. Willmott (eds.), *Managing the Labour Process*, London, Gower, pp. 142–165.

Thompson, E.R. & A. Knell (1979), *The Employment Statement in Company Reports*, London, ICAEW.

Thompson, P. (1989), *The Nature of Work: an Introduction to Debates on the Labour Process*, 2/e, London, Macmillan.

Tinker, A.M. (1980), 'Towards a political economy of accounting: an empirical illustration of the Cambridge controversies', *Accounting, Organisations and Society*, v5/1, pp. 147–160.

Tinker, A.M. (1985), *Paper Prophets: a Social Critique of Accounting*, Holt, Rinehart & Winston, New York.

Tinker, A.M., B. Merino & M.D. Neimark (1982), 'The normative origins of positive theories', *Accounting, Organisations and Society*, v7/2, pp. 167–200.

Tinker, A.M. & M.D. Neimark (1987), 'The role of annual reports in General Motors: 1917–1976', *Accounting, Organisations and Society*, v12/1, pp. 71–88.

Tomkins, C. & I. Colville (1984), 'The role of accounting in local government: some illustrations from practice' in A.G. Hopwood & C. Tompkins (eds.), *Issues in Public Sector Accounting*.

Tomkins, C. & R. Groves (1983), 'The everyday accountant and researching his reality', *Accounting, Organisations and Society*, v8/4, pp. 361–374.

Underdown, B. & P.J. Taylor (1985), *Accounting Theory and Policy Making*, London, Heinemann.

Vinten, G. (1988), 'Behavioural aspects of accountancy', *Managerial Auditing Journal*, v3/2, pp. 28–31.

Wainwright, H. (1984), 'Women and the division of labour', in P. Abrams & R. Brown (eds.), *UK Society: Work, Urbanism and Inequality*, London, Weidenfeld & Nicolson.

Walsh, E.J. & R.E. Stewart (1988), 'Management accounting in the making: two case studies', *Interdisciplinary Perspectives on Accounting* Conference paper, Manchester.

Wardell, M. & L. Weisenfeld (1988), 'Management accounting and the transformation of the labour process', *Interdisciplinary Perspectives on Accounting* Conference paper, Manchester.

Watts, R.L. & J.L. Zimmerman (1978), 'Towards a positive theory of the determination of accounting standards', *The Accounting Review*, v53/1, pp. 112–134.

Watts, R.L. & J.L. Zimmerman (1979), 'The demand for and supply of accounting theories: the market for excuses', *The Accounting Review*, v54/2, pp. 273–305.

Watts, R.L. & J.L. Zimmerman (1986), *Positive Accounting Theory*, New York, Prentice-Hall.

Watts, R.L. & J.L. Zimmerman (1989), 'Positive accounting theory: a ten year perspective', Graduate School of Business Administration, University of Rochester.

Weber, M. (1948), *Essays in Sociology*, edited by H.H. Gerth & C.W. Mills, London, Routledge & Kegan Paul.

Weber, M. (1968), *Economy and Society: an Outline of Interpretive Sociology vi*, New York, Bodminster Press.

Wedderburn, D. & R. Crompton (1972), *Workers' Attitudes and Technology*, Cambridge, Cambridge University Press.

Whittington, G. (1987), 'Positive accounting research: a review article', *Accounting & Business Research*, 68, pp. 327–336.

Wilensky, H.L. (1964), 'The professionalisation of everyone?', *American Journal of Sociology*, v70/2, pp. 137–158.

Williams, R. (1973), 'Base and superstructure in Marxist cultural theory', *New Left Review*, v82, pp. 3–16.

Williams, R. (1983), *Keywords*, London, Flamingo Press.

Willmott, H.C. (1986), 'Organising the profession: a theoretical and historical examination of the development of the major accountancy bodies in the UK', *Accounting, Organisations and Society*, v11/6, pp. 555–580.

Willmott, H.C. (1990), 'Serving the public interest? a critical analysis of a professional claim', in D. Cooper & T. Hopper (eds.), *Critical Accounts: Reorientating Accounting Research*, London, Macmillan.

Wiseman, J. (1982), 'An evaluation of disclosures made in corporate annual reports, *Accounting, Organisations and Society*, v7/1, pp. 53–63.

Wood, S. (1979), 'A reappraisal of the contingency approach to organisation', *Journal of Management Studies*, v16/3, pp. 334–354.

Wood, S. (1982), (ed.), *The Degradation of Work*, London, Hutchinson.

Woodward, J. (1965), *Industrial Organisation: Theory and Practice*, Oxford, Oxford University Press.

Woodward, J. (1970), *Industrial Organisation: Behaviour and Control*, London, Oxford University Press.

Wright, E.O. (1976), 'Class boundaries in advanced capitalist societies', *New Left Review*, 98, pp. 3–41.

Wright, E.O. (1978), *Class, Crisis and the State*, London, New Left Books.

Wright, E.O. (1980), 'Varieties of Marxist conceptions of class structure', *Politics and Society*, v9/3, pp. 323–370.

Zeitlin, M. (1974), 'Corporate ownership and control', *American Journal of Sociology*, v79/5, pp. 1073–1119.

Name index

Adorno, T. 146–8
Althusser, L. 91–2, 95, 148
Anthony, R.N. 136
Argyris, C. 83, 105, 137–8
Armstrong, P. 40, 77, 97, 144

Barber, B. 20
Barnard, C. 108, 175–6
Becker, H. 22, 186
Belkaoui, A. 116
Berle, A.A. 164–5
Berry, A.J. 97, 142
Blauner, R. 75–6
Brandenberg, M. 64, 73, 75
Braverman, H. 67–9, 74, 143–5
Burchell, S. 93–4, 149–50
Burnham, J. 165
Burrell, G. 10, 141, 147

Carchedi, G. 85–6, 167
Chambers, A.D. 197, 198
Child, J. 51, 166
Christenson, C. 131
Colville, I. 141–2
Comte, A. 4, 5, 6, 126
Cooley, M. 70, 77
Cooper, D. 93, 96–7, 140, 169
Cooper, R. 154
Cottrell, A. 85, 164, 166, 167
Crompton, R. 70, 76, 78, 166
Cutler, A. 85, 167
Cyert, R.M. 170–2

Deal, T.E. 175, 176–7, 178
Durkheim, E. 5, 19, 26, 75, 126

Elliott, P. 23
Ezzamel, M.K. 140, 155–6

Fama, E. 162–3, 165
Fayol, H. 80, 135
Flamholtz, E.G. 105, 107–8
Foucault, M. 148–51

Giddens, A. 6, 142
Goffman, E. 141, 186, 188
Goldthorpe, J.H. 80, 83
Gramsci, A. 91–2, 95, 146, 148
Gray, R.H. 99, 101, 104–5
Greenwood, E. 20–1

Habermas, J. 5, 146–8
Harper, R.R. 189
Herzberg, F. 105, 138, 168
Hopper, T. 70, 93, 97, 144
Hopwood, A.G. 93–4, 138–40, 149–50
Horkheimer, M. 146–8
Hoskin, K.W. 149–50, 155–6

Jensen, M.C. 161–2, 163, 165
Johnson, H.T. 135, 151–6, 164
Johnson, T.J. 23–5

Kaplan, R.S. 135, 151–6, 164
Kelly, M. 86, 145, 167
Kennedy, A.A. 175, 176–7, 178
Kuhn, T.S. 118, 122

Laughlin, R.C. 147–8
Lawrence, P.R. 139, 175
Lehman, C. 96
Likkert, R. 105–6, 108, 138
Lindblom, C.E. 169–70
Lockwood, D. 69, 80, 83
Loft, A. 30, 150
Lorsch, J.W. 139, 175
Lukacs, G. 90, 95, 146

Subject index

accountancy associations 26–33;
American Institute of Certified Public
Accountants 32; Association of
Accounting Technicians 27, 62, 63;
Australian Society of Accountants 31;
Canadian Institute of Chartered
Accountants 31; Chartered Association
of Certified Accountants 29, 34, 35, 36,
37, 38, 40, 41, 42, 44, 63; Chartered
Institute of Public Finance &
Accountancy 30–1, 35, 41, 43, 56, 63;
Chartered Institute of Management
Accountants 30, 34, 35, 36, 37, 38, 40,
41, 43, 47, 63, 135; Institute of
Chartered Accountants in Australia 31;
Institute of Chartered Accountants in
England & Wales 27–8, 34, 38, 41, 42,
43, 46, 47, 63; Institute of Chartered
Accountants in Ireland 29, 34, 41;
Institute of Chartered Accountants of
Scotland 28–9, 34, 38, 41, 63; Institute
of Internal Auditors 27, 196; Japanese
Institute of Certified Public
Accountants 32; New Zealand Society
of Accountants 31–2; Society of
Management Accountants of Canada 31
accountancy profession 19–41, 97–8;
women in 41
accountancy as a social institution 1–4
accountants: creative 205–8; public's
image of 37–41; and management
79–87
Accounting: behavioural 137–40;
corporate 47, 51; cost 134–5; critical
93–8; environmental 99, 104–5;
financial 48–51, 113–33; green 99,
104–5; human resource 105–10;
management 51–5, 134–56; political

economy of 95–6, 140; positive 118,
119, 130–3; Public Sector 56–61;
accounting formulae 47–56
Accounting, Organisations and Society
93, 139
accounting technicians 61–4
accounting theory 114–26
activity based costing 154
adaptive rationality 171
administrative man 169
agency theory 161–8
alienation 65–6, 75–6
ambiguity 172–4
anomie 19, 128, 130
auditing 43–7, 180–99; internal 195–9;
Standards and Guidelines 183–4

behavioural theory 168–75
'Big 6' accounting firms 3, 43, 46, 64, 73,
104, 132, 184
book-keeping 113–14
bounded rationality 169
budgeting 137–40

class analysis 83–7
collective mobility projects 23
conception vs. execution 67, 74, 81
conceptual framework 115, 125
consciousness 89–92
contingency perspective 76, 139–40
corporate cultures 175–9
corporate excellence 175–7
The Corporate Report 99–101, 103, 125
cost drivers 154
credentialism 23, 24

decision-making theory 168–75
deskilling 68